The Journal of
Andrew Bihaly

The Journal of Andrew Bihaly

edited by Anthony Tuttle

Thomas Y. Crowell Company
Established 1834
New York

DESIGNED BY JUDITH WORACEK BARRY

MANUFACTURED IN THE UNITED STATES OF AMERICA

2   3   4   5   6   7   8   9   10

Library of Congress Cataloging in Publication Data

Bihaly, Andrew.
  The journal of Andrew Bihaly.
    1. Bihaly, Andrew.   I. Tuttle, Anthony, ed.   II. Title.
CT275.B5724A3 1973   917.47'1'0340924 [B]
ISBN 0-690-00091-X   73-7783

EDITOR'S PREFACE

The Journal of Andrew Bihaly came to my attention through Martha Winston, my literary agent. It had been brought to her by an acquaintance of Andrew's mother, who quickly recognized its profound merit.

Having once been traumatically down and out myself, I was immediately struck with Andrew's journal and agreed to edit his book, not in the strict sense of the word but more in the spirit of a creative brother, since, through the usual process of repetition and experimentation, Andrew had been denied the time to season himself. Therefore, my job was not one of rewriting his book but rather of being his seasoned literary conscience.

What I have tried to do is to maintain the spirit behind his work while cutting some material which I felt detracted from its central intent, which, while doing no real justice to its passion and power, might be described as the effort of one young man, born out of the horrors of World War Two, trying to interpret the country and culture he found himself alive in.

His past was a record of those horrors. To save his life, his mother put him in an old monastery used to house juvenile delinquents, bought him a forged birth certificate, and told him he was not Jewish. Shortly thereafter, his mother became a victim of the first of three concentration camps in which she was imprisoned. His father was murdered during the Eichmann Death March. And at the age of nine years, in that monastery in Visegrad, Andrew, himself, was brutalized by a gang of delinquents.

The past finally overwhelmed him, but Andrew's journal is not a testament of despair. Rather, it is the chronicle not only of one young man's life but also an unintended mirror which reflects the cataclysmic changes, both in sensibility and manner, that in the last five years of the previous decade shook America to its very soul. And ultimately, it is a document of hope, though he never knew it. A testament to the wonder of one man, lost in the agonies of comprehending his aloneness and that aloneness in relation to the world, still and always trying to communicate the feelings of his heart to someone else . . . in this case, to himself only, that solitary bravery and courage his final, irrevocable triumph.

—Anthony Tuttle
NEW YORK CITY
NOVEMBER 12, 1972

The Journal of
Andrew Bihaly

Boy Who Escaped Nazis

June 8, 1951

TODAY Andrew participated in the exercises of Flag Week at Independence Square by telling an audience of 1,000 school children, and the public, just what the American flag means to him.

His address reminds Americans that once again this city will observe the flag's anniversary from June 8 through June 14 with special ceremonies planned as tributes to the symbol of Freedom.

Philadelphia Evening Bulletin

Honors Flag in Ceremony

What the Flag Means to Me

By ANDREW BIHALY

THE AMERICAN FLAG is everywhere; high on the buildings, in the schools, on the movie screens, in the shop windows and in the churches—but best of all it is engraved in the heart of a new American—my heart.

To some people the Stars and Stripes is just a piece of cloth, but to me it is one of the dearest things in the world— because it means America—the place of continuous wonders which delight and surprise me.

In the factories I have seen mass production, cleanliness, speed, and system.

In the school I have learned the meanings of friendship and democracy.

In the courts I have seen justice—a trial by jury—and I was impressed that no man here is guilty until he is proven so. How different from the Europe that I know!

I look around me and see churches of many faiths—the flag means that I may worship God the way I please.

I hear the echoes of great names: Lincoln, Jackson; they were very poor, nevertheless they reached the highest office in the land. The flag tells me that here one doesn't have to be rich nor of high social standing to obtain an important posi- tion—it is ability that counts.

Then there are other names: George Washington Carver, a slave who became a great scientist; Andrew Carnegie, a very poor immigrant who became one of the richest Ameri- cans. Again the flag tells me that this is the land of equality and opportunities.

Most of the flags that I see are new and bright, but I like the ones that I see in some museums—faded and worn because they speak of sad defeats and great victories, of battles, of heroes—dead and living.

The American Flag is everywhere—it is here with us in the park, but best of all—it is in my heart—the heart of a new American.

Part One

INTRODUCTION

My mother told me when I was a little boy and was dumpish and wouldn't talk, that I should express my feelings. "Talk even to a stone," she'd say. Now I talk to my typewriter.

We cannot think of everything that ever happened to us, yet we can recall, in every detail, what happened to us perhaps for five minutes. For example, I cannot remember the exact moment I learned the word 'awkward,' but I recall very well the pride I felt the time I learned that word, even though it was certainly not a word which I considered part of the first things you really need in daily life. Awkward? I learned it when I came to this country, to America. Let's face it, I *am* a new-

3

comer, although often I feel that I am more of an American than a lot of Americans I know, globetrotters, who travel all over the place. Where I came from, when I was a kid, people did not take trips many times in their lives, they stayed where they were, they got stuck in their countries.

And now a little story:

There was a young man, who grew up in the old ways, who also stuck to his neighborhood. He lived in a little house behind the big houses, hoping, every day, to work assiduously in order to make ends meet in his little life. He was parsimonious, he wanted to save a little money to make a darkroom, to take pictures, to become a photographer. That was his 'Plan.' But he wasn't so adept at fighting his anxieties and got bogged down in just ordinary life.

Andrew was his name. He lived on Mott Street, in New York City, in America. The rest of the world was Uptown; he got ghettoized, he became a rebel. And there was a revolution at that time, and other people were revolting against the same thing he was revolting against. He was thinking about the world; he tried to figure out how to make it better. But the world and the civilization that he lived in was in almost constant conflict with his ego, the little boy ego which we all get born with and, I suspect, little girls get born with, too. Everything jived with some aspect of his personality, everything had a precedent, a cause.

This guy had many hangups. He had difficulty relating to people. He never had real friends and he wanted to have them, but he thought that in his milieu friendship was a defunct function—man has to learn to live alone, not to show emotions, not to ever trust anybody completely but yourself. He wanted the things we all want, he wanted to be loved, he wanted to be liked, but wasn't quite sure how to go about it. He tried to become happy but the things that had happened to him during World War Two periodically made him sick.

Not that he was always interested in himself. It was just that he was touched by outside forces during World War Two, by the Nazi occupation when he was young, very young. And sometimes he cries in his emotions over his life; other times he just grooves on life . . . and he has a cat, too, and he loves his cat.

Finally, this lonely guy, who remembered things from his past, realized that he could talk to someone. He was sitting this Saturday night alone at home, alone like almost always, and all of a sudden he did not feel alone. He realized he has someone to talk to, he has a typewriter and he can talk to the world. He did not have to speak to the world in perfect sentences and if he said anything that was not correct, he knew that if the things he observed were true vital things, and if they came from his heart and he could honestly open up his insides the way it really is inside, then he would be a free man even if he is alone.

My little cat sits in my lap, and he gets up and pulls himself up by his nails and puts his head on my shoulder and purrs away. Let me take a few more puffs on my pipe and "talk to the stone."

■ Would it not be interesting to know how man eventually contained himself not to shout? My knowledge clearly tells me that man must scream sometimes.

I want not to live? Or to live again? To go back where I started from and start anew, to be born again now, with all the things that I already learned? Is that what I really want? Doesn't knowledge of the Second World War and after that war, to escape Communism, the dislocations in the refugee camps, getting used to America, isn't that important? I've got to be able to choose in America, in this land of choice, where options are supposed to be the cornerstone of 'the American way of life.'

In this land of personal and group 'liberty,' I made a choice to live in New York, where the hordes have to stand in the subway belly to belly, but they do not smile or talk to each other while looking each other in the eye, where people choose to live next to one another in an apartment building and don't want to know each other, where people are afraid to touch hands, where they don't kiss uncles and aunts, or friends—or do they?

I notice that it was making me sick that I, and none in my 'milieu now,' was kissing, or touching, or hugging. I decided to show my emotions and love for someone by hugging them and kissing them. If they don't like it, I stop, but at least I should try to touch people, and let them know that I love them, the way I used to when I was a kid.

Actually, I made a mess of it on two occasions already. I kissed Lully, and she liked it, and I kissed her boyfriend and he got upset, and I kissed Patty, the woman who owns the coffee shop 'Engage' because I stepped on her foot and she was hurt. But I also kissed and hugged Arthur, because he played his flute and I loved it, and he pushed me off. But I did that before, when I was in the Air Force, at the Indian concert in Frankfurt. I remember how the Indian musicians were hugged and kissed by everybody, and it was friendly and happy and very expressive of people liking each other.

I hope that as time goes on, the friends I have now and the friends I will make will enjoy to be hugged and kissed, and that they will eventually come over and hug and kiss me, if they feel that they like me. Especially I want to hug and kiss and express my emotions with girls. I want to kiss and hug and love all the girls, but never end up doing it. I love people, and I chose to live in a place where I can at least know each one of the people who is in the house, and I have spoken to each of them several times.

Yes, I made a choice to live in New York. There is a New York that is not known to the New Yorkers, a New York that was not known to me in Queens. I never knew that there were little houses in New York where the rent was still 23 and 27 dollars. I never realized that you could get in New York a series of jobs, part-time jobs, and have enough time during the day to get into mischief and to do something creative out of oneself. Or just goof off.

You ask me for some ideas . . . I have many, theories about the world, about what is good, what is bad. Making love is good right now. I haven't made love enough, perhaps ever. I'd like to go somewhere and make love as long as I want to, with as many women as I wanted to. That is what guides me, that is what is most of the time on my mind, especially when I haven't got a steady chick.

Poor Mignone, her mother came to me (she lives in Queens) and wanted me to court Mignone, and I said no. She did not like my clothing, my company, my behavior. Her mother did not like where we went and I told her, "I cannot do what you want me to do. I do not want to put on a suit, always, and put on a special smile, I do not want to be Mignone's diversion, her outlet in your real world." I told the mother she can do what she wants to do, and now Mignone must stay home and act like a good little girl. I haven't heard from her since then.

So far so good, but I lost my keys yesterday and I called Mignone for her set of keys to my apartment. We met in the morning, at Herald Square in the rush-hour. She looked tired and I told her how horrible the city seems, with the people rushing, how tense they were, and I imagined how horrible it must have been for them to force themselves to get up on a rainy Monday, like today, to have to go into the gloomy offices and think about prices and wages. I really rubbed it in. She felt it. She asked me: "Tell me, did you take pot?" but I told her "Of course not," and she said, "Would you like to accompany me to Sixth Avenue?" And at the subway she said "I will call you." I don't know if she will or not.

It is difficult to do what one wants to do. To become a respectable member of society, "You must be able to do something for money." I tried it and all my efforts failed, now I want my life-flow to coincide with my plans.

So I am growing free of society's bonds, awakening from twenty years of dungeoning called a strong mother, and a weak son. I've started to react to the liberating force of the therapy, and here I am, living well, getting all the material goods I want, working gradually into a nice apartment, into a groovy subculture, into groovy people and friends; now I am listening to the rain in the little courtyard, thinking of all the things which will make me happy. I want to live. I want to work for my daily living and to save a little for a photography-studio. I want to take pix, I want to take human beings, and my friends. I want to develop the art of essaying. I want to take a bookful of photographs about some simple bucolic places. I want my pictures to sell, and they'll be sold by my name.

Coming from the museum from work, it was raining cats and dogs, a solid wall of rain came upon me as I walked under my extra large size umbrella. When I came home I changed into something dry (the rain even came through my umbrella) and started to clean up, then cooked something and ate in silence.

I was folding the laundry and Alfred comes in. He brings pot and we take a 'little' drag on the pipe and start talking. By the time we stop, it is darkening already. I said, "I have to free myself from my mother, and it is very difficult to stop believing what my mother told me to believe and to learn to do what I myself want to do." He told me, it is also very difficult to get away from his mother; he often wanted to kill her, now he is glad he doesn't have urges like that. I told him, I love my mother, but I have to be free from her. And he said, some of his friends remembered parts of their mother, a breast, a buttock, and they masturbated while they were thinking about it . . .

This must be just another aspect of some people's lives. Some people dare to be more explicit about it, some people less so. But I am not hung up that way, and perhaps I am just allowing myself to realize the truth, that I've liberated myself from my mother for the first time in my life.

Actually for a while I was thinking about my mother, and what I would say to her if we got into an honest conversation. I want eventually to become friends with my mother.

A whole era of my life was with her and I must have inherited and later had to fight my mother's personality, and still must combat the kind of images she gave me about society, women and principles. The effect is coming out now.

To Chinatown and back. A rainy evening, empty, peaceful streets. As I cross the Italian section neighborhood, I see men standing very close to each other on the sidewalk, like labor-organizations, like a dream, talking quietly to each other, making grimaces.

In Chinatown strange stuff of green, fresh good texture in orderly bins. Chinese vegetables. Flat, humorless old Chinese men. I saunter, I am looking for a certain store where a lantern made of thin strips of wood and rice-paper is sold. I can't find it. Finally I go into a store where a colorful lampshade is a dollar. I shall buy it for my hallway.

The hallway and my house are a joy to me. When I moved into the building the place was open. No one cared about whether it was clean or dirty. People could come and go any time, and they did. There were many renters, people in transit, a constant migration, and I was robbed. Then one day I fixed the front door, placed a new strong screen on the inside, took off the broken lock, disassembled it, replaced the missing parts, and distributed keys (which I bought with my own money) to the tenants. After a long hassle with them they got rid of the renters, and we finally closed the front door. Then one day in early spring, I cleaned the front door. It was practically opaque from dirt, and Ed Regy washed the steps in the hallway. Gradually I picked up my life after a long slumber.

When I moved here the street was dirty. It had no garbage cans. Now it has two and if they disappear, I shall start writing letters and the sanitation commissioner will hear from me acidly again. It took me three letters, and they can bet their ass that if they withdraw them, like the local commissioner said they will, they will have to replace them again, even if I have to go to mayorlindsay.

Winter is coming and I want to have a good life while it is cold outside. I will concentrate on fixing all the windows (they are broken), pad and insulate the window frames so that they will not leak and create drafts. Maybe Alfred will help me fix my fire place to regulate the updraft. I will put down the nice clean newly shampooed rug (which I found on the street), bring home some flowers, and my apartment will be warm, clean and nice. I shall make a lot of good soup; I want to eat well.

Water is dripping from my faucet. I've been thinking about the grooviness of my bachelor life. Making myself a home, finding chicks, getting good and passionate once in a while, not having to be with anyone when I do not want to. And in the midst of all this typing, my cat is climbing up me, like upon a tree. I let him, and I think of my life in the museum, every day giving the girls sensuous looks, working the tables, glancing up the chicks' skirts. Then, after my work, sort of dejected, going through the galleries, walking up to chicks, making remarks about art, trying to pick them up. Being bashful about it, finally meeting and flirting with many chicks and letting them come up to my apartment. Being a playboy, the kind married chicks tell each other about and love to visit.

Now I am doing three things: settling down, building a pad of my own, and doing what I want to do. I am also forming a new identity and I am very much enjoying it.

I have a friend, Alfred. We have been together a lot and he turns me on. He is a friend, and at the same time I wonder about him because I do not trust him. Alfred lives on the top floor. At first, last summer, I saw him often visiting Aly Roul and Willy Merchard. He came with a little fat boy, perhaps 4. He walked with him hand in hand. He was babysitting for this little boy. He took him to the zoo and to the beach. Sometimes Alfred had a camera slung around his shoulder, and had something in a paper bag with him. The boy's mother, Anny, was studying mathematics in a university, and needed someone to look after her son. I never cared about Alfred. Then one day he disappeared. Aly told me later, Alfred went on a business trip to Spain. I never really noticed him going away, only that he wasn't around.

At that time Aly Roul and his friend Willy Merchard were living in the two apartments on the top floor. But Willy moved to Elizabeth Street, and Arthur took his apartment. After Alfred returned from Spain, Aly Roul went to California where he is from originally. Alfred moved into his apartment, and Aly's job as a waiter in the Metropolitan Museum of Art restaurant was left to me.

I just opened up the aquarium that held my white mouse. I hadn't heard it for perhaps two days, and I was afraid it had starved. There was no movement and there I saw a purple little thing that looked like an embryo lying among the folds of the rag. There were nine of them. I picked them out one by one and put them into a white rag; I felt their little cold bodies, they did not have any fur, just thin, purple skin. There were little black nodules where their eyes should have been. I could not find their mother anywhere. She must have become thinner and wiggled out after giving birth. I took the little things up to Alfred, who said they made his skin crawl—that they were his natural enemies. But as I held the little creatures in my hand, they gradually warmed up and began to move and crawl while I talked with Alfred. I did not know what to do with the baby mice. I did not want to try to nurture them. I walked to the toilet but did not want to flush them. I imagined what it would feel like to be dragged down some great pipe and drowned, that cold water frightened me. So I took the little ones over to the A.S.P.C.A.

My cat is sitting in his little box. This morning I was sitting at my desk trying to make order out of my money matters, and he climbed up on me, sinking his sharp nails into my skin (I was only wearing a T-shirt), and I grabbed him as he was climbing up (he did this many times before, I usually had on a thick sweatshirt and he did not hurt me) and threw him to the floor. There was a thump and he ran behind the bathtub. He remained there for a long time. When I went to look at him he was trembling. His leg was dragging behind him . . . I had dislocated it. He was looking at me helplessly and sadly. I felt awful, but what I had done was done, and it would cost too much money to take him to a veterinarian. I put him up on the bed and went out, but when I returned he was back behind the bathtub, so I placed some fabric in his box and let him lie on it. He stays there now peering out at me contentedly, mysteriously.

It is cold in the room; I am hungry and will cook some oatmeal . . . Today is Yom Kippur, the Jewish day of atonement and I am doing so many cruel things on it . . . hurting cats' legs—sometimes I am rotten.

I am not working today. I will put in a wire for my refrigerator, then my electrical wiring will be finished. Next I will put two quilts I bought for camping on the rug and buy some artificial fur textile, and put it on the soft materials, so I can sleep with a girl in front of the fire.

I am convinced that a slum is not a place but a state of mind. It is a limbo, a place where people are forgotten, and they cannot fend for themselves. (I just finished mixing peat moss into the earth downstairs.) When I came to this building the place was a slum and gradually, without giving up, I am picking it up, bringing it back to life, looking at it not as a product but as a process. The rich earth sticks to my fingers, under my nails, black and sticky; it resists my wanting it turned, but yet I turn it shovel-by-shovel and then someone passes by —it is Noah, a friend of Alfred's. He asks if he might help, I tell him, sure. He digs a little, digs shallow; he looks uncomfortable. I show him my blister; he is surprised. He tells about his plants. He is very artificial; square, full of anxiety, the way I used to be (and sometimes still am), I don't dare talk about myself to him. He once told me: when he likes someone it is all right, but when he doesn't like someone he doesn't go the other way, he gets nearer to them and finds out what they are doing. He wants to find out whether I smoke pot or not; he is a spider.

Noah keeps talking. He asks whether he might plant some plants in the garden. Of course, I say, and keep on digging. When the earth is loose, I spread the remaining peatmoss upon it and start mixing it up with the rich black earth.

The tenant from the third floor comes down—Frank with the mustache. He says: "Andrew, you are beautiful. I dig you." I dig myself too. I think of the Japanese people. They make something with the space around them, they love beauty, they are willing to arrange the rocks and stones to form patterns. We should care about our surroundings. We live here, we don't have to neglect our lives. It doesn't matter what we end up with; it is the quality, the feelings that matter, the feelings we feel while we are doing it, the feelings we feel when someone looks at us and we know we are beautiful and it feels good when they say so.

Yesterday I cooked some sausages with peppers, cut some coarse bread to go with it, and a fellow from Frisco who came to live with Alfred was going down the stairway and as I peeked out, he came in. He ate with me. We talked. I described society to him. I told him, I realize

13

that society is divided into a majority who live the American way of life, the kind of life American boys are dying for in Viet Nam. And there are other people, minorities in this land, hippies, cool people, beatniks, bohemians, hippy-intellectuals, collegiates.

Many people merely put on the exterior appearance of hippy-hood. They grow their hair long, wear bells around their necks, do showy things to prove they are different from everyone else. They are rebels. Others look like everyone else, they can't be recognized by their looks. They wear their state of mind in their hearts, in their way of life. They are like me—I am like them. We are quiet about what we are, what we are doing, what we aspire to. We are gentle in our attitudes toward the squares. I understand. We are squares ourselves. We are suffering from the anxieties, from the alienation, which is the lot of modern man.

We ate, and I burned incense, and I felt good.

I just came down from Arthur's, Alfred's next door neighbor. He'd asked me a simple question: "When was the last time you got yourself a piece of tail?" It's been a long time, I told him.

So I take a shave, a nice warm bath and put on something decent and go out to get myself a chick. Like in the old times before I picked up Mignone. Full scale ahead. Cut and dried. Straight. Let's get hot, woman.

It isn't like it used to be . . . I went out but was kind of lost, did not know where to go. I went to the Engage, a coffeehouse I like to frequent because I do not feel it is a commercial enterprise.

The woman who owns the Engage asked, "What will you have?" When I said I had eaten, she told me, "You will have to leave. To-night we have a rule; only those who will eat supper may stay here before nine."

So I left but felt rejected because I had repaired their broken window this past Monday and it wasn't right for her to treat me as a stranger.

I picked the Gallery Gwen, on East Fourth Street, as my most likely place to find tail and found it closed.

As I wandered, I saw two young girls go into a downstairs coffeehouse. I followed them and stood at the stairway waiting for them to choose a place to sit. I wanted to sit at their table, but they walked over to the only occupied one where three young boys were sitting.

The blonde, who looked more mature than the slim brunette, asked in an innocent and naive tone: "Would any of you have some dope on him by any chance?" The boys were flabbergasted and embarrassed. But they liked the girls and when they pointed to me, standing on the steps, warning, "That man there might be a cop," the blonde said, "No, I never get into any trouble. I have all the luck in the world. Even if someone pointed to me and said to a cop, 'Look she is carrying a pound of opium in her pocketbook,' I would just keep walking and nothing would happen to me because I was born under a lucky star."

I, in the meanwhile, sat down at the next table and listened silently, brazenly gazing over where the five were sitting. One of the boys said, "We do have something on us." The blonde asked him to show it to her.

One of them, a youth with a pimply face and angular, manneristic movements and programmatic questions, invited me to come sit at their table and asked what I was doing. I told him I was walking around the village because my girlfriend and I broke up yesterday and I was looking for a new friendship. I had seen the girls go into the coffee shop and followed them because I thought they were beautiful. He seemed to be satisfied with the simple explanation, and I, for my part, kept silent from then on.

The boys finally invited the girls and me to their apartment on Fifth Street to smoke some pot. Before we got up from the table, however, the blonde asked: "Do you fellows have any other motives besides turning us on?" and the fellow in the middle said, "If you come at me and rape me, or pull me into the other room, I shall not resist; but otherwise we shall not want to have anything further to do about making out with you."

15

So we went to the apartment, smoked pot and I went home alone.

There are two I's: one, a hippy-intellectual, the uptown I, who is searching for answers, full of plans, serious, always wearing a shirt, jacket, tie and cleanly dressed. The other I is a beatnik who doesn't like to wash, who is childish, good, innocent and loves life with an exuberance that is delectable for a thirty-one-year-old cat in the America of 1966.

Today I wanted a chick very much, yet, in spite of my great desire, I went to the Museum of Modern Art. In the museum there are photographs which tell so much more than any amount of writing can. Beautiful reproduction books of one modern artist for example, of life and relaxation.

Yes, the Protestant ethic: we grow into it and it overcomes us. When I came home, I swept the steps of the house and afterwards swept the yard downstairs (trying out the new broom I bought). And since I was turned on, I sat down a moment to enjoy the quietness of the little yard, and was thinking why don't I sit down more often and enjoy the existence of existence, why must I always do something, DO SOMETHING? Why can I not do what I want to do even if that is absolutely nothing? I like to do nothing sometimes; that is what relaxation is, that is what relaxedness means. It also means when one is able to sit, just sit, and not say a word, just liking to be with someone, and not having to talk, or for atmosphere—well, do so!

When I came out, the door had fallen shut. I had no key with me, I was locked out of my home. I remember when as a child I was shut out; but now I have only to wait for Alfred to come home, he has keys to my apartment. Until then I wanted to write, so I went to Ed Regy, the peace guy downstairs. He let me have the use of his Olivetti typewriter, which reminds me of Jancsi, a friend of mine who worked in the Olivetti factory. As I was writing that 'cs' a whole cluster of old emotional resonances, aroused by the Hungarian double letter, welled up in me. That was accompanied by the realization that I am Hungarian, and that in turn made me want to cry.

Gee, if I keep on writing, I will have to go through a lot, remember and refeel a lot of ground. You must give me a little time, dear reader, because it is painful to go back to crumby times in somebody's life. When I write of them, I shall have to refeel them, live with them again, and it hurts in me. It is hard to resolve to cry again the tears I had to cry. I will take you into my life, but you must have some forbearance.

My childhood: Ours was a yellow or cream colored six-story apartment house in Budapest. It was a very large hollow box, the way a Pompeian house would look, extended upward six tall stories. Inside were the doors and kitchen windows, encircled with a balcony.

I remember I could never play with other children in our house, I could only play in our apartment or in the park by the Danube. I could never go by myself on the street or in the park. But the Nazi occupation came, I was out of school, and was playing a lot in our big house with the other children. We were allowed to run and play hide-and-seek behind doors, and in indentations. Then I loved the house because we could not go anymore on the street. We had to wear a big yellow David star sewn on our clothing. I was nine years old then.

I remember my father coming to the door and looking at me as I was playing. I see his face, with his dark hair fallen out on both sides of his temples. As I see him tears come in my eyes.

Then came the most salient moment and the time afterward, when I kissed my mother in the hall and left with the nurse. I was sent away by my mother, by my sweet mother, to Visegrad, and ever after I felt that moment, with tears sometimes, with self-pity at others, I never integrated the pain, I can never forget it.

My mother told me how my father sobbingly asked her not to go, "Don't go out of the house, don't go out to the street," how he intuitively knew that mother would disappear. She was caught on the street as she went out for bread. My mother told me about it when she came back from concentration camp. My father, he was good, he was a good man, and he loved me, he loved my mother, he loved us, and they killed him, they killed us.

I realize I am in my room, I am back in my room, and my emotions are in my throat, and my eyes streaming with tears. I can feel again, I can relive myself, bit by bit I can refeel my childhood. But please give me courage, God, if you are, which in my safest and sanest moments I don't believe you are, God if you are, help me continue, let me tell, let me continue writing. I am not too sure because it hurts.

I will now smoke my pot. I want to live a full life. I want to be a writer, I will become famous, but it doesn't matter because it is I who want to get analyzed, self-analyzed.

To live, to LIVE, is the problem. I can want to intellectually, but I became chained. I am at the end of my chains, but I cannot let it go. Why must I now not be average, happy, nonchalant, nonfearful? I want to be just like these guys around me—I want to live, be happy; I cannot, I must try. I must have become frightened, when or where I don't know, I must have become frightened sometime. I am in fright when Visegrad dawns on me.

Yesterday Alfred came and said among other things—about pot—that it lets you out of your cage of anxiety to look around outside, and when you are back in it again, you can utilize some of your knowledge which you gained outside of it. Today, this morning, as I was starting my job, I had a few good feelings—a few notions came to my mind. I wrote them down upon a napkin: "I will find a chick sooner or later; I shall relax; I won't stay lonely. It is only a matter of time. Don't worry. Don't be desperate. Keep on approaching them and, after meeting someone, be friendly at first, but not personal immediately. Then, after talking about impersonal things, get personal, as if she were a man, someone like me whom you would get acquainted with. Then, if and when I am accepted on those terms, switch over to sex."

Today I am having a wonderful day. I was full of passion and masturbated as I have done countless times before, then waited for the sun to come up and played with my cat by my window at eight-thirty . . . As I look at the windows, I see that there is something strange-looking: one window is old-fashioned, the other modern . . . I shall leave them that way. The contrast is good.

Looking at the windows I have been thinking of Alfred. He is Hesse's Pablo in *Steppenwolf*. He is beautiful and ugly, a genius, a Freud, a buddha, a don juan, a jesus, a swindler all rolled into one. He says he was born and grew up in the Bahamas, and he says he also grew up in Harlem. It is likely that he never had a formal education, more than a year or two of college, yet he declared that he went to college and "grad'uated," and went to and flunked out of countless colleges, stud-ied electronics, studied plastics, studied karate. He said he is a sports-man, climbs mountains, tars roofs, drives race-cars. He owned an auto-motive hardware store in Harlem and had a house in New Jersey, was married, is a family man and a bachelor simultaneously. In addition he is a millionaire. He was a policeman and is a connoisseur of drugs. He is full of a hundred enigmatic paradoxes. He is a superman.

Wow! I just got a call from the married woman who visited Frank two weeks ago and waited for him in my house, at which time I told her: I wanted to go to bed with her. We had a delectable time to-gether.

Afterwards we ate in the Jewish restaurant near Pitt Street and I talked up a storm and told her she should start a ceaseless affair with me. Now she called again. I told her if she would come, she doesn't re-ally have to go to bed with me—that we can just talk, or go some-where. "Let me see you," I said. "I want to see you." And she an-swered, "Come to dinner to our house. I cannot leave. I'm too busy with my weaving." (She is like Cely, my cousin, she leads the same type of busy life.) I told her, "I want to see you secretly," but she re-plied laughingly, "that sounds so clandestine, I have to think about it." After we spoke, I jumped with pleasure in the middle of the floor and screamed toward the ceiling, "Wow! am I a male!"

19

I am sitting in the yard in the fall sunshine. My little cat prompted me to come out. He has been playing in the yard all morning and when I came out he actually greeted me. He came to me to pick him up and I was happy to have someone to cuddle to my face. He was purring and rubbed his fur against my face. "You like the sunshine?" I asked him. "I like the sunshine too." He jumped on the table, then upon my outstretched leg and up my torso to my shoulder. Then he jumped among the grasses, and I found a ball for him . . . He played with it, pushed it around, waited for it to stop and attacked it again.

My little cat is not limping anymore. But his leg must be tender—he keeps it outstretched as much as possible. But at least he can use it. He has vomited several times. I haven't been feeding him right; I've been giving him dry food and raw meat, and this past Friday bought some fish and gave him the innards, of which he ate a lot but vomited the next morning. I want to feed him decently. He is such a wonderful companion. He sleeps with me and plays with me. I can talk to him and he practically answers me back. I go out and buy him good food. Yes, I bought him food—and for myself, pears, and I met Tula.

I realize these married women are splendid and if you were with them, all the desires a man can dream of are fulfilled. Tula. She is blonde, very glory-eyed and slender, almost brittle with very tiny breasts. There are women with soft, slightly sagging, beautiful mammary glands, usually women who've had children. Tula has breastlets, so tiny, almost mouth size. She is a lovely girl who is suffering, has many friends and is married to an equally handsome, slender, lean, tenderfaced fellow, named Bob, who is an actor. When I moved into this neighborhood, of course I did not know anyone. Gas or electric range? —none. I ate out of paper bags, salami, milk, grocery-store food, and bread, or bread with bread. Once while eating my lunch from my paper bag, I saw a charming blonde baby playing with her beautiful blonde mother, in the sun, in a large storefront window on the first floor. The baby smiled at me, and I spoke to the mother. She came to me afterwards. But I met Bob, her husband, and couldn't do it to him. It is contrary to my principle. Now we are good friends.

I had a pretty disgusting morning. As I was eating my sandwich, before serving lunch, my new boss, Mr. Melly, said: "Only one sandwich,
my friend." He noticed I was eating two sandwiches. The rotten sonof-
abitches, they expect me to break my back for them and eat the minimum. It reminds me of some kind of brutal penal system; squeeze as
much out of your workers as you can, and pay them the least possible.
Of course I have a good job, cannot complain. I have short hours, and
as long as I show up regularly and do my job, no one bothers me.

But as I was serving lunch, Mr. Melly and Mr. Black, my bosses,
came to get me. They asked, "Have you ever worked upstairs in the executive dining room?" —"I never did, but I can . . ." I took a toke of
pot before I went there and felt calm and confident that I would be
able to learn fairly well. But people started to come in and it became
confusing. I really couldn't handle it, so much was happening at once.
I was out of breath, got almost out of kilter a couple of times. I did not
know what to answer to questions like "What is the special dish for
today?" I explained I was new to this job, I was just learning it for the
first time, and there are things about it I did not know yet. Everyone
was flustered, I did not know what was happening, and saw Mr. Black
serving a few people and he pulled me together. By intuition and a series of people's help the whole affair was somehow accomplished.

It is evening. Mignone was just here for the last time. A big step to see
whether I am healthy or whether I get depressed as when Alma left
me. This may be the last love relationship where the girl was an
image, a beautiful image upon whom I can project the image of my
mother, love them with the innocence and devotion and tearfulness of
falling in love with my mother—I, my subconscious.

The chief activity during these love encounters is crying. I cry because I am happy because I am with my mother again. I feel I must be
protected again because I am afraid in the world. I am still a little boy
and it is difficult for me to make the kind of steps that are possible in

this land and at the same time love a woman with the thirst and patience and beneficence of wow.

Mignone came and packed her belongings in her luggage and took the diaphragm out of her bag and threw it in the garbage with a deft motion, with an intimate knowing smile she deftly put the diaphragm into the garbage bag. My former chick whom I supposedly showed how to make love. She said, "No more, not for me. I will make love again when I am married," she said . . . so, the objective fact may be interpreted as saying: "Andrew, lovemaking is alright but it is not entirely necessary; one can take it or leave it." Then, as she was passing the doorstep, she turned around and said, "Andrew, I only want one thing from you, your photograph; I'd like to have your photo." And I said, "Sure," and kept saying how pretty she was. And she kissed me, sadly it seemed, with her sad, long-drawn silent smile, a beautiful shimmer over her eyes—and I loved that in her, it reminded me of my mother. Now that I see it, I am crying—my mother's face makes me cry. Everything is happening today. Everything is coming together upon me today.

A certain personality character, an identity, evolves during the long-term use of pot. I tend to feel emotionally who I am when I survey my life. This feeling, which is a good one, pervades the other 'unhigh' moments of existence, and self-satisfaction follows.

But now—oh, how can I start to write again? It is a fear, a great fear that pervades me to think of actualities. The only thing I must not do now is to remember the bare fact that I am alone. Some inexplicable mood, which has to do with the absence of Mignone, overcame me for a few days; but it is, hopefully, over now.

The last few days we had were a wonderful erotic togetherness, and then she went with her mother. The feeling of miasma really hit me during my two days off from my work. I couldn't do anything, I felt like going to sleep, felt like dying, felt like lying on the floor and dying, but I must not let myself be overpowered. I must go out and find myself another woman. There must be females who are lovely persons as well as lovely women.

Here comes Alfred, I can hear him—he plays his flute, he is pretty high . . . Today I am able to write some more. For a few days I went out, fled out, almost every night, and Alfred has been getting me high on pot the nights in between. We just sit around and talk. He tells me about his free love theories. He says, "Have many affairs, make love to many women, but do not love them, don't live with them, and let them run around with other men." This means "Be free" and "Let them be free."

I am trying to make headway in the most miserable aspect of America, yet, the most alluring. I am learning, actually, the cultural ramifications of love in the USA from Alfred, and will summarize it for myself:

Man has, with all the other organisms, certain basic needs: water, food, shelter, warmth (or some range of temperature) and after that: someone to love, and someone to love him. I am at this time still fighting to get to the one woman many people never get, and many people postpone . . .

In other words: Don't put all your eggs into one basket. The government knows what decentralization means, why cannot an individual?

Yes, Decentralization. When one woman breaks a man down, he has another recourse: learn the local clichés and masquerade under them. He will have a good time under a cliché-minded society. Wow, I am quite hostile towards this population. I can feel it.

Now it is Sunday. I had a confusing week. On my job I had trouble, Mignone was here, and I had a short 'to-do' with Sally and Adam, the two people I met last week in the East Village Other office.

Sally, she is a beautiful Jewish girl of 20, plump, black-haired, with a beauteous face, and she flirted with me from the start. They invited me to their apartment, we smoked pot, and Adam and I spoke phrases which were full of offensive remarks without any intention; it just came out of our mouths. It was quite chaotic because the chick flirted with me, all the time. I told them I was going to cut wood in the forest next day and they wanted to come also. At home I mentioned to Alfred what we would do the next day, and he said he would come with us.

The four of us took the trip in my car into Bear Mountain. I had a desire for Sally and psychologically couldn't relax and flirted with her in front of Adam. While we were talking, I said repeatedly in a series of funny sentences: "I want fruit, the forbidden fruit, the one Eve gave to Adam."

The beginning of the trip was fun, we were laughing and happy. Alfred was driving; we were looking for a nice place to rest. Finally we found one; it was a fabulous rock high above a valley. We walked around it and Alfred started to take pictures of Sally, helpingly guiding her to stand in a pose and she didn't act as an untouchable. He had his pipe in his mouth, and kept taking pictures—he really looked like a millionaire playboy and I was envious.

Many things happen in my life. Chicks are happening all the time. I work in the Museum, I see a very pretty woman, I talk to her politely. She has an accent and I ask her where she is from, what is she doing in the States. When I quit working, I see her right outside the restaurant, in the Museum. But shortly I have to go meet Kuky, the woman who came to visit Frank one Monday, who waited for him in my house, whom I had told, upon Alfred's coaching, that I wanted to make love to her. Since then she called me up and surprised me by coming to the restaurant. When I was done working, we walked and talked on the grass in Central Park, and, after, we came to my house. Next Monday I am expected to visit her at her house at one o'clock. Probably we'll make love. During the same day, I made a date with Lorraine, the pretty girl in the book shop. She wore a striped sweater; it showed off her breasts beautifully. In a previous conversation I had asked her: "What do you do in your spare time?" "I get high," she answered. She looked straight into my eyes as we talked and did not remove her eyes from mine.

I have been asked many times by women when I meet them, "What do you do?" and I tell them, "I am a waiter." Then for a while, I told them, "I make money. I am a counterfeiter," and the chicks were surprised. Now I say, "I am a waiter but I am writing my memoirs, for a book."

Life is a wonderment. Was it I who lived in that gray old arid dank house in the upper East Bronx? Today I went back there, and a crying was in my throat. I came to this country, and for five long first years I lived in the Bronx—Cely and mother and I. Today I received a postcard from Cuki—he wants to play chess again, as in the Bronx, a long time ago.

All of a sudden I felt that I have to be factual. My life is the life of an inconsequential man who somehow managed to know what the score is, what the breadth and width of human goodness is.

I was in the International Refugee (I.R.O.) camp somewhere in Italy, and we came to this country in October 1950, me, my mother and my cousin Cely. In one of the I.R.O. camps we met a young Jewish man, a little shriveled up man, Cuki. He was young and old, young for his age, and old through his Second World War experiences in the concentration camps. In the I.R.O. camp he made a chessboard out of a piece of plywood. I looked at it as he was working on it many, many weeks. His only tool was his pocketknife. When it was carved, he painted it with green and white utility colors and he gave the plywood chessboard, with his only treasure, a book, the poetry of "Petöfi Sándor," to me as a birthday present. I remember the writing, his dedication. It said: "I give this, there is nothing else I have now."

Yesterday Jolly came over and somehow Alfred got mixed in, and we breakfasted together. Alfred turned on the high-fidelity set. The whole room was afire with exquisitely languorous, caressing and shimmery pop-tunes, they surrounded me with sounds, I felt tingling all over my skin, and I became erotically inspired. One minute before I was writing about the present I got from Cuki in the I.R.O. camp. *I* am the boy from the I.R.O. camp. I must learn to realize it, *I must feel myself,* not just in the present but in my past. I was weak, I was frightened, I was under the shit-heap of the war, I should realize that I came through a hard school, I had so much shit piled upon me when I was younger, and it's taken me a while to get out from under it. The war, the flight from Hungary, then the I.R.O. camps, then America: Philadelphia, and New York—trying to attain a social and economic security. And I failed, but now I am happy again . . . because I am the one who defines my world, not others, because I am living a new kind of life now.

In the old times long ago when I was in the I.R.O. camp, I dreamed special personal dreams. One was that I lived in a dirty slum and scurried around in the city in ordinary clothes but when I turned into a shadowy recess in the wall, the kind everyone goes to urinate in, when I passed a rickety door, I would be surrounded by velvet and laces, in alabaster and marble, in a world of carvings, perfume, incense and beautiful women would wash me and lick me and caress me with their soft white arms. And here I am, surrounding myself with materials I love—but how different they have become: hand-hewn, functional, imperfect.

As you come into my apartment, you come into the living room, and you are in my bedroom-bathroom-kitchen-dining room; my one-room apartment is combined, it has multi-purpose. As you come into my living room you see the rug, it has an early Christian motif: two birds facing in the same direction, and a lamb sits under them. In the living room, to your right, is the gas range upon which I cooked the rice, and soup, and vegetarian foods which I got used to for economical reasons during the first year of my stay at this residence. Please look near the gas range. You will see the black umbrella, the one the neighbors see me with at ten in the morning departing for my job in the Metropolitan Museum. I used it today—it is raining and cold. Now please turn around, completely—you see the bed and the closet space, which I built myself. Now turn back please. When you come in, to your left, you pass by the bathtub. Directly opposite, to your right, is the fireplace.

The fire is beautiful. I sit before the bathtub opposite the fire and I see things in it: Wagnerian operas about Teutonic folks. I see shapes burning, wild hair, the flames remind me of sagas about Brunhilde, and about long, white sun-hair, the way the chicks must have worn it in those Teutonic times. How do I feel about the Germans? After all, they uprooted me, fucked me up for a long time. Apparently I am just coming out of the result of what they did to me; but should I hate them? Shall I hate men for being susceptible to lies? Shall I hate the guy because he belonged to a country which eventually took over Europe? The government, which was usually there to help him make a living—slowly, then suddenly, within a matter of 5 years, 'those guys' took over the government and the government then proceeded and took over the society, the country. But isn't that very similar to what some people think *our* government is doing? Doesn't it seem that this country is being taken over by a certain type of mentality—and this mentality is taking over the government, and the style of life of such men are reflected in the way we all think? The businessmen, bankers, avaricious men who look at you and tell you not to eat two sandwiches, but one. I just do not fit with this type of mentality any longer since I woke up and cut loose from the way you are supposed to think.

Here in America there is an air of sexual malversion. The laws say that we cannot go up to a chick in the street and say, "Hi, I like the way you look." Or a chick is not usually prone to come up to a guy and fondle his ears just because she feels like it. Everyone is a little stilted. No one is free of it. Chicks put on a big act; yet a chick is coming to live with me, an American chick. Jolly, who is an ex go-go dance chick—she made more than $100 dancing in 'The Cage.' She sounds like a B-girl. She is Irish, with reddish hair, and wants to get away from home (somewhere in Buffalo), probably from a *dull* home consisting of father, mother and sisters. She is moving in with me and it will by my third experience at living together with a woman—Alma, Mignone and now Jolly.

Arthur invited her from somewhere and she has been living with him, but apparently he did not feed her very well. He was contemptuous of her! A gorgeous Irish redhead wants to live with him and he is contemptuous of her! He never kept food in his refrigerator. I went over there once and saw Jolly eating rice and beans.

Jolly came over on Monday. She hasn't slept with Arthur at all and hasn't slept at his apartment for two nights. She slept with someone else, she told me. I would like to remember that along with living here, she is a person and can do and should do whatever she wants. I will let her go around with other men. I shall give her exactly thirty days to have relations with me and in the meanwhile I'll try to make love to other chicks. The question is, will my money last? Will I be able to manage to bring home the bread and will it feed two people?

Once in a while I buy something nice or go somewhere I like but that is not often because I'd rather stay home and read or write. I am not trying to eat up all of New York City, and I hope that she will withdraw money in moderation, because I don't have much.

When Jolly was here, Sally came in and we turned on. Sally had a horrid recollection. She recalled that her aunt who lived with them had cancer, and she had to be bathed and cleaned and her mother did it. And Sally had to help her when she was a little girl. She did not dare to cry or scream; her feelings were all bottled up. She screamed inside and when she turned around she had on a beautiful friendly-contorted smile, but behind it she was in terror, in great turmoil and inner pain. Now when she smiles she cannot stop crying. But meanwhile she is smiling and cannot change her face—it is frozen into a continuous smile.

As Sally told the story Jolly was sitting nearby and all of a sudden Sally cried. The tears rushed out of her eyes and I took her in my arms. Jolly jumped up and embraced us, the two of us, and we embraced each other. The moment was very beautiful.

Life has become beautiful. I see people and feel them. We interact. We come together, sense each other and cry for all the lonely hours we spent alone. I realize how we can make something of the life we have and live at this time. We become sacredly humanists.

My life is quite exciting; Jolly makes it so because she might live here. Actually Arthur met her at a party given by a Peruvian fellow. She went to him for a weekend and this is the second week she is staying with Arthur. He likes it but moneywise it tightens him because he doesn't have a steady salary from the part-time teaching job he got a short while ago. I offered to let Jolly move to my house. I told Arthur to tell her I would like to see her.

Jolly came, and I asked her: "Would you like to live here with me?" I explained, she could stay here, I'd feed her and she could clean up once in a while—but she would not have to do so all the time. She could cook for us, but she will not have to cook all the time, I will also cook. She asked, "Would that mean that I'd have to make love with you?" and I said, "No, not necessarily, but eventually I am bound to start."

I explained to her what I thought about her morality, i.e., she thought it was a big deal if a woman has sex relations with a man, but I think a woman gets just as much enjoyment as a man does and that is all that counts.

She asked: "You mean that it is natural for a woman and a man to sleep together and have sex?" I said "Yes, that is exactly what I mean." And she replied: "Why then do you want me to do such an unnatural thing as to get contraceptives?" I answered, "It is like eyeglasses. It improves sex." "Alright, I see," she said.

Now if she comes over this will really be a heavenly place.

I also explained the money situation—that I get tips from the Metropolitan Museum of Art restaurant, which I put into my box without counting it, and whenever I need money I just dig into the box and take as much as I need. My salary—$30 weekly—is for rent, my car expenses, electricity, phone, and gas bills. Whatever overage exists, I use to buy some clothes, or something for the apartment.

Now things are beautiful. They are suspended in the air, somehow the whole thing will resolve. The chick is making up her mind. She knows other boys and might move over with another fellow who invites her, or just stick with Arthur for as long as he can take it. But she said the other guys (five or six fellows with whom she has been living) told her she didn't have to have relations with them when she moved in, but later threatened to throw her out if she didn't. So she gave in, slept with them, and could live with them from then on.

I just emptied the little shelf which I found when I came here to Mott Street, the little shelf upon which I cooked with the cheap electric heater (before that I lived out of grocery bags). After I emptied it, I put a box on it for my squirrel. I had found him in the street and named him Peanuts. He will live here. I'll make a little ladder and bring some pine needles from the forest for him.

Not everybody has the things I have—like a burglar alarm, and a dimming system so the light can be modulated. The place is little, but it has five windows, a fireplace, an inside toilet, a bathtub, a sink and a gas stove—all in working order. I am really making this place into an extraordinary little palace. There is a tree in front of my window, and I see in the next house a swimming pool, a private swimming pool to look at. We were watching with Mignone as it was set up. With her, we often looked through the window to our garden.

I brought this place alive, and it is really showing. This used to be a building, just a building. It was a gray, drab, unkempt place and it was that way until I washed the windows, the six little squares on the front door of the house. I washed them on a coldish spring morning, and gradually things started to happen: I cooked up a plan and promised the tenants I would make a little garden in our front yard, and I made one.

I went to the forest where my cousin Cely has her house. I went deep into the woods and found a bush of ferns with long green leaves. Beads of dew were still glistening on them as I dug them out carefully and brought them home with a big bag of peat moss. I dug up one corner of our yard consisting of gaunt, unproductive soil, mixed into it the peat moss from the forest, and made out of it a fertile productiveness.

Ed Regy, the pacifist who lives downstairs, scattered grass seeds over the whole fertile land, and planted a bushlike plant similar to a marijuana plant. I transplanted my ferns from the forest in one of the corners, and around the garden in a foot-wide strip of soil I planted tulips and four kinds of flowers. It was marvelously beautiful in its own way, a spot of green with multicolored flowers in it. Then I planted a tree (just like I have in front of my window) in the middle of it, a wild tree which in New York grows out of the holes in the sidewalk.

After the garden was finished, I cleaned up the rest of the front yard and washed above my floor all the windows of the house. But people were trying to come into this little garden by breaking our house door but I wore them out. I went there every afternoon to repair the breaks which they made. Afterward we put in the bell. That was the first thing we did, Alfred and I, on a warm spring morning.

And when the spring started in earnest, I had some extremely heavenly days here, falling in love with Mignone. It was so beautiful, my last European motherly-type lover.

Now it is fall, so I brought manure from Cely, and I mixed it into the earth last week. She was here today and brought me some bulbs. Tomorrow I will plant them into the garden, and the bulbs shall bear flowers, and the grass will be green, the flowers will burst into blooms, my tree will leaf out next spring and . . . I hope to fall in love with a girl again like last spring with Mignone. She came last night before going to the airport, and gave me her body. But her mother sends her to France, and I have only a memory . . .

Wow, I am so high!!! For a while at least I shall not have one relationship; I want to have many women at once, I will go to bed with many little birds. But now I will not remain alone, I am thinking of supporting a chick, I will be living with Jolly, and then I will give a party. I will invite everyone I know, and we will turn on with Alfred's best pot, and I will put up as much money as needed to make the best meal for my friends. We'll eat until we can't move; and then we'll listen to any music we want—we can dance—or listen to classical music, or do anything we want. And then, after that party, I will put up my enlarger and make a scaffolding for the trays in my bathtub and take out my camera, buy some film and start taking pictures. I will work and see what comes out. But now I am high and will go to sleep, for tomorrow is another day, my last work day, Sunday, the least-pleasant day of the week. Anyway, good-night.

I had an interesting conversation today at the restaurant; three khaki-clad young army-men, pfc's, sat at a table; I gave them excellent service; and afterwards I asked: "Are they treating you well in the army?"

"Sometimes yes, sometimes no."

"You like it then?"

"No."

"But you like it enough to stay?"

"Yes, but there is no choice about it, we have no choice."

"How about conscientious objection?"

"You see, we are college graduates, and if we plead CO, we shall have that on our records, and we won't be able to get ahead in business, because that will follow us throughout our lives, wherever we may work."

"Then you won't get ahead in business with a conscience. Right?"

"No, not exactly. You see, we are college graduates and we are going into business, and we won't be promoted with conscientious objection on our records."

"But if you have a conscience you cannot get promoted there, isn't that what you said?"

"Yes, I guess that is true."

And that was the extent of it.

Today I went to visit my cousin Cely, and her husband let me feel the difference between our ways of life. But I am much happier now than before.

I had once been a very unhappy young man. Because of my love for Alma. We went to Queens College for two years. We were happy together, but when she left me everything reminded me of her, so I had to quit college, only for a while, I thought. I wanted to sustain my own needs without my mother's help and made my decisions with the help of my therapist.

I started to look for employment, filled out countless applications, searched the *New York Times* help-wanted columns daily, went to employment agencies, all in vain, without success. After I gave up hope of finding a position, I took odd jobs, cleaning offices, being a messenger boy. Then I learned photography, and could not find a job in that field either. I was on the verge of committing suicide. Then I decided to stop satisfying others' wishes and started satisfying my own. I gave up my expensive three-room apartment in Queens for which I had to take my mother's money, and took an apartment on Mott Street because it was cheap. I rebuilt the corroded apartment and decided to make it the scenery of my life. I built my own furniture and I am still building it, and I am proud that I am doing all this by myself. And I am having a better life now than before. There are more people around me, I have relationships with them, and my character is changing because I am loosening up, I am able and dare to reveal more of myself. I can relax and not get upset when someone does not like me right away.

High again, beautiful sensation all over my guts. I am becoming braver for an instant, I am becoming convinced of my convictions, I know I am right and want to live the way I want to. I want to be a lover, a quiet, non-boasting lover who will be craved by the women whom he meets. And I want to be a writer and will write as I go along.

Tomorrow I am going to work again. I work to buy the admission-price into society, the ticket to the great theater of life, the great game. But now I am lonely . . .

33

Today is Thursday. Tuesday morning, on my day off, I went over to Sally with the intention of spending a day with her, if Adam was not home. But he was, and they were very low in mood. I felt they were miserable together and needed a third person to loosen up the gloom that was between them. I was with them almost all day.

To begin with, Adam told me, their lovemaking is not good. He said, "Sally and I are kissing, she grabs my hand and puts it between her legs and says touch me, and I feel I am turned off, she makes me feel unsexy." I just listened. He was apparently still in love with another girl who was religious and 'loved Jesus,' but she left the place they were at, without any explanation or saying good-bye.

Then a year passed, a miserable year; he was lonely, cut off from everybody. When he met Sally, it was a 'rebound reaction,' they never felt surging love, a falling in love, they never felt the sparks flying, but they stayed together and a warm steady love developed between them. As Sally put it, there was no 'swosh' to it. Gradually they were often fighting, and became argumentative, and presently all day they are on the verge of arguments. I felt it between them. Adam said there is a question about their staying together, it has no point to it because they are making each other miserable. He thinks of going to Canada alone and leaving Sally here in New York. As the day wore on, I noticed how little they were in contact.

All together we had a good day. We went to shop, and I made a salad. Towards the evening I built a fire, and Vivian, the little six-year-old girl from next door, Alfred, Jolly, and Willie came over. We all ate on the rug in front of the fire and listened to the Indian music on the tape recorder. I felt happy, sitting around. People just came over, they sought me out. The whole thing arranged itself, and as the moments wore on it was delicious. Later Alfred brought pot; we got high, and Sally said: "Let's go for a drive, Andrew." We went down to my car, but I was not sure I wanted to drive and Adam jumped in and drove us. It was difficult to drive for we were stoned. There was a tremendous tension in the air, and as we were driving, Sally started to sing in that tense atmosphere in the car. She kept singing, and as her voice kept on it became mellower, and more cheerful. It was like a constant protective lightning rod, it dissipated the nervousness that we were all feeling.

After the drive, as we went back to my pad, there was an expectation in Sally that I and she can make Adam jealous. But on the sidewalk, I simply walked alongside Adam instead of Sally. I stayed away from her as much as I could. In my pad there was a complete silence for a long time. We were sitting in the middle of the room, Sally up on my bed reading. As I looked up at her, and saw her round ass on the bed I said quietly to Adam, "Good figure your woman has, she has a marvelous ass," and with a quiet sincere expression he replied thoughtfully: "I'm so glad to know you, Andrew." When they were leaving, as Sally walked out the door, she gave me a significant smile, a quiet kissing look, and I felt good.

After Sally and Adam left, Jolly and Willie were leaving also. Then Alfred told me Willie has plans; he will fix Jolly up with clients and she can make a little money for both, for him and herself. Alfred mentioned that the boys who hang out with Willie will show Jolly what reality can be, and when she has suffered a little, she will be glad to come and live with me again.

Jolly has been living with me for a few days. But after she helped herself to a dress from my food money, and left me with one pound of rice, and she did not want to make love with me, I kicked her out of this place. She left that same night and apparently slept with some guy. I forgot all about it as soon as I calmed down. But ever since she has been calling me up, some of the calls fairly inconvenient; two of those times there were women here, and when I said I could not speak to her long, she got jealous, came rushing here to verify that I really had a chick. But I do not want to live with her anymore.

Alfred is a very nice guy, and I could not have done the things I am doing, the experiences I am having, without his 'patronage.' He understands me, and I am beginning to see who he is and how he loves me.

And I love him. The talks we have are phenomenal, and as I am confronted with his philosophy, many of my own walls of puritanical turpitude simply melt. He says: "People are crazy. Some are happily crazy, some are miserably crazy, some are harmfully crazy . . . Some are helpfully crazy, and that I am." I answered, "Yes, crazy things are done, because people are crazy. If a man tells you he will torture you or shoot you unless you put on this fancy set of clothes made in khaki color, and take this weapon, and kill those men across the sea, people you never knew existed, never did you or your country harm or wrong, then 'he' must be crazy." But he said, "Anything that man does is human. Wars are human. Men castrating is human, priests castrating themselves, they are human."

A human being, perhaps every organism, has its own reality. Their reality is their craziness. Going crazy is volitional. I can be neurotic if I want to by simply doing things which make me neurotic, and follow a neurotic path. It did once and it still could make me neurotic. All I have to do is to start counting my tip money at the day's end, expect myself to make a certain amount of money, and get upset when I do not reach my expectations. Try to boast and to lose the 'respect' of friends when I do not perform according to expectations. Try not to get as much loving and lovemaking as I feel like, considering the chick a hussy, either inferior, or untouchable. To be by myself a lot, I would start to choke again which is what happened to me. Or if I would stop feeling and mechanize my life, develop a dull routine of hour by hour living, rushing around for positions, trying to better my life but starving to death, trying to get materialistic with sole-less shoes trotting around for jobs. To get into a spiral groove, to become other-motivated, to become anxious in other people's company because there is 'silence' between us, if I would look in the streetbaskets for newspapers and so know the news, and read them to impress others, to win them over in arguments, I could become neurotic as I was. Or to bind my attention on books again, to find out about the world from the media, through symbol, to keep learning, to keep taking courses, to know every conceivable answer to the troubles of the world, but not to be able to realize and do something about my very own life. Or, to have mechanical, completely manipulable pleasures, like only classical music, nothing that is a challenge, an original creation. To lie about my past when applying for a job, to try to stop thinking about the past and present and gloss over it. When I do what I did I could simply become crazy again. But I am not, because I don't want to be, and refuse.

And all this, to the best of my knowledge, is part of my therapy, my physiotherapy, and my chemotherapy in the form of pot and eventually LSD. That is where Alfred learned to be such 'fun to be with.' Every man can be a good man, all you have to do is get on a good trip. Many possibilities come to me as I get on my good pot trip. As soon as my trip bears fruit, I can keep writing, I can develop my photography, I can interpret my world, with visuals and the word, or I can become a social worker to help people like myself . . .

Today it looked like, and was, just another ordinary working Saturday. But during coffee hour there was a girl at my working table, a pretty girl, whom I saw as I was expecting my guests. I had nothing to do until then, so I talked with her about many things. She was troubled, lonely, neurotic, and was in dismay several times. I really did not dare to continue at times, and yet went back, and talked the usual meeting questions—about art, whether there were valid standards of art appreciation. I saw so clearly that she was mixed up but did not dare ask her to meet me for a long time. Then my guests arrived. I served them and had to leave her.

After my work she was waiting for me, and we went for a coffee. Then I could observe her. She had shoes with very high heels in which she almost couldn't walk, with net stockings on her nice legs. She wore a brown little tight suit, with a fur collar. Her hair was black with graying stripes in it, and somewhat straightened and put in perfect order. She has a sweet, little-girl's face, a sweet dreamy and innocent little face, and she looked like a little suffering Madonna when she was in torment, in anguish, or she might have wanted to make me have

37

pity on her, which was very difficult to tell from her mimicry. She goes from personality to personality, like a chameleon changing colors.

In the coffee shop I engaged her in real conversation. She responded to me apparently truthfully, but several times I lost what she was saying because she did not speak clearly enough. I knew she was troubled and was on a terrible trip; that is how I know that I am on a terrific trip, because I am able to help a girl like her. She said she is innocent, lives aboveboard as she knows how and has been in mental hospitals twice, tries not to have secrets (her Dr.'s advice). She was rattling a mile a minute about someone who is mystical, who told her all kinds of things, he was superduper, was a genius and a guru and a doctor and a plumber wrapped all into one, and this marvelous person, who apparently is in the underground, had to do with losing money, $2,000, because of some information she leaked about him to some supposed stranger and she felt so guilty. She was making a fantasy out of reality, or reality out of fantasy, or someone wants to get money from this sick girl.

The guy took her to a chess club, and the owner of the place could not match him with any of the players who came in, because the guy won over them all, he knows many languages, a battery of them, and the girl buried me in a torrent of verbiage, never ending, never ceasing verbiage, about this unknown god.

As she was talking I drew her into reality. She said she lives in the Bronx with her mother and is at home by 8 every night. In the mornings, she is a social worker, and after, takes a graduate course at CCNY. As she was talking, her mind went loose towards pleasant memories and she became beautiful. She had trust in me, looking at her beautiful little child's hands, reaching toward me, like begging, 'please help me.' She said I seem very sweet, but I told her, "I am a waiter." She thought I was impersonating maybe a movie director doing research on the details of a restaurant, or I was an artist, but her mind started to cut facts, and went back to her troubles. The waiter started walking around our table. I was nervous, but I kept my cool. There she was talking, and I was selling her the idea that she had no need to be guilty, and she should have forgiven the guy for disguising himself as a doctor, or appearing to be a plumber instead of what he really was, an impostor.

Then the waiter said, "I wish you would leave." He asked, "Will you have anything else?" and I told him, "No, we are just sitting." But I asked him if he needed the table, and he said yes, he wished we would leave. I grabbed the check, but Evelyn smiled, "I'd like to finish my tea." I told him, "We will leave soon, but not immediately." The waiter's lips began to tremble as he said, "You have to leave now. Why don't you leave immediately?" "Because I do not have to," I answered. He said "But you have to leave." "I shall leave soon," I said, "but not immediately." The guy walked away in a silent rage. I turned to Evelyn and she said "tatatata." She continued the conversation as if nothing had occurred. I felt my face whiten but did not move a muscle. I was close to a fight and my adrenalin supply reacted. My heart was racing, I could hear it. Then Evelyn reacted, she started crying. I gave her my handkerchief, and she cried sobbingly, or else was acting. I did not know whether she was simulating terror, or whether she really felt it . . . reality is a tenuous film.

I have to be positive in life, not negative . . .

In the morning, as always on my day off from work, I started a big cleaning job, when Alfred called, excited, asking me to pick him up at Anny's. There I was made comfortable, Anny gave me good pot, and we got into conversation with the guys who were there.

After a while Alfred asked me to drive him and Anny to some places. I drove them stoned to the lower East Side. There Alfred asked me to pick up a box at one address, and then to deliver packets from it to several places. As we went from place to place, we had a good time, I driving and delivering, and then on to the apartment of a 'beautiful' guy who lives in a sunny apartment on the lower East Side. He must pay hundreds of dollars for it, and must have LSD parties. There were clearly symbolized pictures on the wall, war-like destructions juxtaposed with sylvan scenes, men bathing in a pond, a girl in a bucolic scene.

There were beautiful people there, the kind of people I always admire in the lower East Side, beautiful girls, with smooth tan skin. There was one—a little girl with almond eyes and long straight black hair—who spoke engagingly and I felt when she spoke to me she felt what she was saying to me. And there were healthy looking young guys, well fed, sensitive, and somehow natural, not unindividualistic. Meanwhile Alfred and Anny were waiting in my car as I went to a few more places. For last, we all went into an apartment, and there they were talking to a man about some Canadian business arrangement which involved Canadian money. When we came out of there, Alfred asked me to come with them to a "beautiful festive supper," for which they were trying to get money from some people without success, as Alfred explained. And while we were driving, he asked me to "chip in twenty dollars for it." Since I refused, Alfred said, "then we cannot have it." Then I felt they were trying to play with my mind, they were trying to milk me for money. Perhaps they thought: if they indicated that I would be able to make love to Anny or have some delicate and extra sort of psychedelic orgiastic experience, I would give money. Altogether I was wondering about Alfred's having approached me with such attitude, when both of them, Anny and Alfred, asked me to "go change some Canadian dollars to greenbacks" for them. I refused, and then I realized they were using me, the whole time they were using me to pick up, or deliver pot or some dope, pounds of it. The whole time I did not know this, I did not realize it until I remembered last year's packages when Alfred took Anny's little son to places. This is the guy who has my confidence, who can come into my apartment (I gave him my keys), and borrow my car anytime.

Wherever I go, wherever I am, whatever I hear, whatever I see brings back memories from my past.

When Alfred used me to deliver his dope, when the other day I was

40

in that beautiful sunny apartment, I saw an almond-eyed girl and she reminded me of Alma. I remember how I suffered, not daring, not being able to let Alma go. Now, still, after years, something deeply murmuring brings a deep woundlike pain into my lung area.

Alma had almond eyes. She was here on a college scholarship from the Near East. When we met in Queens College, she was boarding in an unpleasantly located house, with a terrible family, in a dark back room with a little sink for a bathroom, and outside toilet privileges. From the ceiling in her room, hanging on an electric wire, was a small, single lightbulb. By that light she did her studying. We had been in love many months when I found out the conditions under which she was living. I offered her to move near me, and she did, but most of the time she stayed in my three-room apartment.

After two years of being together she told me she had to register at Columbia University for necessary subjects which were not taught in Queens College, and therefore she had to move near there. I helped her find a good room, I moved her there. The next day I bought a little radio for her as a present, and went with it to her. I rang the door-bell, I knocked on her door, but she did not open it for me, yet I knew she was at home.

Dear reader: bit by bit, I hope, you will get the picture. You see, I have to refeel some of my life, some painful period of my life. I don't dare poke my head into the past, it is too daring, it will hurt and I am postponing it . . . But I have to go back into my past, to 1944. During the Nazi occupation I was nine years old. On a hot summer day my mother told me that I had to leave home with a lady for a strange place, but she would come for me in a few days. She kissed me and hugged me and gave me a big bag of delicious candy. And I saw her smile as I went away with the strange lady, who was a nurse.

The nurse took me by train from Budapest to a place called Visegrad and from the train, after a long walk up on a hill under the hot sun, to a huge, strange-looking building complex. There I saw priests in long robes, and many boys dressed in long gray uniforms which were too small on some boys, on the others too big. All the boys had

41

their hair almost completely cut off, but not evenly cut. It was cut so that their hair looked like steps on their heads. I had on well-cut summer shorts with sandals, and my blond hair was cut in style.

The lady who took me there turned me over to a priest, and she left.

The priest told me to go to the boys outside, and I did. When the boys saw that I had candy, they all asked for it. In the evening we went to sleep and nobody kissed me good-night. I cried in the dark.

I found out the boys there were delinquents and I had been left in a reformatory. I was waiting for my mother to come for me, but she never came. I was punished there, so I thought I was a delinquent, I must have done something bad, that my mother had sent me there to be punished. She sent me away from her, she did not love me, she did not want me anymore. But what did I do? I didn't know.

After the war, I got back to our house. I rang our door-bell. A strange lady opened our door, and when she saw me she said to me, go away. She didn't let me in. And Alma didn't let me in either. I knew then that she did not love me anymore. But why? What did I do to her?

Today after I came home from work Alfred came into my home. I told him, "I really did many favors for you, but I will stop doing them, especially driving you around. As your philosophy goes, it takes time for them to get hooked, but once they come, they continue coming." He made himself comfortable and asked, "What are you talking about?" Looking at me with the presumption of innocence, he said, "First take a good breathful of smoke." But I told him, "I am done with wondering about the world, I am done with understanding you, and taking the frightened little boy position with the idea that I do not know what it is all about." And I told him, "I know what it was all about with the packages." He tried to interrupt me, but I continued, "For me to live with a life-philosophy which is not rooted in truth is a burden. Whatever a life-philosophy is—it may be a religion, or a belief of triumph of power, or hedonism, or action à la Mussolini, or any ridiculous neurotic set of dogmas—first of all it has to work for the man who espouses it."

Alfred listened to me and said, "Basically the human being must be 'happy,' must think well of himself, and must maintain himself in the future." I told him, "My philosophy declares: Be honest. Be good. Be kind. Give." And he answered, "For me it declares: Receive, do what you want to do, and do not make self-sacrifices. Andrew, it is better for you to conform." I thought and answered: "I am beginning to see that well-being is a matter of attitude. Attitude is a matter of what I believe is true for me. If what is true for *me* and is not true for the reality around me, human as well as natural, and if I would conform, I will start going 'crazy.' " Alfred interrupted me and said, "Unless you rearrange your life in such a way that you conform to a new identity and reality." I told Alfred, "I will never do that. I am not adopting a new identity. I am happy with my own brand of Andrewism and the slogans from the previous periods in my life. I want and will stay honest." Alfred was angry and said, "You adopt my sex theories." I answered: "Sometimes you restrain people, and sometimes you maintain a great deal of force. You make them frustrated, you titillate them with sex, you frighten them with it, you use it constantly in imagery, you substitute images for the sex act to aid in selling your products, your dope." I told him, "You can influence people to take your dope. You can force some people to conform to your standards, and they are willing to spend their lives with it and then their scenery becomes a perpetuating force. They build buildings, get power, interrelate with departments of the nations wherever they are, and sanction wars in holy names—and perpetuate the Bowery. They are priests. But is it good for humanity?"

And Alfred left without an answer.

But I met Alfred a little while ago: he looked at me strangely. Anything may happen at any moment, but I have answers for most eventualities. I seem to keep my mental life in remarkable equilibrium, as my living forces shrivel under the burden of "our way of life." I'd like to sink back into pure existence. From the point of view of a child when I wanted things, then my parents gave me what I wanted. Now I must learn to accept people for what they are.

Days go by. Sally called me this evening; she said Adam does not want her . . . he wants her to move out. So while Adam and Sally fight, while they realize that they are not mature enough to arrest the perpetuation of their hangups, and while they decide to separate, I can be a good guy, I can be the man who waits, who helps, who is magnanimous and most likely will get to live with the darling calendar girl, a most beautiful Jewish girl and twenty, all aflame, with a mane of thick black hair, sizable breasts, a lovely round plump ass, probably white and full of little unpredictable dimples, a chick who spent time in Israel being the 'woman' of a kibbutznik, a chick who will follow me over hell and high water, a woman who is using me to get her husband back.

She wants to live here, nearby, and have her husband get jealous because then she can make him more servile to her wishes. The guy is working for her without her getting a job. Sally feels that there is an endless supply of beautiful things in store for her, that men are angels who hold a conelike basket from which endless amounts of diamonds tumble out. All she has to do is ask, and take them. She does anything she wants and nothing that she doesn't want, and Adam supports her. Since he is too sick mentally to pay attention to her, she goads him on, she makes him jealous. This might be Sally's game, but if she plays it skillfully enough, I will engage her in it, and love her up good, and if she wants, we can play jealousy trips with Adam's head.

Yes, I am insane too. I just noticed how I slid from a nice humanitarian healthy trip, how it changed in my mind, into a cool calculating Queens trip, the kind of a trip from which I had to go to psychotherapy. I really want Sally's body, but there would not be anything unpleasant about that as long as it would really benefit Sally and Adam

. . . Still . . . I will be cool and gainfully calculating, using situations to be able to live better . . .

Yesterday, when I was writing about Sally and Adam, I went back into the past.

I remember the last semester with Alma at Queens College. We attended day classes together, but Alma needed one subject which was not given there, so she decided to take it at night at Columbia University. I took her there by car and waited, each session, for her until her class was over.

In the beginning she would come out right after class; but later she had laboratory experiments to do, she said, which took two-three hours to complete. I would wait, feeling sorry for her enduring those long study hours. When she came out, we'd hug and kiss and drive home tired, starved, but happy. After our meal, she made passionate love to me. We were very happy together.

But soon I moved her near Columbia the following semester, she did not want to speak to me anymore. Finally, I was able to reach her, and she told me she did not love me anymore—not since she had met her teacher at the beginning of the term at Columbia. She said she did not stay there those long hours because of laboratory experiments but because she was making love with that man. Then I realized she was gainfully calculating, using me to have a better life, a better communication medium with my car, to have good warm meals which I prepared with love for her. All the time that she was pretending to love me, she was using me.

I must tell you people, I felt so cold, so ice cold after Alma deceived and deserted me. Once, I was so lonely that about three in the morning, I called the telephone operator, and asked her to speak to me for a moment, because I felt I was going out of my mind. And she did. She asked me where I was studying, and where I was living, and she said, "I have a daughter studying in Queens College," and then I felt better.

Yesterday, remembering all that, I had to stop writing.

I turned the clock around this morning and decided to live the day unaccountably, on subjective, 'natural' time. I started to play with my own head. I would like to get lost in life, like a doe in the woods, like when I was a child and a moment could go on forever. I must communicate with my child self . . . I must forgive my mother for sending me away. I have never forgiven her. I love her and at the same time hate her. I must relive the times when I was sent away to Visegrad, I must speak Hungarian again, "beszélni kell magyarul," I must remember my friends. I must remember Köves Tomi, and Köves néni. Who were these people? I must remember the people who were around me, I must recall the names, or at least the images and character of those priests, and I must understand how I felt there. Where was I? Where was I really? Do I feel any of the things which I felt then? Why? I must refeel the things that happened, that is the challenge. This would be 'beneficial,' but will I ever be able to do it? It is possible. I must go on writing, I must describe myself and consider my health. I must create something out of myself, I must become well again.

I went over to Adam's. He was in torment and told me about his life of misery with Sally. She did not accept him. She did not accept his love. She did not want to make love to Adam. She emasculated him. There is a glass wall between them, "so I kicked her out of the house." That was what he said. But his world is coming apart, because the government is after him. They want him to do something irrational, they want him to get into khaki uniform and fight those thin little men in Asia, the Vietnamese, he told me all this. And I said, "The world wants to tear itself apart, and if you start tearing yourself apart because the world is doing it, you do not help matters, you just add to the misery." He agreed and calmed down as I continued: "You cannot change the world, so the best thing is to fend for yourself, maintain your own integrity. Live in society but do not subscribe to all its tenets." He was more relaxed then, and I said, "They are crazy in the world, 15% of the people in the world are crazy, they are preparing to burn us all up, and the only way to contrive to combat them is to start to be happy. I am taking kids to Chinatown tomorrow—come along with us." I came home, went up to the Negro family and asked the mother of the three children if I could take her children to Chinatown tomorrow evening and she said happily, "Yes." I will take some children, somewhere, every month to begin with.

Today, after my work, I went over to Adam to talk with him, and ask him to come to Chinatown. In his apartment the air was thick with pot and cigarette-smoke. Sally was just sitting there, and as I talked with Adam, she hugged me. When Adam saw that he tried to freak me out by staring at me. I looked right back at him and said, "Hey, I don't want to take Sally away from you. I like her, but she is yours and I am a good man." He answered, "Take her away, she closes up as soon as we are alone, she doesn't want to make love to me. I kicked her out of bed last night." I felt very friendly towards him, and asked whether he wanted to come to Chinatown. He refused. But Sally decided to come.

I went up for the three colored children, Joseph and James and the third, the 'little' one. Their father said, very calmly, their (the children's) mother prohibited them from going, and she was out at this time. I urged him to let me take his children, I would take care of them, it would be safe, and we would have a lot of fun. He repeated the mother's wishes. The children were polite and calm, but somehow pathetic and sad. Their eyes said, "We are only children, we would like to go very much, but crazy adults do not have any sense," and I left. I was somehow depressed and decided to find other children and take them places.

Little Vivian was waiting at my door, and Willy was coming too. As we were walking in Chinatown, tension crept into me. Perhaps because I was jealous of Willy who was getting along so nicely with Sally. He simply took Adam's place and she let it happen.

47

By the time we got back to my house with Sally, I was tense and nervous, and she started to behave like a little girl, saying, "I am so unhappy." She told me her side of their life. She said, "All of Adam's frustrations and tensions seem to come out through his sex. He forces me to make love to him, and I feel nothing. When he makes love to me, I feel I am making love to someone anxious." Then I honestly wanted to have sex with her. She said, "Build a fire." I built a fire, took off my shirt. We were close together, and she asked whether I had some music. I turned on my radio, and she said, "It is too hot." She opened the window, and then said, "It is late, I have to go home." I offered to let her sleep here, but she left. It was late and I did not walk her home.

Last night went as follows: at eight o'clock, as I was writing, Alfred pounded at my door. We had a man-to-man talk about honesty and how he used Anny and me to deliver his dope. I told him, I want to relate to chicks but to their benefit in a completely equalitarian, humanistic and man-woman oriented relationship. Alfred and I cooled out, when Sally called me and wanted to come over. She was very tense, and Alfred offered her a drag on his pipe, but she refused, and Alfred said, "Just one little drag." She took it and gradually relaxed. I started a meal. We were making conversation and Alfred took that little girl and softened her up. We threw compliments at her, she believed them and was encouraged at every instant, and took over the cooking. We had green peppers, onions and cabbage, all fried. After the meal she felt like writing a poem to me. This is what she wrote: "With an umbrella for a parachute,/ Andrew Bihaly you dropped into my mind/ you had to move through a hurricane/ and a jello-a swamp/ Andrew Bihaly/ but twinkly-dinkly/ My third eye turned all over/ And saw you landing on a Hors D'oeuvre."

When the place was in a terrific mess from the furious cooking, and after we ate, Alfred slipped out. I fixed the tape-recorder and we started to sing, Sally with mellowness, and I felt a childlike happiness as we sang well-known Hebrew songs, which I learned when I was a young boy. I told her that my father had a nice voice and I sang a song which I learned from him. She liked it. I told her, "I will preserve this tape which will remind me of our togetherness."

We were lying on the rug in the middle of the room before the fire. I kissed her. She said, "I don't feel like kissing, Andrew." I snuggled up to her but she pulled away from me as soon as she noticed that we were close to each other. I could not make love to Sally, although everything, the mood, my feeling, and her provocative behavior, was perfect for it. I took her to the subway, and as she left she told me she felt happy and romantical.

My squirrel, Peanuts, is here on my shoulder. He sits peacefully, a little frightened by my cat Tom, but not by my typewriter. I think gradually they might make peace, the squirrel and the cat.

Sally came over again. I cooked a good meal. She coquetted with me but when I moved toward her she moved away. She was teasing me. So I said to her, "I am a human being and I have needs too, and I am not going to sacrifice myself for you as Adam did." She said, with angelic innocence, "I don't understand you, Andrew." But I continued without excitement, "Whenever we are with Adam, you are flirting with me to make him uncomfortable, but you made me that way also." And she said, "Andrew, I don't want you to think that I've been using you," and I said, after a long silence, "I don't want to think that either." So the conversation ended. We finished our meal, but she washed the dishes, and after she made a phone call to her parents, she cooked "for you the supper for tomorrow." I was sitting on the rug and she came to me, bent down to kiss me, and I felt a warm delightful thrill as she went back to the stove.

When Sally finished the cooking, the cleaning up, she came back and put her arms around my neck. I reached my lips to hers in the dark, but our lips did not meet. Then the desire of the hungry male animal for the unconquerable she-animal came over me. I didn't feel love for her at that moment. Frustrated, I was seeking only my satisfaction in that villainous bitch. I stood up and kissed her. She could not resist for I was strong, but her lips were cold and I let her go.

It was late, near midnight. The night was beautiful. I felt that it covered us with its blanket of darkness as I walked her to her house. There she said, "I'll visit you tomorrow." When I came back I felt I was hearing the echo of my loneliness in the quietness of my room.

I am learning to be a lover, but I am confused.

I met Diane, a lovely chick, through Sally, and we met often afterwards. We were very positive about each other, and she came over today. But Alfred came in, and when I bumblingly introduced them to each other, Alfred took things in hand, and is now making love to her. How did I bumble? And how did Alfred do what he did?

In the afternoon, as I was cooking, Diane came, surprisingly, and told me she had been looking in the museum for me. She was told today is my day off, so she came. I told her she must stay for soup-dinner. She was fascinated by what she saw, the furniture which I made, the reproductions on the walls, my plants and my fireplace. She seemed pleasantly impressed. We sat on the carpet before the fire, she, smoking pot, and she said, "Take a toke on my pipe, feel it, it's nice." I asked her, "You know how it makes me feel?" She asked, "How?" and I kissed her, first tenderly, then kissed and kissed her. She said, "I like your lips, Andrew." But then Sally and Alfred came in.

Alfred went to Diane (she was at that time practically sitting in my lap) and admired her hands, admired her ring. I saw the soup boiling, went to the stove and as I was dishing it out for everybody, I saw Alfred still holding Diane's hands. I gave soup to everyone. Alfred was sitting close to Diane, and I sat at Sally's side. There was tension between us.

After we finished eating, I squeezed myself between Alfred and Diane. I felt miserable. Alfred crept over to Diane, who was cuddling my cat. Sally sat alone and proposed to go for ice cream.

We went down to my car. When the two girls went to buy ice cream, Alfred rushed away. He went straight to a flower shop and came back with a white bag. As the girls came back he placed the paper bag into Diane's hand. Alfred made quiet remarks as we drove past a sports car. "That car is a very good car," he said. "It costs 28 or 30 thousand dollars." After a few minutes he said: "I used to race those. I used to race cars."

We drove to Sally's apartment and she went upstairs to pick up Adam. I remained in the back seat and watched the following: Diane asked, "Can I open this?" And Alfred said: "Open it now, it is for you." She found a red rose in the white paper bag. She flirted with the rose, she touched the rose to her lips, then to her throat, to her cheek. He was watching her constantly as waltz music came over loudly on the radio, and Diane got more and more sensually involved in the dreaminess of the situation. I was watching them with an indifferent feeling, with a numbness.

Alfred opened the top of the car and said, "Not too many stars tonight." Then he said, "That would make a sensuous photograph," and pointed to a woman in the washeteria. "It is very beautiful and stimulating, that woman bending." He held hands with Diane, and she seemed to caress his hands sweetly.

When we arrived home, Alfred invited us to his pad where Bill and Anny were waiting. We all went in and Alfred started to clean some pot. I sat next to Diane. I wanted to speak to her—and perceived that Alfred was gaping at me.

My feelings, stemming from humiliation, came to a collision within me and I grabbed and pawed her hands. I pawed her shin, I put my hand on her thighs. I felt like going to bed and making love to her. Then I realized, "I am not alone with her in my room." I put my hands behind me. I became bashful, stood up and jumped back. From then on she did not look my way.

Alfred passed a pipe around, and we all smoked. Then he took some pot and started to process it with a sieve and asked Diane to help him hold a pan under the tea strainer while he dumped the pot into the strainer. What they were doing was not important as long as they were doing it near each other. Alfred meanwhile found the *Four Seasons* of Vivaldi on the radio. I saw them pass the pipe, which was filled with much milder pot than the kind I smoke. I saw them talk softly, I saw them place the red rose into a battered coffeepot, then into a better-looking one.

The light bulb, the naked light bulb, was lit all this time. He stood up and lit the old-fashioned petroleum lamp, which I had given him, and put out the naked light bulb. They talked quietly, and I saw Alfred caress Diane's cheeks, the side of her mouth, very softly, barely touching. Probably he paid her a compliment, while I was watching. Everyone was quiet. We were all listening to the beautiful music. Then Alfred gave us the signal to leave. I left immediately with Bill and Anny, and returned to my pad. Sally and Adam came down later and went home. Out of my frustration, I relieved myself sexually.

Now I know what Alfred did. He copied and did almost exactly the same thing Albert Ellis described in *Sex and the Single Man.* The thing for me is to get my teeth fixed, get a nice set of fashionable winter clothes, buy some mild and powerful pot to mix into a good brew, and a good pipe to smoke it from, and tape a selection of music to coincide with my need to bring moods about. Also, I need my radio back from Alfred.

I have health in me and sickness in me. The health is emotional, positive, straightforward, imprecise, even ambiguously vague. The sickness is factual, intellectual, a dull-feeling. I become gradually sick from the outside and only wake up during the two days of freedom, Monday and Tuesday. My home self looks a certain way, and my Museum self, my uptown self, another way. My home self is unkempt, and the Museum self is rigid, shaven. I comb and brush my hair carefully, but when I come back home I dip it into hot water and go over it with the towel.

My Museum self is a mechanical dummy, meticulously calculating every move by serving the guests, yet my impersonality is an awkward mask. A lot of humanity shows in my job. I have a chance to pick up girls while I work. But I'm cool. I think, "What does the scene look like from an employer's point of view?" So, when all the tables are bussed off, and there are no guests coming, and there is a good enough looking woman around, and she happens to sit at a table where nobody can hear our conversation, I converse with her. I have a chance there to enamor some chicks with my talk.

Things are really happening. In the museum on Sunday, the last draggy day of my working week, I was very tired, I was very wrought-up, I was very agog, but I swung with it. I had chicks, I had hussies, but I haven't had a woman since Mignone left for France. I was telling myself that everything, everything was alright, things are looking up, I have something to look forward to Tuesday. I will be with a woman all day, a beautiful woman I met in the museum, and she works. What does it matter that she works? She is a dazzling woman. It happened this way:

As I was working yesterday, a woman came in. She was beautiful, but her beauty was uncommon in every detail. Everything was perfect on her. Her long hair was pinned up meticulously, her eyebrows arched and lined, her lips carefully made up with specially selected cream-like lipstick. Her dress was designed meticulously and in exquisitely selected colors, especially made for men to look at her—a woman who really tries very hard to please men with her beauty.

She sat at a table, and I went over to help her. She got exquisite service, because all single women become a beautiful affair for me. I flirt with every one of them. I told a few young college girls how beautiful they were, and they giggled. I try to talk to every beautiful woman. I say to them: "Hello," in a most sensuous, inviting manner, yet carefully modulating my words and carefully sticking to the routine of my job as a waiter.

I walked over to this woman and she talked to me. She said, "We all are so lonely, I'd like to see you again." I wrote down my name and

53

phone number and gave it to her. I said, "I'd like to see you; if you call me, you'll make me happy." She said, "I will come back, I will come back another time."

I was called away, did my job, and she was left alone the rest of the time. When she left, she kissed a piece of paper. I was convinced she would leave my address among the napkins on her table, but no, she took it. Now I realize, she kissed my name on the napkin. She left me a note saying: "Want to be with you Tuesday." But Roselle called me up that same evening!

She called me from the Village and said she saw two very sad movies. She cried and she wanted to talk with me. I went right over. She was waiting for me in Nedick's at Eighth Street and Sixth Avenue. I invited her to my pad. She was somewhat anxious as she came to my apartment. When she hesitated, I told her not to worry.

I prepared a meal: fruit salad with sour cream and honey dressing. She talked about Anais Nin and her books. I told her: "You really are involved with symbols," and I shifted our conversation away from symbols, away from negative things like *Guernica*, or *To Die in Madrid*, the two sad films that she saw. I brought it back to ourselves and told her I like to write, and she started to talk again. She said she herself wrote journals when she was in therapy. Her therapist was very handsome and she wrote her thoughts and fantasies in a diary. She fantasied that she became intimate with him. I asked her, "Tell me, did you know anything about him as a person?" She said no, but expressed in so many words how she loved his body, how she liked being with him, but thought he did not like her looks. I said, "I desire you, you are so beautiful, I would love to make you feel good." I wooed this most beautiful woman. I reached out, I kissed her, but she did not want to get into it. Her face was watching me, her eyes were cold, but I kissed her again, and again, and said, "I love the way you are, I want to give you roses, but I only have daisies." I took a flower from the pot and gave it to her. She touched it and kissed my lips, and I caressed her back, fondled her ears. She started to love it and took off her dress for me. Her breasts are little and soft. Her body is soft but brittle. I described to her how she put me aflame, how I desired her, and how I would like to make her happy. We found satisfaction in each other, her knowing lips were making a dance upon my lips. She became a female animal, eagerly finding the kind of pleasure she always wanted. I screamed in ecstasy. The room was spinning, I was dazed.

After a while I woke up and took her home to 77th Street. There I ran into Willy, Alfred's friend. I introduced them and was so proud to be seen with her. We went to her apartment. She had fixed it up artistically with carvings and statues—a little room but she made a beautiful illusion out of it. She has two cats. She told me she was a dress designer before, but for the past two years she has been a nurse. She is doing cardiology and X-ray work. She was vibrant and happy and said, "When I went to your apartment I did not want to make love to you; but from now on I want to. I know I will enjoy it."

Now I have a woman. I must put my place in shape and plant the crocus bulbs which I bought last week. We will have multi-colored flowers with my tulips in the Spring and life can become beautiful again.

I just had another toke and now I am a cheerful guy. This is a wondrous substance. I did not have any yesterday, and tomorrow I want to start a two day's fast. I told Alfred, "I want to establish a sort of pacing-plan, whereby I can enjoy pot to the utmost. When I have enough of it, it stops tasting good—I do not appreciate it so much." He said, "Baloney." I told him, there are many stories afloat why people should not smoke pot. One says that anything artificially induced is undesirable. He said all this is "hog-wash."

He explained, as we were again smoking: "There is an argument for you smoking it, Andrew. You are let out of the dullness that you have been in, your mood changes. You feel comfortable. You become an insightful, sensitive, positively living human being, who likes the company of other human beings. Your thoughts range far and wide when you smoke pot, my pot."

Yes, I am apt to write well when I am high, or perhaps I like myself and I liked the reflection of myself in writing when I am high. That is what may have happened to a girl I once met at a ballet, who gave me *Steppenwolf*. She was a painter, she painted at Cooper Union, and she smoked pot. She said that she started to paint very badly, but meanwhile thought she was painting very well. Then her teachers told her that she was awful; then she stopped getting high, and her painting improved. But Alfred was right: "You are let out of your cage."

What does it mean to "be good?" I want to be good. I want to do good. I decided a long time ago that it would be a regular part of my life to be good in some manner. I do good deeds, but they are sometimes selfish. But aren't all good deeds selfish? Here I live. Should I live for myself? I do good to others inasmuch as I give their lives a lift. They see what ideas I have, I help them and they beautify their homes and their lives. Now Ed Regy is painting and refurbishing his home (with my help), Alfred makes his house into a palace (I gave him my plans, and worked with him), and I am thinking of painting the hallway white. Would these people ordinarily refurbish their houses without my being here?

Alfred. He made $10,000 off dope smuggling. I saw it. It was in a paper bag. He also wants me in the business. There are five of them in the scene. Whenever a run is made, with a rented truck, everyone makes a couple of thousand dollars.

He came down in the morning. He was sweating and told me he needed money—he could make money with truck deliveries. He told me he needed a truck for one day, for which the rental was $15.00. That much he had, but the deposit was $50.00 which he couldn't raise, so he came to me for it. I had the bread. Altogether I gave him fifty dollars—all my money. I trusted him with it and he left.

Later he returned with four other men. He told me the truck was rented. He said he was worried about getting caught. One of the men said, "Go on the route twice. Once with a dummy load, then with the real load. If they catch you with the dummy load, it won't matter." He looked relieved and they all left.

I was home, and it was late, when he returned. He showed me money in a paper bag. He told me it was 10,000 dollars. After telling me the whole story, he suggested that I go into business with him.

I was awake long into the night, I meditated. *Alfred has troubles, he cannot exert sustained efforts, he has claustrophobia. It does not let him hold a job!!! He could hardly build his apartment, except for my help. But why does he hold me back from my plans? Do not worry, do not strive, he says, do not work for the future, do not think of it, enjoy!, enjoy!!, enjoy!!! He enjoys games. Do people play these kinds of games?*

Facts don't come to light by magic; they come slowly, and I realize the truth about Alfred.

Last evening, I went up and told Alfred, "There is a time when men lose their identity. When I cannot feel who I am, who I want to be." He said, "Identity is what you feel yourself to be." I asked, "What are our true needs?" and he answered, "Food, home, sex, clothing, luxury." I declared, "My true needs are food, shelter, warmth. Human contact. Honesty, regard for my fellow-man. Without this, man dies." But he answered, shouting, "*You must* have money, and you must get things for your money, and you must make a big wonderful show, to impress all your neighbors, so they can admire you, otherwise they will not know you, they will not respect you." I told him, "Buy! Get! Spend! Show! Look at you Mr. American, you super-avaricious bastard! You delude yourself into thinking that you can leave humanity, the trust and love that we all need." Before he could answer, a voice in the hall called him out. I came down to my room and locked my door.

He thinks he lives in a world where he can rear people to disregard each other, to conquer each other, instead of to touch each other and to be good to each other. Life can be so lonely. There is so little friendship in the world. And coldness can freeze a kind man. There is such anxiety everywhere. People give bad vibrations to each other. They make each other pretentious. They hide their true selves.

Still I will try to guide him in my way of thinking. I have to try again and again to be sane about life.

Alfred and me, we became friends. It became a beautiful friendship, a friendship which gave something to my life, which was when I was 20, when I was young. But I never have been in a crisis like this! My life is very complicated. There are so many people around me now. Life is lived at so many levels. The people around me are so different as I migrate from my culture into Alfred's. But I so want to live my life, not to lose my human dignity. And nobody, not even four strong guys, can guide me to a different path.

Beth, Anny's roommate, called me up, and she came over. I treated her beautifully. I placed on the tape recorder Renaissance music, prepared gourmant food, and put it down upon the rug. We ate and conversed in a pleasant way. But gradually something went wrong, I did not know what, but something was wrong with my mood. I got a sleepy, listless, sad feeling. I became glum. I stood up and moved the dishes from the carpet, and lay down next to her. I put my head upon her thigh and looked up at her; she reminded me of my mother. I wanted to tell her that but at first I couldn't find the language to say it.

I tried. I explained that this is one of my greatest troubles and I am trying to get over it, that whenever I am under a strain or tension, I look up at a woman and, no matter how young she is, how unlikely the association, I feel she is my mother, she reminds me of my mother. She held my head close to herself, caressing it. We made a date for the following week at her place.

I became emotional again after Beth left.

It is a religious morning, made religious by incense and Baroque music, and a beautiful stream of white light streaming into the room from the window, my window, the window that somehow means life to me. My tree is alive in the summer with its green leaves just under my window. I feel closer to myself gradually, at certain rare times, and it is always at the window. Pleasures somehow coalesce, to create a desire in me to be myself, I feel the existence in its most genuine form, that of pleasure, not orgiastic, but quiet and inner. Life at such times touches us, and our emotions surge forth. Now in the gleaming sunlight I perceive the tiniest Daliesque details; and everywhere I look my eyes become like magnifying instruments. I see the tree; now it is dizzy-looking in winter nature. I see the droplets of condensation upon the glass in which I poured the cold milk for my breakfast alone.

This morning I could not find my shoes. I panicked (having only one pair) and searched for them in both Alfred's apartment and mine. At nine o'clock, unable to find them, I called up the restaurant that I couldn't go to work. From then on I told myself, "Today I will do what I feel like doing." I fixed my door outside. I screwed upon it a large metal sheet on the area they had gone through with pliers, when I was robbed. This nobody can go through. Upstairs I fixed the light into which I plug in my heater to heat my room. I steal the electricity from my landlord. I did not turn on the whole day. By evening time I was tired and took the vitamin capsules which Alfred gave me last night. Then I started to get restless, sexed up, and later, evening time, I was half mad with loneliness and a ceaseless sex-obsession. I started to call chicks. They were not home. Then I started to call women— they were tired. And every five minutes I called Roselle. But I saw that I could not get her and I was angry at myself because I couldn't buy shoes today. Around ten in the evening Alfred came down, gave me pot, and we turned on. He asked, "Did you take my vitamins?" I said, "Yes," and then he told me, "Those capsules I gave you, they are supposedly producers of male semen. How do you feel?" Then I laughed at the whole horrible day and said, "Now for the first time I know I am a pothead, I accept." Oh yes, later, finally Alfred brought down my shoes. He found them in his apartment.

I want to will myself to focus my mind away from the fuzzyness which surrounds me when I am anxious. To think myself out of being mixed up. Is it possible to mitigate everything? to believe people? I am consciously trying to get over the experience with Alfred, and the things that happened to us. I needed someone to show me that love, or a semblance of love, still exists among people, that people are friends, and they can be comfortable with each other and can loosen up at the time we need them, when we are anxious, when we feel lonesome. I am predisposed to go through anxiety; this anxiety, which I am feeling, is then to be expected. That is perhaps the reason people today remain as lonely as they seem to be: they are reluctant to expose themselves to greater levels than they normally would. Bad situations should be avoided. Bad people can be converted to go straight. We can be happy in this world; people must try to make each other happy.

I made a visit to Roselle. She likes to make love to me. But the night before yesterday things did not go as well as they used to. To begin with, she started to emasculate me and I played right into her hands. I told her I wished to be in forestry, but I am only a waiter. She said that my way of life is delusionary, I should be doing something else, that I am wasting my life. I answered, "I accept you and do not judge you. I think your life is beautiful. I love the way you fixed up your room. It is a beautiful illusion." But she said: "I wish I could be as tolerant as you are, but I am not." She would want me with a stable and romantic position in society.

Yes, I am a waiter in the Metropolitan Museum's restaurant but I am left alone by most people here. Each of them tried to give me a hard time in his own little way the first day, the boss calling me by my first name. I asked him whether I might call him Tom. He said "No," and I then asked him to call me Mr. Bihaly. That stunned the entire office.

But I perceive a schism in me, a schism between my Uptown self and Downtown self. I would get boxed in my home were I not forced daily to "go out into the real world" and take a periodic whiff of reality. At home I am somehow masculine, bushy-haired, a little slovenly, but I feel secure. And just before leaving for work, I plaster my hair with a wet brush, put on a clean shirt and tie. The transformation is electric. It is a jekyll & hyde . . . I feel dismayed, neurotic, hung-up when I feel myself in this Uptown image. Nowadays if I weren't high, I'd cry because I have to go into the unknown as to Visegrad. And yesterday I fairly obnoxiously tried to pick up a chick in the food line. That can be bad. It is not cool. Unless a chick passes by me or gives me the eye, there is no need to act out a Lothario image. When the hostesses noticed it, they kidded me about it. They wanted me to feel uncomfortable, but I felt a fright as in the monastery . . .

Phyllis, a slim chick here in the Museum restaurant, often wants to pick me up, but I watch myself not to get involved with any of my co-workers. I want to continue to seem the smiling, healthy young man I appear to be while, in fact, in my head the memories are teeming.

Now, after my work, and a half hour of peaceful writing here in the Museum, the fountains surge skyward and bring the place alive—the water echoes in the huge chamber, muffles the voices. And in me my past echoes and I cannot muffle its voice. In the summer I try, but if I cannot go somewhere, I stay here in the air conditioning.

I often see people on my job who want to meet, and could meet, but there remains an icy silence between them. A woman and a man sit down to a table next to each other, and the woman buries her head in a book or a newspaper. The man does not have the nerve to interrupt the silence. I've been that way too.

A visitor from outer space, Lattman, my landlord. He called me "Andrew." He was bugging me about the electric heater being plugged into the outer socket. But when I told him straight it was cold in here, he turned on the radiator, and when I showed him that the electric heater I was using is thermostatic, that I was not wasting any electricity, he was really friendly. "It is alright now, it is alright," he said. So he recognizes that I've improved this place.

Today is such a beautiful day. It is starting to get cold, and the rains of autumn have put droplets of water on the branches of my tree, the tree which makes my room a happiness to be in. The droplets change color, like prisms. I see them fall and behind them a backdrop of mist creates an effect of rainbows in miniature. It is warm, sleepy and comfortable here in my room, and it is good to be home on this autumn rainy day. I enjoy my weekends, having a day or two to myself. I will not see anyone for a few days. Even when I have women to visit me, I will pack up once in a while and go out to live by myself, and feel good again, like I did when I went to the mountains. This summer I have not been out of the City.

I am going through a concentrated phase of exuding a lot of energy towards women. I am conquering my ever-present hunger for the other side of the world, the world of silken bodies and panties, and a lot of coquetry which is fun to be with. I want to relate to the most beautiful females, as with the less beautiful ones. I want to be able to court and know them intimately, and make their lives beautiful and enjoy their bodies freely—as I can.

I want to see women as they are, wild happy-sad creatures. I will not run around at night at concerts any more looking for a woman, being lonely for months on end, fearing that I was going crazy. That is how I met Mignone. Mignone is my last mother. I do not want to meet my mother anymore.

I want to have a harem of women. One for every night. I want to meet new ones, I want them to want me. I want to go with wealthy women, poor women, educated women, I want them all to want me. When they reject me because they want to play games, like Kuky or Sally or Roselle or Beth, that is alright, I must educate myself against being hurt. I have to educate myself to make them remember me as a nice guy, so when they will be lonely in the world, they can come back to me for good loving.

Alfred was here. I told him to stop his dope business. Then we spoke again like before.

We spoke late into the night and the subject was women. He told me, "Do not get bogged down in arguments or negative topics. Glide over these. Talk about your good times, Europe, Spain, Italy, Sweden, Switzerland, Norway, wherever you have been. Tell them Mexico . . . Please her . . . buy her something. When she is thrilled, kiss her. Find music she'll like. Create a strong masculine image, then project it, like foreign affairs, or with knowledge of racing-cars, art. Have an assortment of music, enough pot, and the n e r v e and s o p h i s t i c a-t i o n to use it all. When you see a chick, go over to her and look deeply and warmly into her eyes, say in a friendly, relaxed smiling way: 'You are so nice.' Use your eyes! See whether a woman looks at you. If she does, flirt with her! Give her the impression that you want to, but cannot keep your eyes off her. Look her way constantly, but when she looks your way, quickly look away. Do this once or twice, and appear to be furtive. Keep your eyes on hers and when they meet, glide slowly from her eyes to her breasts, then to her body: allow yourself to think you are undressing her. And let yourself be turned on by her. Look at her ass! Thigh, and legs. Rest your eyes on her, and blush . . . tell her she is very beautiful: her figure, her skin, her teeth: find something lovely about her, and tell her so. But keep your mouth shut! Whatever you say to women will be the only things they'll know about you. This includes chicks. Wait a while after meeting them, until they accept you into bed, before letting them into your life; but still better not to let them know about you at all!"

I went over to Anny's house to speak with Beth. As I was crossing the wide Houston street, Anny was coming out of her house all dressed up. I kissed her on the lips, and she said: "Beth is not home but Honey, my new roommate, is. Go up and make yourself comfortable, I have to go out for a while." I did. Honey talked quite a bit about herself. Being the daughter of a marine officer, she got married down South to a man she felt good with; she thought he knew so very much. But they cannot get along in their marriage.

I got smitten by her, and paid her compliments. She poured a very special ginger wine. It was delicious, for my throat was dry and nervous. I saw her face from very close, she has a northern face (she is American), it is clean skinned, no makeup or any kind of stuff on it . . . but lovely. We were sitting and kissing. I felt an ardent keenness for her, I touched and held her face, and a stiffening dread grasped me. I held her, but couldn't move. I couldn't act. I kissed her quickly, and she said, "I'm sorry," and I, "That is alright." We were not connecting, she did not look up, her face was beautiful but tense. There was nothing I could think, or do. I could only say, "It is alright . . ."

Do I have an inferiority complex when I am with USA girls? I might have hit something potent here. An inferiority complex plus hate for myself. I came here when I was 15 and we did not have any money. I think we had $20 with us when we got to the docks with tickets around our necks and went straight to Philadelphia. Then we came to New York the next year and I was sixteen, and I had to go to work. I got a job in a summer camp. That was the first time I was away from my mother since she found me after the war.

Most of the kids at camp sang in a play, *Brigadoon*, but I could not because I was a worker, doing the heavy work in the kitchen. I was the boy apart from everybody, who played harmonica. Then . . . I fell in love with a little girl. She came to me. We went and sat on the grass, I, playing my harmonica, she, sitting with me, holding my arm. And that was my first acquaintance of American woman. But someone saw us and drove me away. I wasn't supposed to be there, I was a Kitchen Man in that summer camp. I was supposed to be there to make money. Money I had no idea to live by, I never had a dollar, we were dirtpoor then. And after that summer I went home with $600, and gave it to my mother.

Who am I? Where have I been? I push away the layers of memories. I repress them, I do not want to see old visions. I do not want to remember the summers with my governess in Hungary, in Budapest, our home there. Is it alright to remember? Is it alright to love your mother? Is it alright to remember the pain when my mother left me in the monastery? Is it alright to cry when the past hurts? Is it alright to cry when you feel the warm tits of a woman? No more sitting around. I want to do something about my life. Where am I? What am I doing?

A few nights ago Alfred told me his plans, our plans. "You will not paint alone the hallway, we will do it." But we did not paint the hallway of our house, as he planned. He did not clean his pad as he planned, nor did he knock completely the dividing wall of the two apartments. (After Arthur moved to his girlfriend, Alfred moved in.) He left, because Arthur came in and started knocking him. I let him, and did not respond. Arthur said Alfred lied, his pot was not good. Alfred told him the police were after him and he was afraid to go for his shipment. So he bought it from someone who delivered to him.

Afterwards, he told everybody that the police were after him. To me he said: "Only you know that is not so. Here is $100 for the landlord, $100 for the man fixing my high-fidelity components, and here take this to Anny, take it over to her tomorrow. I'll call you from California. I'm getting out of pushing pot. I might as well have a vacation in the meantime." No farewell remarks, no arrangements. And he's gone.

The next day, I went over to Anny's with the money from Alfred. Beth came in and apologized for treating me horribly, and she talked about herself: "I need an analyst, because I need someone to rely on besides myself." I listened as she talked, as she said: "You know, Andrew, there are so many problems, so much unhappiness in one's life." I said, "Yes, the world is full of problems. Unhappiness is the biggest of them, and to escape from it we do many silly things." Beth said, "We do silly things when we are unhappy. I like you Andrew, you are my friend."

I was at Beth's for a long time. It was around midnight when I left. Of Beth I thought, "I meet a girl, but I don't make the girl *my* girl, I made the girl my friend." And came home into my loneliness.

Kuky called. The married woman, the one I dared to say to, right after I met her: "Let's make love. Now. Right away." This idea was put into my head by Alfred, to get me not to be afraid of women. At least that was accomplished. I told her that. She liked it, I put her into bed, and followed up with action. Not even having curtains.

The following day I called her and told her how much I enjoyed her love making, and she came again the next day. Still, my windows were bare. I found a little shop around the corner on Mulberry Street and picked up some beautiful material, coarsely woven white shades, especially made for each of my windows. It cost me $23, but I said to myself, "I do not care, only the best goes into this apartment." Well, as soon as my shades were made, whenever she could, she came and we made love by shaded windows.

The last time, though, I was at her place smoking pot, and she threw me out.

Now who calls me but Kuky, and spoke with love and openness. She explained that her grandmother was sick a long time, and died. Now she has to work day and night with her weaving, and she cannot come. But next week, after her work is finished, she will come to me, and we will be happy.

Can a Jewish refugee become a healthy lover?

Will I be happy? Will I dare to be a man with her? I want to become a lover again.

I am the Jewish refugee displaced D.P. boy, who came to America, and couldn't get on his feet for 15 years afterward. I am the Jewish boy who at nine and a half was persuaded to go to a 'boarding school' by

66

his mother (out of a middle-class "assimilated" Jewish family), and was promised that the following week she would come and if I didn't like it, I could go back home. And nobody came. I found myself in a prison for young delinquents. The name was Visegrad Reformatory. I was little. I want to cry at every step, but I must translate and refeel my feelings. Priests. They were Franciscans. Assisi, Francis Assisi. "Assisi Ferenc." And I think only the head of the Visegrad Reformatory knew that I was Jewish.

In a boy's life, growing up has many phases. The learning period, the boy-girl relationship, is a normal part of every man's life. Kids date in some way during their growing up, but I did not.

I had my first experience girl-wise during the Nazi occupation. I remember how we were allowed to run and play in the building. We were playing hide-and-seek, I was hiding with a girl, and there behind the door she showed me her breasts. Then she pulled down her panties and told me how it is done. My childhood ended there.

After the war, we escaped from Communist Hungary. We became refugees, Displaced Persons, D.P.'s, and we were always with other D.P.'s. I never had friends my age. I had only one friend for a short while, Cuki. He was 6–7 years older than I, and he was in transit. He came to America, and I was left without a friend. In those years, I was always root-less, friend-less, girl-less, date-less, until we came to America. Then in America, I met some girls but couldn't speak with them. I had first to learn the English language. After I could speak it, my head was full of thoughts, but I could not put them into words. I was ashamed of my Hungarian accent. So again I was girl-less, date-less, and, in the presence of girls, speech-less.

When I was in the Airforce in Germany for four years, I had many girls, was in love with some, and some loved me. Back here in America I had my ups-and-downs. So the learning period which I am going through now is a normal part of every American's life. I am not 'making up for it' but rather am taking a concentrated course in an adult frame of mind.

Life has limitless possibilities. Alfred called from San Francisco and said that he will settle down there to study sculpting in a school on a government grant.

I told him I was happy about what he was doing but I feel his absence. He spoke to me encouragingly, suggesting, "Take life easy, do only what makes you happy and try to be happy." Now I am sure; he got out of the dope business. Maybe I gave him the conception for it.

After I spoke with Alfred, Kuky called me up again and said to rush over to her, she was hungry for love. It was Monday, my free day, and I went racing to her. I was sexually aroused, was hankering for a woman. But when I arrived at her house at first I was without strength to make love. I have been with this woman many times. She has shown me, like a thermometer, her ecstasy and she has waited for the same. I felt so cold and frightened in my impotence. Her healthy body seemed so white and bleached, like the figures in a Bosch painting. I was horny as hell in my mind and body, but I could not raise my invalid male-hood. She kissed me expectantly and finally her flaming passion restored my masculine pride. I did not leave my woman in her ardor unquenched. She became content.

Kuky. She is tops in womanliness, but also on the practical ground. After her satisfaction she showed me her work, her weaving. It is gorgeous, the colors warm and lovely, organic, and the material she weaves becomes a little man-made animal, soft and beautiful. Then she saw the clock and became tense. I told her that I would bring her some warm soup. Maybe we can be friends and add friendliness to each other's lives.

But is it an illness I am facing? A shriveling away of my membrum virile? I feel as if I was wearing some enormous impersonal magnifying glasses, and can see myself, sickly, like pieces of flesh. I feel cold as a piece of stone. I am sick at these times, and become hostile against myself. I say, "How dare you exist out of flesh and bones? Why are you not like before?" But I am cold and tired when I feel the warm body of a woman, and when we talk, certain subjects or gestures or certain movements, bring back visions from my past. I become paralyzed

68

with fear that she will leave me, that she will abandon me, that she will send me away from her. Visions blow my mind, I become desensitized by my fear and discomfort. That disconnects me from her, and thus I do not and cannot feel, and I am out of contact with her. I want something but I cannot reach out, out of fear. I become paralyzed.

Now I can put it into words. Can it be a backlash from Visegrad this fear that I am feeling?

What was my sexual history during the time I was in Visegrad? In the Monastery, the Juvenile Penitentiary. Some prohibitions? If I could just remember what was done to me in Visegrad by those priests . . . Does it have any effect on my life? My sexual history—how was it formed?

I must go back finally to the realities of my life, to the realities of the war. If it has to be, I have to intentionally bad-trip myself, because now I can do it. And if this is the thing that I need, let it be. Perhaps it is the way it must be; self-knowledge is freedom. But I was a little boy then, and yet, that is the thing, I still am the little boy. But I do not have to be that anymore. I can be a man now. But first I must describe as much about the war years as I can remember, and the more I feel the more I will benefit by it. The first thing that occurs to me is to cry, to desperately cry.

To begin with, Hitler fucked the shit out of me. One man channeled the ferocity in his fascist Germany. He created enough death waves to reach me as a little boy. I was nine and a half. Born in December 1934. He created deathrays, human vibrations of hate and death, which was called the 'secondworldwar,' "Másodikvilágháború."

This is all with hindsight. To me the war seemed very exciting. It was full of march music and serious intense looks when the news was heard. Everybody was scared, everybody was scared: the w a a a r! The news was all of a sudden a matter of life and death, and my parents did not allow me to say anything when the news was on. It was all very weird, the radio was so low and my parents sat so near to it. Cely and I, we played and we were laughing and happy, and all of a sudden the news came, and it was about the war—names and people who made no sense to me, Roosevelt and Churchill and Hitler and Goebbels, and Horthy—and it was strange, very strange. In March 1944, there were the German soldiers everywhere. The Nazi occupation! And my life changed completely. I did not go to school anymore, and we played around the house. Never was there so much freedom, and then I discovered sex. I met a girl who was bombed out of another house, and in our courtyard we chased each other round and round, out of hallways and into other hallways, and when we caught each other, we felt each other up, we liked the contact. Immediately, I could feel that I was a horny little fellow. I remember in their apartment I was allowed to touch the nipples on her little breasts, I was allowed to touch her between her legs, and it was hairy. She explained to me how it is done, and the same day I had to go to Visegrad. In the monastery I had to go to confession. I was told I have to confess and shrive my sins. "You must rule yourself. You must keep your hands to yourself!!!"

Let me not write of bad things, let me write of interesting things, beautiful things . . . beautiful things in the air. I am finding out all about women.

Oh, no one can nullify my past, the past trails me, catches up with me and haunts me. I have to crystallize past events myself. I have to work at my troubles alone. There is a chance that I will go on a mescaline trip. Or an LSD trip. I think it would help me. Probably it will manumit me from my yoke.

Oh, I'd love to be free, as free as when I was a child. I hate to be afraid of life, I hate to be afraid of impotence when I am in bed with a woman. If I can live my life just one year, no matter how old I am, sexually free, really free, then I have worked for good ends. But let me see how I feel about such things in one year. Life will pick up, there is nowhere for it to go but to pick up. My fear has to give, I know my fear will give, as I try more and more to relax, to make love perhaps to the same woman repeatedly . . . When I am confident, I will be confident always. But I must keep working at it, every day, and then I hope that by spring, when everything in nature is in love, the sun with the sky, the earth sucking the raindrops, the birds calling for their mates in my garden in the spring, then I will be free for love, I will be a good lover.

It is Monday; I start my weekend with writing again. I want to talk to myself. To myself? To my stone?

Yesterday I had a very strange day at my work, because I stood up against Earnest Willers. He wanted me to get up from my meal (for which I have only a few minutes) and help him with the pouring of the salad dressing for his section. I got mad and told him, "I will not work for you and for the house six hours on an empty stomach," and he, threateningly, "For that I will put you on condiments from now on," and I said, "Now we go and face the boss." As we were walking towards the kitchen, he said, "Forget it" but he came back to talk to me about it again and again. The third time he came I started to shout —the first time in all my working experience. Alex Rokowich, whom I always liked, but who was always cool towards me, came and pulled me by the arm and asked me a neutral question, "Where is Lilian?" The cycle of viciousness thus came to an end, and the danger of my getting fired for shouting, or physically attacking Willers, or starting to cry in his presence or walking off the job was averted. I am grateful to Alex.

About ten minutes later Willers came over again and tried to ride me some more, but I simply said, "Look, let us speak about it when we aren't on the job, like human beings! I would like to work now." And I walked away while he was in the middle of a sentence. I worked, but I was tense all day.

I want to retain my job. I need it desperately. I will try to maneuver and avoid Earnest Willers; he wants to be our supervisor, he bothers us oldtimers. But I will stay on this job, I will be able to save enough money for photography, while I flirt myself out of the Museum.

After work I called Cely to speak with her, but her husband criticized me. If others look at my trip from the materialistic point of view, from a critical point of view, from the point of view that "Look son, it is nice to play around, but look at my mansion with the big trees," I will tell them, "Baby, if you do not like it where I am, stay where you are." Because there is no use judging myself by other people's standards.

I am on a good trip, so I decide. The idea is to make a strong enough illusion that what I am creating is the fulfillment for my particular needs. I see the beauty in my life. The sun is shining through the window. I see my tree in its winterish hibernation. Winter is approaching, my room is warm. I planted tulips for next spring.

Yesterday, from the museum I went into Central Park, where children were playing around the Alice in Wonderland statue. I found a bench around the rim of the statue and there the park was quiet and dimly lit. I turned on, smoked from my pot pipe and it was a beautiful moment. Soon my insides relaxed. The world turned peaceful and romantic, I saw a woman who smiled at me when I came into her eyeview, and she embraced me with her smile. After my walk in the park I was in a good mood, it was a beautiful experience.

Alfred is back and is a terrific liberating force. He is health, sanity and it is beautiful how I respond to it. He arrived on my birthday night.

In the afternoon, I'd fled from my room to escape my solitude. In the streets I wandered aimlessly and as the darkness fell, I viewed the glitter of Christmas in the store windows, like a child gazing at sweets. But I was alone this day, which was so special in my childhood.

When I came back, there he stood in my room, glistening, on his arm this gorgeous chick, Alba. Both were smiling and there I stood. But when I saw them I became happy. It was a birthday present for me. Later Anny arrived with Willy (who opened an art gallery in Englewood, New Jersey, where my mother lives). He has a mustache now, and with them was another man I had never seen before. Anny brought me a book, *The Book of Tea* by Okakura Kakuzo, wrapped in this beautiful purple paper. Anny said, "This book is for you. Start reading it right now." And I did. It was beautiful, it was life, attitudes, philosophy. We put on the tape-recorder Indian music, and I cooked swordfish with new potatoes and babypeas. There was plenty for everybody.

It was bewildering: I realized people came to visit me on my birthday. After we ate, Alfred left with Alba. I found good music on the radio. Willy left for a while with his friend and I was alone with Anny. She said, "Andrew, I am not good for you: I am a destroyer." The two guys came back but left soon after. I wished Anny could have stayed, but I couldn't tell her so. I kissed her and found myself alone. And I became thirty-two years old. I thought, "I am I-er than before." It was the 16th of December, 1966. I told the people before they left that I had come alive when I moved here.

Alfred gave me hashish as a birthday present. I got high. And then things started to happen.

Papo, my next-door neighbor, came over, and said he was moving away, that his apartment would be free and if I wanted it to make him an offer. I offered him $100 cash and will go to the landlord and ask for a duplicate of the lease. I will have to pay $37 a month, which is ridiculously low rent in New York. I am going to try to rent it to a beautiful girl, and if not beautiful, at least one very good for me. I will have a chick living next door to me, groovy and unbelievable.

After Alfred left, Arthur came with his girl, Joan. Arthur said, would I tell Anny that he wants to buy pot from her. When they left, I turned on, shaved, and called Anny. I asked her about Honey. She said, "Would you like to talk to her?" and Honey came on. I suggested pretty directly that we get together. She said not until next year because her husband will be coming and staying with her through the holidays. Then she said, "unless you would like to see me sooner." We made a date for tomorrow evening . . . Now I'm high, high from life, and hash. My dying days are over. I still have a chunk of hash which I am saving for tomorrow, when I will be at Honey's.

And now I'm turned on and listening to an early symphony by Mozart on the Bill Watson radio program, the marvelous announcer on WNCN. He is like a friend, for he shows me good music consistently.

Middle-class boy trying to play it cool on pot, and now on hashish, after he couldn't play it 'straight.' That is what I am.

73

Emigrant boy, making it, after a long time lost in the war.

I had Honey here, and I was frozen. She is so wonderful, so exquisite. She was so beautiful in her little Indian sweatshirt. She is so open-minded, so knowing, or so I'd like to perceive her. I would like to take LSD with her. She took it already, and she I could trust.

The details, yes, the details: Honey came after five. I showed her my squirrel and my greeting-card collection which I collected from muse-ums all over Europe. I cooked swordfish and a lot of good things. We were eating and she told me how much she liked my card collection. I gave her Christmas cards, which she admired especially, and she seemed so happy to have them. She said she would like to mount them section by section, upon a beautifully stained piece of fruit-wood. We sat across from each other, and we talked. She told me about herself in details: about her sordid parents, of whom she is afraid because they could 'come and get her.' She has dreams about them. She spoke about her married life, her sex life. Her husband could not wait, he had chronic immature ejaculation, and when she told him about it, he got angry, in a rage. We talked about the senselessness of anger. She said, "Tell me whatever you want about yourself." But I was quiet and she said, "I am a warm human in my body. My warmth is underneath a thin shell of ice." I could have been in love with her at the drop of a hat, but I was scared. I told her: "I feel sometimes that I'm a little boy." She was nice. She said she was a little girl. But when we sat next to each other by the uncomfortable bathtub (which will be my next project: making it into a padded love-seat) I felt cold, ice cold, and I was frozen. My joints became stiff, I became partly paralyzed. I couldn't think clearly and forgot things, commonplace things which I prepared, like lettuce in the refrigerator.

But here I am, having had a beautiful woman in my room—she was friendly, telling me her most personal inner worries, and she listened as I tried to give her a soothing answer from my personal point of view. She left me with an inner quiet peace which she said I made her

74

feel, and to extend my hopes, she kissed me warmly before she left. Yet why do I run from the realization that I become gloomy with women? My gloom, in spite of all my efforts, pervades the atmosphere and reverberates between us. It is fear in me. Fear also makes me insensitive to the reactions of women. I cannot sense how they feel, so I cannot easily respond to, or judge their reactions. I have a notion that I leave a woman ice cold sexually, because *I* feel ice cold. It is the effect of fear. But what am I afraid of? Am I afraid they will run away if I touch them, that I will be left alone, like I was left alone by my mother when she was taken to concentration camps? Then I had the awareness, 'I must have done something wrong,' otherwise she could not have left me. It is like an echo, "Chicks must be on a pedestal, not to be fresh with. You must keep your hands to yourself," and I feel the pain and I cannot touch the girl. I hear a muffled echo, I cannot cry, the pain chokes me, I am left alone . . .

And the fear descends upon me like a net, pulling my head downward, to my limbs . . .

Pot does not elate me the way it used to. But today Alfred gave me more hash, and it is delicious to get high on. It calms me when I am tense, encourages me to speak fluently and allows me to be happy.

Last night I was terribly miserable, and Alfred lifted me up. He repeatedly talks me out of my sadness and misery: Yesterday he said: "You know, there is no need for you to go back into the past and hang yourself up with all the shit you went through. It was bad. No doubt about it, it was bad for you. But that does not mean that you should continue in the past and constantly revive it. You can get it better." He then repeated, "You can get it better." He will get me LSD. I gave him $10 for pure crystals. They are the best for me, he said. I am going to cure myself this Christmas. I am thoroughly in contact with its reality. I will take precautions, I will leave the windows open. I will prepare good rice, eat plentifully in order that I have something in my stomach when I take it. I will put on the music I like very much. It is called Yusef Lateef, and it is in my veins. I listen to it over and over again. This happy music will be my liberating music, because I know that when I cure myself perhaps I will write down all that I have in my subconscious, what I felt, and feel and remember. LSD will free me and I will be more confident in the world. I will be more comfortable with girls. I will look at them as women, delicious women, rather than the one woman, my mother.

When I was little we used to live in Budapest. I went to a German-language school, and I got sick with ear trouble many times. Later I went to a regular school, wartime it was, I think. And in the beginning of 1944 the German Nazis came to Hungary. Then I was hidden in Visegrad in a reformatory on a mountain. The Russian soldiers liberated us there. For a long time we had no food, and when there was no more food at all for us, the head of the monastery took a bunch of us boys to Budapest. He let the boys loose, but he took me to our house where we lived, 40 Jokai Street.

I went up to our apartment where we used to live. The door was shut in my face by a stranger. I was crying on the steps when a neighbor on the lower floor by the name of Köves found me. She took me in and fed me until she could find me a place on the roster of an organization called National Help, 'Nemzeti Segély.' This organization distributed the parentless and homeless children from the city to the farms of Hungary, so that they could stay alive. There was starvation in the city. I was 'adopted' in a little hamlet, in Apagy, and lived with two women, a mother and daughter. One day in the summer of 1945, when I came out from the school, there was my mother, she came back—my mother came back and I did not want to recognize her. I said to her, "You goddam liar, you are not my mother!" And she took me by my hand and we went to my adopted home, and I immediately went up into the attic and did not want to come down. But my mother called me, she called me, and when we were in the kitchen alone, she heated some water, poured it into the metal pan, called 'lavór,' and started to wash herself, half-nude and I was crouched in front of her on a chair. And she said to me, "Andrew, come here, wash my back," and I went to her, took the soap, and washed her back. I touched her naked body and then I recognized her. Then I started to cry. I think my mother turned around, and I cried mother, and she clutched me to her bare breasts, and I kissed her, and she picked me up. She held me in her arms for the first time in eleven months—she had been in the concentration camps for eleven months. I cried for a long time in her arms, I kissed her, I felt her body.

But my mother said there were no places to live, no way for her to make a living for us, that she would eventually come for me. Then my mother left. We would have starved. So I stayed, but I do not remember what calamity drove me to run away from Apagy back to Budapest on a railroad train. (I sneaked to the top. Almost fell off twice.) I found my way home. I was welcomed by my mother, and the first thing she did was to heat some water and put me on a stool, and wash me and scrub me all over. It was delicious. And then she fed me, and then life began again.

It is night. I started my Christmas by going back to happy years, happy memories, and I am having a Silent Night with my cat Tom, and my squirrel Peanuts. I took out my squirrel from his little box. He has developed some kind of shakes. I will get some good food for him in a pet store. He puts his nose between his front paws and turns his head inward, stays that way for many minutes. My cat and my squirrel are the only living things in my reality whom I can touch, besides my own body. Oh, I need someone to touch!

Tuesday I will go to Dr. Ellis, for psychological help. I want to start up my life again. Sometimes I feel like a big tearful phallus. I feel I can't continue this way. I must become engaged in the practical world. I must finish my apartment now as soon as I can, for I have to be free. I told Alfred, when he gave me the LSD, "I cannot take it now, I feel too weak." And I need a woman to be with me, someone who will love me.

I screwed up so many relationships. Bungled them one after another. And I am lonely. Unashamedly lonely. Above me are three symbols: 'Hi,' 'Let's love one another,' and 'I only followed orders' with Eichmann's picture on it. But where is my father?

Life is moving again. Today I bought the next-door apartment.

I was worried that I would not get the apartment, because Papo moved out of it. I looked for him yesterday, with the $100, and could not find the address he had given me. Alfred said, after we got high: "Do not worry, Bihaly, the apartment will be yours in due time, smoothly," and Papo knocked on the door. As he was coming in with his wife, Alfred asked: "Have you turned him on yet?" I realized what he meant and said: "No, I didn't turn him on yet." I decided to make up for it and turned them on, with good food, which I cooked—for the three of us.

After we ate, the three of us walked over to the notary public and made out the document of the apartment transfer. Papo is a little skinny guy, true and innocent, with wide, large brown eyes. He struck roots in Puerto Rico but couldn't find work there, so he came to New York. Now with his only money he goes back to his Fatherland. But having had two homelands, he fears that he will be a stranger everywhere.

He explained his fright with limited English. And all of a sudden a great warmth overwhelmed me for Papo, who was my neighbor for two years, but who I hardly ever spoke to. Now he is my friend and I offered him my two tangerines. Now he has sold his place to me, and I feel that things are going to start for me again. This death phase is over because I will rent the apartment to a healthy girl. I will find a girl who will be without tension, without the need of any kind of hash or pot. I will do it this coming year, then I will be my own self again. I will not see symbols in everything.

New Year's eve. I was lonely. Not catastrophic, like Christmas night when I had a great desire to die.

In the evening I cooked a good meal, ate, and forced myself to fold my laundry. At ten o'clock I went to the Gallery Gwen, a place on East 4th Street. There was poetry reading. It was one of those dreary events where each of the smoky room's occupants gets to a little table and reads his poetry.

I stayed in one corner where I could see the whole room, and there she sat. There was an empty seat next to her. I found myself sitting and talking. Her name is Mira. Other guys came, and I thought they might take her away. I asked her to dance. We danced, she noticed things about me: that I was unshaven, paint was on my pants, and on my shoes. But she said: "You make sense to me."

She must have liked me, because after we had tea, she asked whether we might go somewhere else. I proposed we go to my house. To my surprise, she asked: "Why not to mine?"

It was a long walk. All the while I did not believe it would be possible for a woman to take me up to her apartment. In front of her door, she said: "I hope you do not expect anything."—"Oh, it is alright, I know, we are just friends, I won't expect anything," I said. For a few minutes she was shuffling around, making tea, and then she was next to me. We adjusted the pillows so we could sit more comfortably. With childlike charm, she said nonsensically, "You are now like a strong brother, big and broad." I reached over and kissed her, gently, just our lips touching.

It was midnight. Holding our teacups, we wished each other a Happy New Year. Our good-wish kiss lasted long minutes into 1967. She said, "Funny, I did not find you sexual when I met you, nor when you kissed me before . . . I only started to feel your heat when you kissed me 'Happynewyear!' " We kissed a long time. Our lips became sensitive, we couldn't part from each other.

It was difficult to undress her. She wore a really pretty dress, with the waist high under her little breasts, and a zipper at the back. I realized I will have to learn the mechanism of a woman's dress, maybe in a department store, where dresses are hanging on rods.

Undressing her was a hilarious game. We were laughing, she with amazement over my clumsiness, I with a curious amazement over the complicated mechanism of the hidden locking device for the zipper. Finally I found it under the collar of her dress. But there was still her girdle. It was so tight and stretched so closely about her body that there was no way I could get hold of it and still keep kissing her. We were both hot. Finally she went into the bathroom and liberated herself from her armor.

When she went into the bathroom, she shut the door, and a fright and cold beset me. Finally she came out. I tucked her under the blanket. She started to kiss me, but I felt frightened and cold. I recall, at one point, being completely aware of what was happening. She was lying in my arms, I felt her warm body, I felt it radiating warmth through me. I started the kissing all over, I felt her little breasts, her whole body. I desired her, but I did not force it. Sampling her, I brought her into a sexual trance. It was thrilling as I held her in my arms, feeling with her her ecstasy. Then my arms supporting her started to tremble, then my shoulder. I was in a sexual twitch, a tremor, but by that time I was withered and cold.

It was difficult to fall asleep. In the morning we talked. She never has been with a man, she feels herself ugly, she thinks she has huge big buttocks, a deformed body, an ugly face. She served me breakfast, but I couldn't stay long afterwards.

In New York, a tree is so precious. Out there in the woods, where I went today to get some acorns for my sick squirrel, Peanuts, out there where my cousin Cely lives, there are many trees. Here there is one, the single one which I planted. How I love it. It is 'my' tree: I have *related* to it. I don't just *own* things, I love them. Before I just lived someplace. Now I know the walls, the lights because I made the installations, I know the warmth of the fire for which I collect lumber on the streets. I love objects. But not with the perverse pride of Cely's husband who gets more and more involved in the exterior and formalities of his life, i.e., telling me of *getting things*.

In college there was a joke in one of the classes. A man was given an experimental government program in which actual samples of cases had to be observed as to how people react to the lowering of the working hours. When the first 'case sample' was interviewed, he was asked: "What will you do now sir, now that you have all that time on your hands?" "I will get another job, of course, so we can live better."

Yesterday I saw Dr. Luria for the second time since I graduated Queens College. The first time we met accidentally and I told her that I stopped studying because books no longer made sense to me. I told her I was involved in slum clearance. That on the Lower East Side I taught men and women, anyone who wanted to learn, how to repair their homes. I told her I helped people, taught them how to better their lives. I sounded very positive and enthusiastic. I did not tell her that I was working in the Museum restaurant as a waiter, until yesterday when she came there and saw me. She sat down at a table and called me over. I told her, "I'm still helping people." Her expression showed that she disapproved.

I have learned a lot. It doesn't help me in my daily living. Now I am learning how to court, how to make love. Some men never learn this. If they could learn the secret of true courtship, maybe more unions would be happier. For me, many things are very difficult because of my many hangups. But I will learn how to get rid of my hangups, I will learn to endure the slurs against my life-style. I will have to catch my own brand of happiness which means: help people.

It is strange to walk into the new apartment. At first it was Papo's. Now it's mine. I can do with it whatever I want, whatever pleases me. I had the notion to rent it to a girl, to a beautiful, to a semi-beautiful, to a non-beautiful—it doesn't matter—to a girl. But I rented it to a man, to Alan Doner. He had been living haphazardly, a few days here, a few days there—then he stayed with Arthur a few weeks. But Arthur moved away, Alan had no place to sleep, so I rented the apartment to him for $40, 3 dollars more than my actual rent, but I furnish the gas and electricity. It is a good feeling to know that I still can help someone.

Mira had her 24th birthday. I brought her flowers, and after she opened the box, she kissed me lusciously.

She was waiting for her brother. Her brother is an actor, and he was supernegative. I tried to be superpositive (although I was painfully hungry), and it worked. I kept being nice, in spite of all his efforts to establish an upper-level attitude. I kept being myself. Mira carried the conversation when there was a lengthy silence.

After he left, we went to buy posters, a birthday present from me. She couldn't decide on which she wanted, but finally she bought an illuminated manuscript. I was very hungry by then, and ate a roll on the street. We bought frankfurthers, rolls, and oranges for home. For me it was a festive supper (and I told her so): I was eating in human company, in a girl's company, a girl who seems to be balanced, undisturbed. She accepts me for myself, as I am, and not for what I should be or could be. She told me: "I don't like to do housework, I don't like to cook, I like to eat little tidbits, I want to lose weight." Then she told me how happy she was over the birthday present, that little gift I gave her, which she herself chose from among my suggestions—her thrill over the first present she ever got from a man. Mira's talking is like a little bird's.

After our meal, we started kissing. I felt pins and needles all over my body, and as we kept on kissing, she offered herself to me. She said: "I am 24, I think this is a good time to do it, it is better you do it than anyone else." A feeling I hadn't experienced for a long time came over me. My body and soul glowed with vigor, and she became mine on that beautiful night. I kissed her into a lovely dream, and I felt very relaxed as she slept beside me.

When she awoke she had doubts as to whether she had done the right thing, but I told her: "This was the night for it." And she said, "It was time for me to become a woman. Now I will be free."

We both were going to work the next day, and we did not want to stay awake most of the night making love. We arranged the lights, we covered ourselves with the blanket, and when she put her arms around me, I started to cry.

I came home and started to paint with Alan Doner, who surprised me with his tremendous energy and knowhow. He intends to transform the apartment, which Papo had left in a shamble, into a habitable place. Alan has extensive plans to bring out the beauty of 'his' home.

Alan is a fellow who did not have a home for perhaps two months, and was invited from house to house. He was quite distraught about not having a permanent residence. I had the apartment when he needed a place most urgently, when all his friends were tired of him. He is a unique person. He has conflicts within. He is bisexual, but likes to be with girls. He was with two very pretty model-like, cool, so-phisticated uptown girls all day. And in the evening he fell asleep while we were sitting around the fire. Alan is an artist, he goes to art school. It was there he met these girls.

Alfred came back late at night and started to lament about his cab fare. Then he started to push hash on me—"if not for tonight, then for the morning." But I told him, "I am going to work, and hash makes me jagged." He became quite aggressive and domineering, and when I told him, "I don't want it," he became cool and left. I had 'defied' Alfred!

Since then, when he sees me, he is curt. He does not come in like he used to, to cook or sit by my fire and just talk. Now he is building his apartment according to my plans, but without my help. Meanwhile some very beautiful things were delivered to him—ornate furniture, sculpted fineries, carpets in daring colors, pleasurable to see but too loud from my point of view. He does not wait for a chance to get high in life. He rushes, he plunges, he takes chances to get what he wants.

When Alfred called from Calfornia, he said, "Try to be happy." But when he came back, he elaborated. "Figure out what this life-style is all about. Listen, get something good out of it for yourself."

"What are you talking about?" I asked.

"Money."

I didn't answer, and after a pause, he said, "What about your writing?"

Since then I've been trying to figure out what he meant. I start feeling a tension whenever I sit down to write about it. The tension increases whenever I think that someone might "inspect" what I have done. A long time ago I said to myself, it is best if you do not show whatever you are writing to anybody, because whoever you are writing about might pick the damn thing up, and you may not see him the way he would like to be seen. Right away there can be hostility. So no, Alfred, you cannot see what I have written. (Anyway, nobody can see my manuscript until it is worked over.)

For what if Alfred should see how I describe him? He would say, "What a sonofabitch!" How frightened I am. God, how frightened I am of this world!

I am getting an abundance of sexual satisfaction nowadays from Mira. We kiss and kiss for hours and after a certain point I cannot feel anything but her lips. She holds me tightly. Her tongue travels around and my body becomes more and more sensitive. She makes me warm and hot. In her eagerness she becomes ferocious. She makes me cringe with pain in my ecstasy. She does not let go, she keeps me in ecstasy, and when I become surfeited she switches into a soft, gentle caress. She nurses my languorousness into pulsating erectness again and keeps edging me into one phase of rapture to another.

But she entertains the notion that her enormously big posterior is a hideous spectacle. She told me this yesterday after we came back from the movies. I told her: "I accept you because you are you. If you had a

'Pinocchio' nose, or a 'Donald Duck' beak, or owl-like eyes, as long as you are you, your ass is ditto for me."

She is not really beautiful to look at but I turn her on, not finding fault with her little breasts and big behind. And when her moist and soft lips and mine meet, it becomes the most exquisite, overwhelming wondrous experience. It is good for me when I am in a state of rigor, like I was yesterday when I went to her after the funeral.

My little squirrel, Peanuts, died. I brought him acorns from the forest, I bought him a piece of fur. Did I neglect him? I found him stiff in his little fur-nest. Before daybreak, I took him down to the courtyard. I gave a funeral, a personal funeral in the garden.

Yesterday Alfred came in. He radiated friendship. I told him I had to eat fast. "Can you not wait?" he requested. I told him, "Hunger changes me. When I am hungry I am hostile, tense. I must not be near a woman when I am too hungry." Yesterday, I went to wash laundry, and Beth invited me for supper, but I said, "I must eat now, I have to have something in my stomach." I bought borscht, with boiled potatoes in it, went to her and started to eat voraciously. She was angry and said, "You will not eat my dinner"; I left immediately with the container. I couldn't think straight from hunger. She called after me, "Do not come ever again."

Alfred calmed me down, gave me hash and I felt better. I asked him: "Why do I want to eat whenever I see a woman? It seems, when I meet a woman, I become fearful, hungry, and I start eating. Eating too much. Full of anxiety, hunger . . . I know what it is. I was hungry so many times."

Life is magical again. There is sunshine streaming into the window. Alfred is here. He cooked sausages and the eggs that he fried slowly turned white like an organic transformation. The mind expands under the lucidity of pot and hash. Things have a texture, I am conscious of

85

textures. We go to the window, we are looking at a prism and rejoicing in the colors. Outside hang the colors on Neapolitan clotheslines, the laundry fluttering in the fresh cold breeze, in the clear azure of the sunshine, and the sound of the song on the radio is made of glass: *Ninetyeightpointsix—I'm glad to have you back again.*

Erotic comfort shimmers in every one of my ligaments. I remember Mira. I told her last night, "Your ass is oval, white, gently curving, round with little cheeks, and I love it." She is so girlish, a little girl-woman. I told her about the war. She understands me, she is Jewish. She listened last night as I told her about my life. She held me tight. I writhed with my memories for a long time. But slowly I became tranquil, and gradually I began to tingle with passion. It was phenomenal, I enjoyed her so much. And oh, it was an erotic night. In the morning we took a bath and she caressed my softly washed hair, which brought back memories of my childhood. While we were eating breakfast I told her, "My personality disintegrates if I limit myself to an exclusive relationship with one woman; I become frightened that she will leave me, because of my bad experience during the war with my mother. I become insecure, I become impossible to relate to." I talked about my writing, how it had a therapeutic value for me.

We walked the few blocks from her house to the subway with a friendship bond between us, a love. She was wearing a nice, warm wintercoat. But I kind of like the feeling of disintegration in clothing. Torn things are somehow nice to wear, it represents your sentiment.

A few days ago I was so lonely that I froze inside. It was a great public loneliness, a freezing non-recognition of the person in you—you could be a machine, or a monkey, or a slave, you start to feel lifeless and ashen. This happened on my job last Sunday, and I turned ashen. I tried to wiggle out of it but felt myself turning catatonic. It happened after Earnest Willers had asked how long I intend staying on the job. When I answered, "I will stay on," he started to laugh. Alex was not working Sunday, and I felt alone, like in Visegrad. After work I hurried out of the restaurant in such a haste that I left my tips (very little) in my pocket in my locker. Out in the park afterwards, although many people were walking around, I turned on, and everything went all right. And the beat goes on, and on . . .

I am sick. I am becoming sick again, like when I had to go to Dr. Binra after Alma left me.

The same old symptoms with the same old feelings in new guises are taking over my body, my soul. I try to modify my consciousness in several ways: 1) Walk away from it whenever I can. 2) Turn on. 3) Write.

1) I shall try to be less nervous, not just mentally, but physically too. My body tenses up. It is a Reichian nervous tension. I am sick mostly from work. If I could just stop what I am doing when I tense up, try to relax my muscles and reason with myself while I am in that state, try to actually relax my stomach and my back and my neck and my shoulders. In the restaurant, I try to walk away from this feeling, but I can't, not when my throat starts to get dry and my head starts to get mixed up. I only get relief when my lunch break comes.

2) To "get high" relaxes me. It helps me to control my emotions, but only when I am high, only when it has its effect, and how far can I go with it?

3) Writing might be the best method to ease my tension. Maybe turning on and writing could help me. Self-psychoanalysis. You learn more about yourself, and while you learn about yourself, you continue searching for your own self. It is like you were blind and you reach out and learn to know a person for the first time by touching his face. Now I'm high and I feel my own person and I think that my own face and all the associations that go with it are very nice and I love that person. For a moment I loved my own image, as I saw myself, even though I know how mean that face can be. Yes, sometimes I hate myself! But what are these standards by which I love and hate myself? And what makes me love myself after one encounter with reality, yet hate myself after another different one? Oh, this is deadly, my feelings are all cramped up inside of me, I am just as tortured as when I lay on the

psychologist's table. Dr. Binra asked something from me and I didn't want to answer—strange, the images I get from seeing myself on Dr. Binra's chair. I imagined that I was lying on top of a table, the kind of a table a butcher works on, and he cuts you open, and your red blood is pouring out, and you see yourself butchered. It is terrible, this image. I know that in my childhood I was terribly afraid of the operating table. When they were beating me I thought the beating was the same as an operation, and the whip was a razorblade held by a surgeon and cut into my hide. I feel this hurting, I feel this great sorrow for myself as I lie on the whipping table and see myself whipped. I know it has something to do with my childhood when I was in Visegrad. But the question is, who was the one who was beating me?

Thoughts, memories, memories I haven't had in many years suddenly come as visions. My mother wanted to give jewelry to a lawyer man, in Modena, Italy. The man did not take it from her, the man dropped the jewels, platinum bracelet, and other gold bracelets on the ground and walked off. My mother begged him to do something to prevent my being sent to some infirmary or hospital where the I.R.O. camp Doctor wanted me to go. I was sick with jaundice, and my mother wanted me to go only to a private hospital. I did not understand what was going on. I never understood what was going on. All that I can remember is that she gave this man the jewels. She wanted him to take them and he dropped them on the floor. I do not remember the facts. My life in the refugee camps in Italy sounds like a police report to me. I am alienated from myself. I blotted out parts of my life, but now they come back in my memories, and I do not want to run away from them anymore. I am tired of running away from my past—I feel very tired and apathetic, I shall go out somewhere. To a museum or to meet Mira—maybe we can talk a while . . .

Now, a good fresh garden salad, with bologna and bluecheese, as much as I could eat, and more left over for later, in front of the window, the lifegiving window. The oboe practice swirls from window to window, hour after hour, rote learning, but with exquisite perfection, never letting up until the passage becomes a part of the background noise, then another theme . . . Now, on to the Pierpont Morgan Library. I haven't been in that part of town in a while, and I'd like to buy several of their cards. They are very beautifully printed. I will give some to Mira, and some to anyone who looks unhappy on the street.

Holy smoke! My life is a little life, and when I concentrate on trying to get that old feeling of knowing where I am, I have to ask the question, who am I? where am I going? Why?

I will stay on my job (it is only part of my world) and decorate my house. Spring is coming and with my flowers blooming I will love and be loved by the women of New York. There are so many strands to my life now. I have made a whole army of contacts with girls.

I had a wonderful day in the museum, just as wonderful as yesterday. Earnest Willers had his two days off, his weekend, Wednesday and Thursday. Alex told me he heard of the intolerable intimidating remarks which Earnest Willers made to me concerning my job. He declared, "We cannot be pushed around any longer." But I told him I need the job, I have to pull my tail in between my legs.

But the day was wonderful. I noticed that a slim lovely girl, who had sat many times before in the area where I work, sat there again, but with a very beautiful woman. The woman smiled at me while I was working at the other tables, and it felt good. After five o'clock, at the bus stop, I saw her. I said, "It seems we are taking the same bus." She picked up on my little remark and started a conversation. She said, "You are so original." We got on the same bus and she started asking me questions. Her friendly smile, her smooth face with tender blondish fuzz on her skin, excited me. I was turned on anyway because I had smoked two breathfuls of pot and to lull my hunger had bought two rolls (now that we don't get anything on the job to eat after work, I was very hungry), so I was in a high mood. I told Carol, "I am going to buy an English paper near the library." "May I join you?" she asked. It was a lovely ride, and we made a date for next Sunday after my work. I am so happy.

My meeting with Elsa was also fortuitous. With my English news-paper, I was walking down McDougal Street and saw her ahead of me. I turned as I passed her and she smiled at me. I smiled back and began a conversation.

Elsa. This blows my mind. 'Tante Elsa' was the name of my Aus-trian-German governess in Budapest. She was big-breasted and blond. She loved me. I could do anything and she never was angry at me. Tante Elsa just kissed and cuddled me against her big breasts. And now I met Elsa, who is also from Austria, of Jewish Austrian heritage. She came up to my room. She has long goldenbrown hair, she is sol-idly plump. Her ass is round and soft and O lovely . . . and she has large breasts. She is marvelously sexual and seductive. Elsa—all my erotic dreams have been fulfilled.

I laid myself between her breasts, played with them and enjoyed them. She took me into her arms, and I went to sleep, a sleep that was like a beautiful trance.

But she woke me up from my dreams. She did not say much. She was looking at me like a psychologist would. I told her about Tante Elsa, the Hitler war. She listened, I fought within and struggled, re-membering. She looked up at me and said I was like David, not Joel, which is my Hebrew name. We made love then.

It was lovely last night and today during my work hours just think-ing of Elsa made me want to rush to whereever she was, undress her and make love to her. I am going to meet her next Saturday. I antici-pate an attack of paranoia, but I am going to laugh in its face.

Saturday I went to work, early as always. Earnest Willers called me over and ordered, "Andrew, clean all the tables." I did. I was with him all alone. Not even Alex was around to grasp his wink for consolation. Then, after I finished preparing my section, placing the salt and pep-per, mustard and ketchup, the sugar bowls on the tables, Willers called me over again and told me: "Andrew, you take number three, this is your new station from now on." This is in the back of the restaurant, the hard section. But I obeyed and prepared my new station too. All day after that, I could not come alive. I felt sick to my guts and I was close to collapsing from the pain I felt. I sat down to a table and Gina, Alex's friend, helped me just by talking to me. It is said that among the Incas, if a man wanted to die, he just sat down under a tree, and died. The Spanish could not make slaves of them, they could commit suicide voluntarily.

But today. Oh, today! I started out well rested. Alfred woke me up by tapping on the pipe which is near my bed. (We set up a communications method.) We are real friends now. We need each other. He gives me warmth and friendship when I am in need of it. He is a wondrous teacher, giving me advice about women. He knows when I am sad too, when I am insecure, when I need help, when he can help. And I am learning the same thing about him. I give him a plan and a solid center. We are dissimilar, yet we like to be with each other. He is wonderfully shrewd and discerning, yet sometimes very much like a child —a very wise child. He is able to shape his life to his liking. I am apt to believe that at least—at least some of what he says about himself is true, for he sometimes repeats himself, what he said before.

He is an amazingly versatile person, and I knew he liked me very much when he lifted me up out of my depressions. He must have liked me to have been able to help me through my crisis when I re-experienced the onslaught of the breach I suffered when I was left in Visegrad in the juvenile penitentiary.

Of course, I realize Alfred's insincerity, and furthermore, his morality is disputable, but his hedonism has an ascensive influence on me. His superexistential roots in the present, his awareness of the moment of my mind at the time, his ability to say the right human word at the needed moment, all these work for my benefit.

Alfred had seen me in my leadenness after Earnest Willers plagued me and it sucked me into despondency. I told him how it demoralized me to the extent that I couldn't meet Elsa and Carol on the weekend. But Alfred said, "Don't worry, Andrew Bihaly, that pus-pocket will burst, he is ready to split, he will drop dead pretty soon."

In the morning after he woke me up, we cooked each other sausage and eggs for our breakfast, and we left the house together.

A misty, balmy evening. A walk down Mott Street, then McDougal. The fog is full of the yawnings, the melancholy calls of the tugboats towing oceanliners past the tip of Manhattan.

Now I sit in front of the window, my lovely window, and eat cottage cheese and bologna salad with coarse brown bread. Loneliness awakens a pain in my breast. Life is magical, it can be magnificent—it can drive you mad.

Earnest Willers: an actor, has six children, is rapacious and conscienceless. His only motive is to make as much money as possible. When I eat my sandwich, he is there, saying with a metallic voice: "Only one sandwich," while he stands there, eating like a disgusting animal, sandwiches, pies—milk. I was paranoid today when I heard his voice. Every little difference in his resonance made me shudder. I know my job is threatened. There are ominous signs.

After work Alex spoke to a group of waiters. They don't like Willers. He will take legal steps against him with the backing of all of us.

When I got home, I placed my flowers in a vase. Alan Doner has settled down, cleaned up his apartment and is working on the walls of his pad. He came in and said, "It smells good." We ate together and afterwards he watched me as I fixed my toilet. I fixed all the walls and plastered around a plasterboard which I'd nailed to the wall. I painted it black for my darkroom and framed the inserts of my toilet window with Christmas cards: reproductions of the window of Notre Dame cathedral, and of Strasbourg. "It is beautiful," Alfred said, "even for lovemaking." But it reminded me of a church—where I was in a state of captivity in Visegrad. The day I was taken there was the last time I saw my father . . .

I am learning to be a man with Alfred's help. After growing up with a background of war and the psychological screwed-upness that comes from a fatherless home, I am learning to act like a man. There were not many men around the two women I grew up with. My mother and Cely, but no father. But I am learning to be a man. Now I am learning . . .

Many nights have passed in succulent lovemaking with Mira, who I am beginning to be in love with. She loves me. She is hooking me and it is delicious. She is grabbing me by my most logical and sensitive spot, between my legs. She is my sweet virgin. Mira Kling, average American girl from Boston Mass. with amazingly iconoclastic notions. "I have such a huge swaying arse, and sooo tiny breasts." That is her self-description. She cries when a great emotion grabs her, and she laughs when I sing kudos over her glorious body. Mira Kling sweetens me up for the museum.

Part Two

Contributor: Andrew Bihaly

Former Employee of: Cafeteria of the Metropolitan Museum of Art, 80th Street and 5th Avenue ('service entrance')

Manhattan.

SPECIAL: TO WHOM IT MAY CONCERN.

■ This is a true story. It happened at the museum. Before I went there to work I was jerking from job to job, just keeping my head above water financially, but teetering on the brink of financial bankruptcy. I had no food. One of my friends who worked at the museum left for California and got them to hire me in his place. The Metropolitan Museum JOB was a godsend. It was a good place to work. We got treated well by the Day-Dean's restaurant-catering firm, the managers of the restaurant. The pay was good.

I was working there more than a year when new managers took over. Then Earnest Willers, who had come to the place as a waiter long after me, convinced the new owners that he could save money for them in different ways. He was assigned to a semi-supervisory position, becoming the overseer of the waiters.

We were ordered not to eat more than one sandwich. We were ordered not to eat dessert after our working time. And, finally, we were ordered not to eat during the six-hour double-shift serving time. They were more than orders—they were warnings.

I made an issue of it. I brought it up at the next employee meeting. The answer was still NO. The outcome was that when I got hungry on the job, I had to pay for my food.

We oldtimers knew that it was all the result of Earnest Willers' special brand of politics. Under him the old crew left, one by one, and he brought part-time actors in to work as waiters. They were made "Earnest's crew."

Alex Rokowitch and I were the only ones left of the old crew—and Earnest Willers fumed about it. He couldn't stand us. He made new rules: we had to arrive before eleven A.M. if we wanted to eat. He boasted to one of his crew members that he kept his new job because he found new ways to get more and more work done by less people.

One day our porter quit. No one was hired in his place. The porter's job was, instead, parceled out for us waiters to do.

Every one of us were fed up, we formed a waiters' committee. Alex made a call at the union, the union men came to the restaurant every day. The union men called a meeting at the union building. Seven waiters attended and the union decided to organize in order to deal with the conditions in the Metropolitan Museum of Art restaurant. One of the waiters squealed to Earnest Willers. I was fired the same afternoon.

The next day I went to the union building and made an appointment with the chief organizer. But when I got there at the given time he flatly refused to see me.

It seems like millions of light years away from the security of a steady income, I am UNEMPLOYED. On unemployment benefit.

The status of unemployment, the request for Unemployment benefit at the Unemployment office, the surroundings and the proceedings have all sorts of strange connotations. Standing in line, answering questions, filling out the application forms with provoking questions. It brings back unpleasant memories.

Now I have to answer questions verbally. I try to play the game, to put my head, my brain where the clerks in the employment office want it to be. It makes me paranoid. Nobody sees it, but I feel it. I can't take a strain job. I am frightened to death one moment, anxious the next, sensible at others. I am afraid to spend money, therefore I walk home. I am afraid to buy food, I buy only potatoes but I hesitate to eat them. Then I become hungry and weak. Then I get depressed and lie down and withdraw into myself. Later I turn on and become calm and I say to myself: "I must get hold of myself. If I don't examine my problem from the point of view of solving it, nothing will change, nothing eases; so the idea is, whenever fear comes upon me, sit down and examine the situation without panic. I now have $140. When I pay the rent, gas and electricity and telephone I'll have $60 left. That will have to last three weeks, until the unemployment checks start coming. That equals $20 per week, three dollars per day. Not enough? Not enough for carfare, eating and smoking habits? Ridiculous? No, for I can eat for one dollar a day—comfortably. What am I afraid of? Nobody is after me, I am after myself. I am scared of nothing and running from nothing. Insecurity? The future? Each day will take care of itself. I do not have to badtrip myself. Instead, I want to get into action. I will make extra money, I will make money by writing papers for college kids. I will find some income no matter how little. That, plus the unemployment checks, will be enough. "You have nothing to fear but fear itself." Fear can paralyze me. Paralysis can choke me. So this is a condition of which I am in control, because it is only within me, no one is outside of me.

I haven't written for about ten days. Now I am writing because I do not want my life to slip away, because I want to preserve my life. Is that what I am writing for? Or am I writing because I need to talk to somebody in myself?

Vivian, little Vivian who lives in one of the nearby houses, came by. She is a little girl, she has Indian in her genealogy. She is bronze-skinned. In her little face everything is tiny, her nose, her mouth, her forehead, but under her beautifully arched eyebrows her fawn-like eyes glow with large pupils. Her velvet look is so innocent, but I seem to see a shadowed sadness with a spark of wisdom in it, which is uncommon for a six-year-old child. Why is it that the touch of life is always so painful?—like we feel our body only when it is aching.

Whenever little Vivian came, I gave her some fruit, which I kept specially for her. But will I be able to do it in the future? Little Vivian lives with her grandmother. Her mother lives in Brooklyn, and her father lives in Chicago. Her mother and her father are estranged. The child has been coming here, I do not know why. She feels something here, maybe, like all the children who came here before. When I moved here into this house, they wanted to come up, 'to see my house,' they harassed my kitten all over the room; I had to stop them from doing it, and they stopped coming. But Vivian, whom I didn't notice, who might have been among them, came up frequently. I was kind of afraid that her parents would get worried, so I told Papo, who was Puerto Rican, to ask whether her parents knew that the little girl was here. He said, her grandmother said it was alright. I started to talk to her about little things. I taught her English and gradually she has been thawing out. She started to speak English to me, and now she wants to marry me. She came out with it. She declared, I need a woman to cook my breakfast, wash my dishes, and she said she knows how to do all that. She saw the daisies on my table and said flowers are beautiful. She saw a photograph of a loving couple in the bushes. I told her the name of the greenery, I told her it was by John Brook. I told her the name of the magazine—*Life* magazine. But pointing to the couple, she asked, "What are they doing?" I told her, "They love each other." The next day she said, "The grass is green, the bushes are bushy, roses are red, violets are blue, tatatatatata, and I love you." It startled me, because on one occasion when people were in my house they made a snide remark. I said, "My view of her is quite innocent and friendly. I love children, I only let her near me because I know, I would never touch her." But everybody laughed. Today little Vivian shook me out of my lifeless meditative doinglessness. She said, "C'mon let's do something," and 'We' started to clean, and 'We' rearranged the shelves.

I am feasting on oatmeal and rice. It is good food, it gives me strength. I am eating well. But since I do not buy eggs and sausage products, Alfred doesn't come down for 'his' cooking nor is he pushing me to "get high." The other day I went up to him and asked him to give me something on credit to get me high. He said he didn't have anything.

And today something happened between Alfred and me—I was unable to be myself. "Myself." What is myself? A man holding onto his own sanity? To his own life?

Put simply: After I asked for credit the night before last, Alfred invited me today very early to make money with him. He said that if I were to become his 'stash,' then he would become a 'pusher.' It has to do with conning me into actively selling dope. I was struck with terror. As I hesitated, he let me out of it. He left my house without another word.

Today for the first time in my life I smelled gas. For suicide. It does not smell bad, but it made me sick, it still does, the idea of it. It is so easy, and so hard at the same time. Alan Doner and Alfred drove me to it.

In the morning, after Alfred left my house, I had to go to the Unemployment Office for a morning hearing. When I came home, after a long walk in the bright sunshine, I found the wall between my apartment and Alan's in shambles. I asked, "What happened?" Alfred said, "You cannot keep up your apartment without a job, so Alan and I will take it over. We threw down the wall to make it like my apartment upstairs." I couldn't believe it!—I have no where to go! My home is part of my life . . . Life? What is life? Hope? Trust in Humans? Love? Honesty? Security? What works?

When Alfred moved into my life, I was fascinated by him, I saw possibilities of life which I'd been missing, and tried to make my life more versatile. I declared to myself, "I want things to be different," Alfred helped me. He introduced me to pot, I've gone along with him on his 'trips.' He became my friend, my Friend. He showed me many things, how to love life, how to have confidence in life, how to approach chicks with confidence, how to brighten up my life with chicks, how to navigate with more than one chick. Some of the trips we took, I didn't know what kind of trips they were. But when I found out, I said to myself: "He shows me his consciousness, but I will teach him what consciousness is."

And now he showed me how it is possible to show someone that he is loved, by taking over his life, his home—by breaking down his wall. And now that I am liberated, I am also weary. And lost. I must pick up the pieces. I will! I will pick up the pieces and learn from it. I must act. Not write, act! Not think, act! My house is my home. I will re-erect my wall.

My apartment is mine again. I erected the wall piece by piece—as I would like to pick up myself again. The wall protects me. The wall shuts out the invaders . . . it shuts me off from the world. There seems not a soul a mile around. I imagine that I am on an island. I imagine that I am able, that I *can* do, all the things that I'll need to do, plant and reap potatoes, go fishing for perch, bringing it home and cooking it for myself over a woodfire. But right now I am with the memory of a dream I had last night: Alfred brought flowers, many flowers, and there was a lot of light in my apartment and in the luminosity everything glowed. Then he got up, gathered up all his flowers and left.

In reality, he came in today, asking, "Why the big rush with the building of the wall?" He didn't notice my emotions. He told me, as usual: "When I see a woman, and I like her, I look her up and down, and stop at the right places. Her tits, her ass, and in my mind I visualize how lovely her body would be without clothes. I try to talk to her, and during the conversation, I tell her, 'You are so very lovely, I find you so very beautiful, I would very much like to make love to you.'" I couldn't get with it today. But he said: "Take flowers to girls the first time you see them, a red rose, and when they hold it, ask them to stand still for a moment so you could look at them for a while. When they stand for a second, kiss them on the lips." Then he instructed me how to make love to a girl, even when she doesn't want to do it.

"I am alright the way I am," I said with finality. "People like nice people, and if someone doesn't, they will eventually."

Today, for the first time, I turned on with bananas, and got a significant high from it. I read about it in the *Village Voice*. It is a godsend substitute. It was difficult for me to come to my right consciousness in the morning. But as I got on my banana-high, I turned on the radio, and did my Canadian Air Force exercises. My anxiety let up after I did that. I ate a hearty breakfast of oatmeal with honey, then went job hunting. All for nothing, and I had to spend money for two newspapers and carfare. On my way home, I shopped for potatoes, cabbage, bread, milk, tea, and my cake, the bananas. For the city diet this is magnificently frugal. I am trying to get used to a simple diet, so I can have some money left over from the unemployment checks. Perhaps I can buy some lumber so I can finish constructing the bathtub cover. It's a wooden structure, simple, sturdy, which will hold my photo enlarger, which I hope will help me get orders, so I can make some money.

I am beginning to see a spaceship swooching through time, and I am building it right here. A one-man spaceship, which is going with my life. My spaceship is my house.

We are in slavery, slaves of the economy, slaves of 'The Man.' There has always been The Man, the one who can force you into his mold. He has power over you. He holds you by your balls. I recall the ads for guard jobs in this morning's *New York Times*, "Married men only." I went for the job anyway, from early morning till four o'clock. I did not get the job . . . Why Married men only? To make sure they will be on the job for a while? Yes, The Man got you by the economic strings. The only way to get out of it is to become an independent photographer. I will call the prices, and nobody can fire me, nobody can kick me out. I have to get into photography this year.

I lack self-confidence. Self-confidence comes from self-reliance. I think of the attitudes of my parents. "I will do it, and if I cannot do it, I will learn to do it," said my mother. I remember the words of my father: "When you think that something cannot be done, try and figure it out. If all possibilities are exhausted, when you at least examined the possibilities, and cannot figure something out, then ask for help." But they killed my father . . .

At nine-fifteen in the evening, I had a pleasant meal of fish and boiled potatoes. While washing dishes and listening to a violin concerto, I uttered the words, "There is nobody there. My mother isn't there. There is nobody there. I've grown up. I am alone now, and it is all right." And my pain stopped. When it hurts that way I know that I am all alone.

The Be-In: March 26th—Sunny Sunday

My night left me in stupor, I could not move, my head, my whole body was so heavy. But eventually I got up and did my exercises (which I am gradually catching up on). From the exercises I started to warm up to the feeling of life. I ate my breakfast, and as the minutes wore on, I felt beautiful by the time I got out into the street, into a cool, bright, friendly day. I felt full of expectations as I took the subway to Sixty-eighth Street on the Lexington Ave. line . . . and went to the Be-In.

I got off the subway with oddly dressed young people, in fur coats, fur capes, high-heeled boots. They wore necklaces and yellow flowers in their hair. People were filtering towards Central Park in holiday spirits. In front of me walked a young man in a burnous, with a prayer-rug rolled up, and a small drum. He looked like a native from Turkey, or Arabia, or Persia. Some men carried babies on their shoulders. Some women carried their babies in bundles in their arms, and some girls had little dogs on leashes, but everybody had flowers in their hair, and I was drawn with them towards the park.

People were spread out on blankets in the green grass, where the snow had not completely melted. They were sitting on benches, on rocks, scattered in the park. Finally, after taking many paths, I saw beyond the trees and bushes a shimmering crowd of people gravitating around a rocky abutment. It looked like a swarm of ants, with little heads sticking out. As I got among them, I saw that everyone wore strange costumes—some very elaborate and expensive and studied, some from the East Village, who lived in their costumes, which were part of their personality. Many boys had painted faces with intricate designs, some had bananas scotch-taped to their heads. There were men in business-suits, very neat and dandy, even somber and estranged, out of place in that crowd. And girls, girls, pretty girls were swarming in pairs or alone in zigzag aimlessness.

The Be-In was a flux of images, chance encounters, meetings—new meetings and remeetings—of old friends. A friendly girl said, "Hello, there" and gave me a balloon. I said "there" and gave her a kiss. From then on I kissed girls, some kissed me back, some pulled away, some pointed to their mouth, some to their cheeks, and I kissed them wherever they pointed. I met a girl I had already kissed and she said, "I cannot be with you now, but call me," and she gave me her phone number. Her name was Susan. "Don't forget me," she said. I found someone else, a little almond-eyed girl, slim, creole-skinned with short curly hair which hadn't been straightened out. She wore old-fashioned wire-rimmed glasses, very clean and shiny, and had two front teeth sticking out in front of her mouth which gave her a childlike appearance, belying the big earrings in her tiny cute ears. When we met, she said, "My name is Anita, c'mon," and hand in hand we walked around. We met Joan and Arthur, and they asked if I had something on me. I showed them and we got them high on bananas. They said it is legal, bananas are legal to smoke, and I felt the way a liberated slave might feel. There were others in the middle of the Park smoking bananas. We handed the pipe around, and I told them: "I made it yesterday at home from bananas. I made it myself."

After a night of loving with Mira, my long walk home from her place was preoccupied with looking in the trash cans for daily papers. Now I am searching—I try to find a job in the help-wanted columns. I'm very hesitant but pack two sandwiches and an apple, I spit-shine my show-shoes, put on my cleanly washed shirt with a necktie, and start out for the day's hunting expedition.

Coming home, I said to myself, "Life is life, and nobody can live when they are unhappy." I have to look for my happiness, do something worthwhile! The world is beautiful. But it isn't beautiful if garbage is strewn all over the streets, my street, my neighborhood, and not placed in the garbage cans. Everybody is blaming everybody else for throwing garbage all over, but nobody wants to clean it up. Everybody wants the authorities to clean it up, and the authorities don't want to do it, the superintendents don't want to do it either. The superintendents here are fat ladies who hate to work, and work as little as possible, because they are fat and sick. They are apathetic too, because as soon as they clean the house-front, people throw beer bottles all over again, so the superintendent-ladies sit on their fat asses and don't clean up, so I have to clean up. I will go out tomorrow and count the houses and shops in our block. Monday I'll get mimeographing papers, write a proclamation, then post one on each door and shop window, alerting everyone for the street and block cleaning next Saturday. It will be a good experiment. It may work, maybe I can do it, maybe it will be a job . . . That means "Dropping in," versus "Dropping out."

Little Vivian came by, and asked what I was doing. After explaining what I intend to do, she said, "Let's clean up the streets tomorrow."

Today, after a long time not speaking to me, Alfred woke me up quite rudely and demanded a sewing needle. While I was looking for it, he saw my banana tobacco and asked, "What's that?" "Instead of pot I turn on with bananas," I said. "You deserve that shit," he said. Then I realized he wanted to sell me pot, to have some money from me. He couldn't say it out straight, so he demanded a needle first.

He talked about money: "I have $7,000 owed to me, but I cannot get my hands on the money. I cannot go to New Jersey to get it because I am afraid that the police will follow me." He offered me money to go to New Jersey. I told him: "The way to get people is to get them hooked. When they are hooked . . . you send them on a mission." "So don't you want to go?" he said. "You'll be sorry!" And I answered, "You are willing to risk my freedom, you want to send your beloved friend to fight for you, but you forget my 'I', my ego." He said, "That's ego-games," and stormed out.

Rainy day. Drizzly and cold, and everything has a brownish coloration. Brownish industrial, a haze in which I feel myself blending. In this mood I went to the Unemployment Bureau and signed for a check. I got one in the mail, $38, and cashed it. I need it for last month's rent and electric bill. And what about food and spending money? If I could only do it. Go and tell people that I can do anything, that they should try to give me a chance, ask them whether they have anything around the house that needs to be done, ask them whether they want me to do it. Jobs around houses. Gardening. Or perhaps cleaning an office. Watching somebody's children for a while. And if they want to pay me or offer me a meal or give me something, I will accept anything.

What is your modus vivendy?

I got some flowers for my room from the East Village, where I've been looking for work, and on my way back through the Bowery, I saw two girls in bluejeans and army summershirts. They had satchels on their backs. I thought, how lovely it would be to make love to one, especially the chubby one, and afterward to sleep with her in my house.

I walked after the two girls. They stopped to price some warm jackets. They were cold, the April wind chilled them. I asked whether they had a place to stay. The skinny said: "Yes"; the chubby said: "No," and I invited them to my house. They asked one question: "Is it warm?" I said: "Come look at it, and if you don't like it, you may leave with no hard feelings." They came. I was tense but quiet, and they stayed. I was hospitable but neutral, gave them tea, and left to visit Mira.

I hadn't seen her for a week and I got to miss her. She has another boyfriend, an architect, and she didn't want to make love with me. We talked for a while, she telling me about her new friend, and I, about the two girls at home. But when I told her I missed her, she kept quiet. I didn't make any further allusion in spite of my desire, and came home.

Ruth, the chubby girl, was reading in my bed. Her friend was not there. I asked her: "Where is she?" She told me they had a place to stay and the other girl went back to the group who they are going to Europe with. They are leaving on the twenty-seventh of April. I said, "That is fifteen days from today" and told her if she liked it here, she could stay in my house until then.

I cooked boiled potatoes, prepared good coleslaw with garlic dressing, and, before the potatoes started to boil, ran out for some old lumber which I always find around the corner. I lighted a fire, spread out my nice print-cloth on the carpet, placed my flowers in the middle of it, and we ate a festive supper by candlelight on the carpet.

After supper, I blew up my air mattress and gave her my bed. I had a great desire for Ruth but made no advances, being happy enough that a girl was here with me in my home, since with Mira I am always at her place.

Ruth went to bed as I prepared the air mattress and after saying goodnight to her, she climbed down from the bed and we made delicious love. I tried again to make love to her but my anxiety stopped me. She asked: "What are you thinking?" I could not answer. She asked me again, "What are you thinking now?" I started to talk but when she said how she would like to stay with me but must go to Europe, I broke down. And she dried my tears and caressed me. I started to make love to her again but somewhere in the process the malediction of the past overshadowed me and my anxiety didn't let me feel. I became numb.

I'm searching to find a girl whom I could love and not be lonely.

With this consideration I went to the April 15th Peace demonstration. I walked to the park carrying my umbrella, and there among all the Be-In people was a girl standing with a young fellow. She had on a thin dress, sandals on her stockingless feet, and a movie camera hung from her shoulder in the cold rain. When she saw me under my extra-large umbrella standing alone, she came under it, snuggled up to me and gave me a kiss. Her name is Recia. As we were waiting on the wet grass among the people for the start to march to the U.N., we listened to some of the speeches. Those talkings made so little sense. Words were few between us, because what our lips were saying was so much better.

She was here from Antioch College for the Peace demonstration. She was with a young fellow she met on the way to New York. She arranged that he go somewhere to sleep where she could reach him, and she came with me. On the way home we smelled something good, went in to buy the strawberry shortcake, and ate it here. She was so hungry that she didn't dry herself, her dress was still clinging to her body, from the rain.

I put down a blanket and started to dry her, unzipped her dress to dry her shoulders and was amazed at her having no brassiere on. I dried her legs and was more amazed to have touched her flesh when I expected to feel her panties. I undressed her. She didn't want to make love but let me kiss her little breasts. In the twilight, my room became cozy. She stood before the fireplace and warmed her legs. I took out a sparkler which I lit and Recia held it, gently swinging it up and down in front of her, around her, not moving from the spot. After the sparks of the sparkler died, her body became rigid, a standing silhouette in a fire-frame. I became mesmerized and cried out loud, "I love you."

In front of the fire, the blanket on the carpet became our bed. I kissed her and we made love passionately. After I opened the window we slept intertwined until the brightness of the sun awakened us.

She left me no address. She didn't use many words, except to say: "I will remember you all my life." She left me a little black bead from her string of beads. It is black with many beautiful patterns, uncertain shapes in silver, white, red, yellow and blue.

I took her to the railroad station. She stood by the window as the train started to move and soon she disappeared in the distance.

I went back to the park where I had met her. I sat down where we had stood and I started writing on the still-wet grass.

Peaceday

> I found her at the Be-In, we met
> With a kiss of surprise and revelation,
> Our lips danced.
> No one was out there but our feeling
> On the wet grass.
> Words didn't spoil our poem for us,
> Under a big umbrella we homed to love
> Hand in hand.
> It happened on Peaceday yesterday
> And tears flowed inside our throat
> Today.

Had I had a dream? A phenomenon? But here is before me the little black bead. In it I see her, her body, the blue and silver sparks from the sparkler.

Fuck you books! Fuck you 'EDUCATION'! Fuck you phony verbalizations!!! College, you whore, you keep people on the shelves, don't you? I pull out my books, out of those boxes in which I put them when I moved in here more than two years ago. Now I line them on the floor, and I will give them away . . . away, let anyone have any of them. I take the pile of books and with venom and fury I throw them into the corner. They are meaningless hogwash, useless dead symbols!

I asked Carl Retsel for a loan and now am reading his oversimplifying answer . . . Yes, I am a grown-up, yes, I should stand on my own two feet, yes, I have education but without any achievement, yes, I should have more pride than to look for manual work.

Have education they state, and you will succeed! It is more complicated than that. I fill out applications for jobs without result. You don't believe me? Go read the book!!! You need author and title . . . You don't get it? I will lend it to you. Read my book, you will see that I am right.

I know in my guts that books are not what I need. A smile, a caress, speaks! A helping hand speaks more than all the books in the libraries. Reader, don't stay with books. If you are in them, don't stay vicarious!!! And if you want to tell me something, tell it to me nicely, and if you want to give me something, I would like to feel your vibrations. Give them to me.

The buds of my tree are sprouting. I saw the first flower at 6 A.M. this morning when I got high. This is my third spring here, the pipes are still knocking. It is cold today and the heating is pleasant. But the flowers are beginning to bloom.

I often remember sleeping at Carl Retsel's house. I remember his father. Where is my father? Why was he killed? Why?

Yesterday at nine o'clock, after a terrible rainy day of depressed hibernation, I called up Mira. I haven't seen her for a whole week, and she said, "Come over immediately." She was beautiful, her hair cut shorter, and was gorgeous in her pink-orange nightgown. As soon as I got there I kissed her, gently, barely touching her lips, but she kissed me with her open mouth to greet my tongue. She was sensitive and sensuous to my touch, and she aroused my fervor. I knew just how to touch her into culmination, and she gave me pleasure because her lips were so familiar and knowing . . .

After a slumbering repose, I took a shower with her and powdered her whole body. Mira, her upper torso is slim but directly from her waist down it becomes instantly round. She is like a fecund queen-bee.

Her hips are created for bearing, for motherhood and she is so soft. I massaged her powdered body and when she said, "I'm so plump-assed," I told her my observation about that 'ass' and she caressed me from scull to thighs, under my hair, my neck, my shoulders and my spine. "I love you," I said to her, these three little words that are so difficult to say. Afterwards she embraced me and held me in her arms. I kissed her endlessly and said again and again, "I love you." And the incense I took her as a present filled the room with mystical, gentle perfume.

In the morning I served her breakfast in bed, and she told me about her new boyfriend. He is a tall Californian, an architect. She is trying to get used to him. I told her about the Be-In, and Recia. She was amazed and fascinated, especially about Recia's having no underclothes on. She asked me to help her next week with cooking because she is expecting her parents to visit her from Boston. Before I left her she gave me $25, which I said she was lending me, but she gave it to me. Then I walked her to the subway. She went to work . . . and I to my landlord with her $25.

When we are kids and our minds run away from us, everything is mixed up without any sequence. In our grown-up state our mind meanders the same way, but we try to deny it, and afterwards we force ourselves to get educated, our 'education' helps us to deny it. Thus we live in a myth, self-created.

It makes no sense to listen to the radio, because it is like a child's mind. It runs wildly away from us, because the performances are begun, interrupted, and ended by commercials. It says, "Ten—Fifteen —Twenty Minute news time, "supposedly 'reality time,' but whenever reality is talked about, commercials are pumped in between. There might be a million men thinking: "Say, why do I have to put up with it?" but . . . we listen.

We are psychologically trained to associate with feelings of unreality, i.e. commercial-like language. They are formulas, pat phrases, limericks, teasers, dronelike verbiage interwined with sexuality. The announcer is talking about serious things, like: earthquake—(then the commercial) 'Take Dancing Lessons!'—underprivileged—'Take a Vacation!'—the distractions of the bloody war—'Buy a New Home for the Future!'—hunger—'Open a Savings Account!' This I hear on the radio, with music in the background. These things are really happening in the world today.

In the headlines we all read about 'the work situation.' But the reality of it is not the same. Somewhere in the back of our heads, we feel that something must be changed radically in our heads, or in The Man's head:

You're going for an office job. There's the first question: Previous position? You've had none? The Man needs someone with experience. Or you're going for a job where 'No experience is necessary'—but The Man needs a young person. Or you're applying for a waiter's job, The Man is in need of one but only from a good house. Take manual work and the other workers will think you are disdainful of them, or they will think you are a bum and The Man has to fire you. You don't believe me? Go and try.

There are two alternatives for me. 1) Make a living 'catchascatch-can,' wrestle with existence whereby I can find a way to hold *jobs* consistently, because in *one* job there will always be behind you The Man, and his behavior depends on how much you depend on him. To counterbalance these concepts, I discovered the agency of 'Everything for Everybody.' I registered there, and hope to get four or five jobs simultaneously. I will take odd jobs. "Have you no pride?" I ask myself— "No. Pride is ego and it limits me." I will take any kind of work, anything. I will have adventures . . .

Happiness in any kind of job depends on how The Man talks to you, and how you can talk to him. You may be equals, each having a service. He can give you money, you can give him cleaning his apartment, but you can talk as equals. If he fires you, you have two or three more jobs to work. (You survive a little less regally than before.) But you pick up another job to replace it. If you work in more than one place, you are freer from The Man.

2) I am grappling with a way of life. What kind of life do I want to lead? Right away there is a division for my future: Do I want to get into Alfred's hassle? follow his line? "The best man is the one who can make the most money." And live my life accordingly? He is the one who has the duress. Selling drugs and getting rich—accept *that* as my credo? The other part of the division: if I cannot get *jobs,* then "You are tuning out, becoming a character, a drug addict." Other people call it "deteriorating," "wasting life in this Land of Opportunity."

After a hearing in the Unemployment Office, further payments were denied to me. But in the mail I received last week's check. I took some of it to Mira, repaying her the $25. She was expecting her parents, so I cooked the meal, and while it was cooking, cleaned her house. Her parents arrived too early, unexpectedly. They are old-fashioned Jewish people, Mira, larger, taller than either of them. The Mother, a little Jewish lady. Her father, an angular tough-sounding gentleman, who wanted the womenfolk to behave themselves, to give him respect. He asked me with a statement-like tone, "So you are in charge here!?" I said, "I only cooked a meal." And he asked: "How do you know how to cook?" and I answered: "I like to cook, and I like to eat, that is why I cooked the meal." I watched Mira feeding her parents, and feeding them bits of questions just to keep them occupied with conversation. After Mira's brother arrived I left, without eating the food which I had cooked.

I AM LIVING HAND TO MOUTH

Rotten life. Money and getting a job is obsessing me.

Today I begged my first three dollars on 16th Street and Eighth Avenue—in two and a half hours.

I found a pickaxe in front of Sally's house, almost new. I will try to sell it.

I go lower and lower and now have to follow my father's advice. I remember it distinctly: "When you are swimming, and a whirlpool gets you, you start to spin in it, and you cannot swim away, then stop trying, struggling. Curl up in a ball, take a deep breath, let the whirlpool suck you downward as fast as it can. You will hit the bottom soon. When you feel the bottom touch you, kick out with all your might, and you will find yourself liberated from the swirl of the whirlpool. Then, only then, swim upwards to the surface."

Tomorrow I will look for a porter's or a dishwasher's or a busboy's job. Meanwhile, every evening I will try for a dock-worker's job. That is a well-paying work, and as soon as I get it, I will call in the next morning to my ill-paying job, and say I'm sick, and cannot continue my work. I will stay on my dock-worker job, and scrounge some money together, then I can go for something easier, better paying or of some intellectual trend. I would like to find some night job, to have some daylight hours free to do some research work for my 'project.'

But until I find something—anything to have some trifling income —I'm begging. One dollar a day for food, one dollar a day for shelter, one dollar a day for spending money: "Can you spare a nickel?"

As I was coming home from Eighth Avenue, I saw a lanky young man with a very beautiful young woman, both on roller-skates but she was being pulled by a huge Saint Bernard dog. I was amazed looking at them. They gave me a happy hello and I greeted them back. I spoke some words to the woman, who was cut off from her man by a red traffic light, and she said, "Would you like to come along?" "Yes," I said, for I was quite lonely. We went on to 16th and Third Avenue, to an empty store with dirty windows, with a sign: "For sale, call CL5-0210, Mr. Feldman." Someone opened the door. We went behind the store, which was fixed up helterskelterly into a place to live. There was a lot of room and it was owned by a young man who is working for IBM. There was a girl, Pamela, whom I had previously met at Everything for Everybody, the employment agency, where I was promised jobs—jobs—jobs, but could get only one hour in Queens, two in

Brooklyn, and when I worked three hours I had to travel six hours, and had to spend money on travel expenses.

We hugged with Pamela with pleasure. She told me that I was "at the family." And I was. I found a bunch of Young People, beautiful people who are themselves, who smoke pot, who like records, who can make music by hitting wooden sticks and wooden spoons together, who like good healthy food, lots of it. I was treated most generously by the people, and got very high, on meat, meat for the first time in a long while (kosher salami), a strange experience on an empty stomach. I met Pamela's man friend, who told me about himself. I told him about myself. I was truly happy, I was in a group of people who happened to be together because they wished to do so. I was invited there again, and I gave them my address. They might come by, and I have no idea how my life might change from now on. If only I could have better clothing. When they come to me, I wish to give them some food.

Today I found myself again, after losing myself in the quagmire of fear and uncertainty. I got started at six o'clock in the morning for job-hunting, but I could not walk any longer—I was tired and hungry, so I started the begging on Sixth Avenue. Got $1.50, bought a quart of milk and two rolls, and ate my meal at noon in the library park under the glorious trees in the shade. From there I tried again to find some work, but without any luck. It was ten to seven when I got home, and felt horrible, drank a heavy load of iced coffee and it turned me on. Cleaned my apartment and the lower part of the house thoroughly. I worked on it like a madman, moving at top speed, and did everything in three and a half hours: put the house in ship-shape. I realize that coffee is a chemical, like pot, and if something is to be done, it is very helpful. After cleaning, I boiled some scorched cabbage and ate it with the watermelon I bought while coming home.

I'm like a somnambulant. I know I have to look for a job and the fear of going for a job returns again and again to haunt me in several forms. An intestinal liquidity overcomes me, and I have to race to the bathroom. Or I become very tired and sleepy all of a sudden. My mind starts to zigzag and darts everywhichway, involuntarily, as if in a spasm, or quake. I force myself to go for a job but on the subway I cannot help but be very distracted, easily and obsessively, by beautiful women—I leave the subway—I'm not going to look for a job, I'm going to Eighth Avenue and Fourteenth Street . . .

Just came back from Mira's.

Last night when I went there I was tense, and kept standing at her door. She sat me down, massaged my shoulders, and rubbed my back, scratching my skin with her nails. She kept doing it, and gradually I relaxed until I was transported into a dreamworld which had no division between wishes and reality, where what you want came true at such a rate that it was fulfilled immediately—I 'went away,' back home to my mother where I had much caressing and never had to worry. Just like when I wake up in my lonely room from a daydream, my hand over my eyes, my face all messy from tears. It took me a while to open my eyes. But I was not home, alone. I woke up in Mira's softly lit room. She, in her lovely white nightgown, sitting beside me, looking with wonderment into my face with her knowing smiling eyes, her womanness, her motherliness was in that smile.

Afterwards, we took an oily bath together. She put her breast over my face, and I grabbed the soft suppleness of her body, and squeezing her I said, "Mira, you lovely bitch, I love you!" I kissed her body all over with such gusto that we found ourselves touching each other and every movement sent electricity prickling life-currents through us both. Such is sex when it is good, and thus it was last night.

Now I came from walking her to the subway. She went to her $90 a week job, to a special meeting of teachers. She was in her pretty new spring-coat, and I was walking next to her homeward, with my hair curling up beside my ears, in my dirty navy jacket, my black pants with paint on them, on my feet my high boots and sweatsocks. I was glow-

117

ing inside. After we parted I thought about begging but first came home to eat the food which I had found.

A long, long time ago, when I arrived at Visegrad, the correction house, 'Javitointézet,' I had candy with me. The boys, who were marched in columns, seeing that the priests said it was all right, surrounded me, and I gave away all my candy. A whole bagful. Some of the boys stuffed candy into their mouths and stuck their hands repeatedly in front of me for as long as I had candy. I noticed it because one of the boys had tar stuck to his hand and I saw that hand stuck in front of me several times. But when I did not have any more candy, I was alone for the first time in my life all alone and I was only nine, a little blond boy, skinny, frightened. I needed a friend then very much. And a boy came over, put his hand on my shoulder and acted as my friend, and soon he asked me: "Do you have any more candy?" and I told him, "No, I gave it all out." He turned immediately and left me standing. I had friends later, but it is hard for me to trust anyone, and it is very hard for me to give anything to anyone, to share my things.

Anny and Honey and Beth came to visit me. On the way, they met someone who claimed to be a millionaire. He drove a Cadillac, drove them around, then stopped for a minute at the Waldorf Astoria. He gave them each a box of all sorts of rich, expensively wrapped candy. The girls brought them here, ate a lot of it, but of course couldn't eat them all and left them here. As I was unwrapping and eating the candies, gradually the past started to haunt me. They were the same kind as those that my mother had given me before she sent me away. And I remembered the pain those candies caused me in the correction house.

Yesterday I took the candies and walked with the box through Christy Street, one of the poorest Puerto Rican slum streets. The box fell and all those beautifully wrapped candies scattered upon the gray, dusty sidewalk. I picked them all up and gave one to each of the kids who came over to watch—they were dressed up prettily for Sunday. Their mothers stood close by, gossipping together in a little group.

They stared at me. I was rich and they were the poor, since I gave away the shiny candies. But then I became scared and started to run—running out from the monastery . . .

At Tompkins Square, breathless, with my heart throbbing, clutching what was left of the candies, I gave them to the young people who looked like hippies, and I became calm.

On the Lower East Side, boys and girls, 'hippies,' who have long hair, sit in a group in the middle of Tompkins Park. When they accumulate, they sing and get high. Then the cops come. They don't like what the hippies enjoy, it does not suit them and they pull these young people apart and drag them away. The rules do not have to be so exact, friends. Fellow species, the rules can be looser. We must give freedom to hug and kiss. We must speak to each other, and laugh together instead of being strangers to each other; we must be able to look our friends eye to eye, we must not teach that you must mistrust your brother, he might take your candies away, or the man might rape you . . .

LOVE IS LIFE—Hate and Fear is chaos.

A very eventful life. Having determined not to strive anymore for jobs, I was begging for a while . . . without looking for any sort of work. I really tried it, but gradually I pushed myself into the realization that I must get a job—so I can pay my rent and have a little money to go into the mountains to trip on pot, then hashish, and then on mescaline. Maybe I can cure myself from the past-pests. If it will not cure me, then: LSD. But not yet.

In the evening I went to the docks, worked there, and afterwards I found work in the fishmarket, cleaning and loading for the regular workers, who paid three dollars for five hours work; altogether I got home with six bucks. I slept a couple of hours, and after, tried to type some. I want to learn it professionally.

Two evenings couldn't go to the docks, because my back hurts from the previous loadings.

Today I went to look for a job again. I could not find one, after applying again to the Doubleday Bookstore, the Bell Telephone Company and the Museum of Modern Art. I became panicky because I only had $3, and I needed more money to look for jobs the next day. I was even tempted to go to the welfare department for help. I also begged while going from job application to job application. And before going to the unions for another factory job or dishwashing job, I bought a large manila envelope and a drymarking pencil. On the steps of the New York Public Library on Forty-second Street and Fifth Avenue, I wrote on it in block letters: "PLEASE HELP: I NEED A JOB." I sweated for 20 minutes, at first in embarrassment, then in defiant animation and expectancy. While I walked slowly down 42nd Street towards 6th Avenue, I was telling myself: "Will stay the afternoon!!!" I stood on the corner of Sixth Avenue, in a stiff, palpitating sweat for a timeless-time, and a young man dressed in blue came over: "Looking for a job?" "Yes, I am . . ." "Look no further, put down your sign." I followed him to 50 W. 44th Street, in a medium-fancy office area. He was either a vice-president or a personnel man—for me: Salvation.

He offered me a salesman's job in a human way, salary guaranteed during the training time, a weekly draw of $150 and, after training, a commission of 8% on everything I sell. It will be lots of money, and that is what I need. I have to buy some clothing and a pair of shoes most urgently, pay my back-rent for last month, pay the electric bill so it can be reconnected—all out of my first week's salary. It will be fun having light in the evenings, after not having it for six weeks.

From my first salary I will buy one hundred eggs and will give them away at Tompkins Square Park. With hard-boiled eggs maybe we can put a smile in people's hearts next Sunday. The hippies are returning to the bucolic because they enjoy being with each other, and they want to communicate better.

Emerson said that: We are divided, and we disagree, but in times of crisis we are united, and we are always on the side of truth. It is on the wall of Hunter College. But this time we are divided in national crisis, and we are not on the side of truth. This time crazy men have seized the machines for crazy values, and they play inflexible games.

Our history doesn't teach us the sordidness of what is happening; we are taught false things, we are told: our country is great, and because we are on the side of truth, so we are led to fight. Do not listen to those leaders! People! don't you see there is no real reason for our boys to be in Viet Nam? People on this Globe, don't listen to your leaders! There should be no such thing as a nation. People wouldn't hate each other, but they are given an identity, and this identity tells them that they are Germans or the Jews, or Turks, or Russians, Yugoslavs, or Rumanians, and there are slogans, games, ceremonies played out for them on a stilted level, all in the name of power for the leaders. They don't want peace. And, now, the Arabs are at the throat of Israel, and we have new carnage on this day.

By the time we become adults we have to go through such an inhuman training. We are made mad with national slogans by those who tame us, by our mothers and fathers, by our teachers and leaders who forget the pain of their training. *They* trained us but they shackled our generation. The young can feel it. They rebel against it, they want to go back to living like a tribe. But if we are a tribe, we must tame ourselves by letting ourselves return to elemental life habits. We must make this earth habitable for all humans. This is the wish of the young.

Mother wrote. A postcard in German. Its evocatory power from the past shocked the soul out of me. She writes that she writes many letters to me, puts stamps on them, and tears them up. But now she will send them, her every thought is with me. Oh, the lumps in my throat. The front of the postcard, which comes from Portugal (mother works while traveling), shows old women in black clothes, talking. There is hard, white, clean stone all around them, the cobblestones of a street, not the cobblestones of the courtyards in the correction house in Visegrad where we had to walk in pairs. Or someone had to kneel as punishment. All is tranquil and well ordered on this postcard, clothes are white and hanging in the sun and boots hang in a frame to the left of the door to the house. It looks like advertising for tourists. But there is aridity, suffering and resignation about the scene. The stones show a certain silent pride, a classical, Monastery-like timelessness . . .

And I am lonely. I am wretched. I don't know who I am anymore, I've been so many persons within the few months since I lost my job in the museum. I was a busboy, a bellboy, a delivery boy, a shoeshine-boy. A storecleaner, a factoryworker, a dishwasher, a dockworker, I was a beggar and, in between, hungry and lonely.

And now I am in training to become a salesman, and what I have to do is avoid getting muddled up, forgetting where I have to go, and why I am doing these things which are so foreign to me. Because this whole state of mind and corresponding state of life is a hopeless mire, a quicksand that tries to swallow me up, licking at my feet sometimes with voices, sometimes with visions of memories from my past. The office where I work is the cause of this. My new job consumes my life and I am still new on it, after being at it for 10 days or so. I am trying to be free of the vicious spasm of anxiety, my eyes teared, my throat for hours constricted by a muscle contraction, as if strong fingers would choke my throat, whenever I remember that I am Jewish.

Alan Doner from next door made a move for his pleasure, which disturbs me.

To begin with, Arthur called me up, saying that he would visit me with his girl friend Joan, and we would spend the evening together. Alan was here when they arrived, and I had not taken a bath yet, and felt hot, sticky, for I had sweated all day on my job. I asked Joan whether she minded if I took a bath before we ate. She said no, so I took a bath. During it, Alan said, "Would it not be fun to suck milk from a cow's tit?" After I finished the bath, I dressed myself in summer shorts and Alan gave me a suggestive long look. We ate supper, and I gave Alan milk from my large round jug with a straw and we were laughing. We were high on pot, especially I, smoking plenty in my try to feel elated.

I showed Arthur and Joan out and when I came back, Alan was still here in my room with his back to the door. When he turned around he was exposed. I just stood there. He came towards me, grinning. When he was near me, I said go away. He projected, I shuddered, I became disgusted and said, "Go away, go away and don't come in my room." He left, closing the door behind him. I locked the door, tore off my shorts and scrubbed myself. After a long while I wrote a letter saying: "Don't come into my room. I don't want to go that way. It is not good for me. Please remain kind."

Cely, my cousin, and her husband came over Friday and surprised me ten minutes after I came home from work. Since I just got paid, I invited them to Chinatown to eat. We talked over other people's talking, over the noise of clattering dishes.

I told Cely how I got my job, and said, "After my training, my work will be to contact landlords, wherever they may be, and pay them money to permit TelePrompTer Company to connect their houses to a network of cables which leads excellent TV reception into the TV sets of each tenant. I work out of 44 W. 43rd Street, an air-conditioned large office, where 'we' salesmen, called 'Real-estate Representatives,' are at work around a large conference table, with three telephones in the corners. I was placed under a District-Manager, his name is Charley Keith." Cely asked how do I adjust myself to my new job? "The stress I feel in the office is from the strangeness, the unfamiliarity of the milieu."

I have to grasp the motives for the unceasing wretchedness which crumbles me. I try to categorize them. 1) The pain of loneliness. 2) Longing for my mother. 3) The parallel of my childhood with today's situation.

My mind keeps wandering and all sorts of mental, theoretical figurations evolve but I am trying to read the three painful situations and prescribe solutions for them. I am beginning to feel not only the intellectual beauty of the solution but I am beginning to emotionally feel the beauty of it.

1) Loneliness: Peaceday was April 15th, and my meeting with Recia on that rainy day left in both of us a profound admiration for each other. I thought she disappeared from my life forever when the train rolled away. But she wrote me and since then we write each other, and would like to be together. Now I called her: I just spoke with Recia. She cried with pleasure, and I cried with pleasure, too. There was an intensity of experience. I told her, come to New York to live. She said she will have her wisdom teeth removed at home in Massachusetts and, as soon as she can, she will come. She told me, after her semester ended, she lived near the beach in the sand dunes with her dog, in a dream, in a dream of being with me. And I realized, she is for me. I want her next to me to experience the world together, the discovery of being, to enjoy the being, I want to tell her all my plans and dreams.

2) My mother: At my work especially did my anxiety mount when I received my first paycheck, a booming $159. Of course, the reason for my feeling so ill was, basically, an unconscious, subconscious fear of the independence which this money would allow me, which went counter to my subconscious dependence on my mother. I did not succumb to the pain, but followed Dr. Ellis's advice of keeping right on working, doing the best I could with the limitations at hand. My pain will subside, he says, as soon as I get used to the situation. I hope it will.

3) My work in parallel with today's situation: My District-Manager is head of the Harlem District. The area he asked me to research was in a good and wealthy neighborhood but was taken away from me as soon as I completed the research on it. He promptly put me to work on wasting time and gave me five corners of 2nd Ave., from 109th to 123rd Streets, where I was to get as many permits for the four corner houses as I could. I am still at it. This is a poverty-stricken section of Harlem close to the East River. I've seen at least ten landlords and had

no results yet (no sale), for they're taking their time deciding if they want to permit TelePrompTer to connect their houses to the network. I offer money to them, so they have nothing to buy.

In the first few days, my conscience bothered me, for I knew that as a result of my work, the rents in each apartment would go up $2 each month, plus the $5 charged for the service from each tenant per month. These people are in a cruel machine-society, which urges them increasingly at every turn to get into more expenditures, which doesn't really improve their lives, for they are luxuries. I mollified my hurting conscience by planning to fight society by giving needed stuff to them as soon as I can afford it.

My tree, the tree of life, has been attacked outside my window by a horde of caterpillars. At first they were just larvae. When I first saw the tiny white tents on the twigs, I knew they would hatch. I tried to pick them out one by one. But I couldn't do it on the whole tree. Those which were left hatched and began eating the leaves. I marvel at the durability of these tiny creatures, they endure nature's vicissitudes. I tried to fight them with a sprayer which exuded poison on them, but they are still feasting on the leaves. But certain branches which I cleaned are not attacked and the leaves on them are a lush everchanging green. I stand on a high ladder and wash them with a protective solution.

My tree, surrounded by concrete, grows with a slim body, stretching arms for light, air, rain and sunshine. This tree reminds me of so much. Of novels in which heroes looked out their windows. I used to read many novels when I was a child. Then I didn't have to borrow books from libraries, I had my own. I read stories of heroes who looked out their cell-windows and saw a tree. My tree became my friend. I grow like this tree, hurt, wounded. Yet it grows, but now it is different. My personality is different, too, more and more so . . . I am not unique. Or am I?

I can hold my job. Now everything is transformed. With my high salary, I am building a life. I can do many things, many real things. I am discovering new spheres of sensibility, and the more I allow the real, spontaneous part of me to live and feel, the more I feel at one with myself.

I am giving out food, at the present, eggs, hard-boiled eggs which I boil and take in a bag to Tompkins Square Park. A few weeks ago I was begging there but now I give out eggs, and find relief from that moment in the reformatory which was the shock of my life, the first touch of reality upon my good little boy self, when I was still innocent of the injustices of life, when I was still unhurt. And that day, when I got to the reformatory, I stood at the white stone wall with pretty, colored broken glass sticking upward on top, and a priest informed me it was there to cut the delinquents' hands if they tried to escape over the wall.

I couldn't believe the glass was meant to hurt. It glittered in the sunshine. It was too pretty to hurt anybody! I stood there with my bag of candies looking at the pretty glass, and a crowd of big boys wearing gray uniforms surrounded me. The boys stuck their big hands in front of me, and took the candy from my hand one by one, and then there was a rush of hands, a fervent hunger for the candy. And then I noticed the hand with black tar on it . . . and then the third time, the black tar . . . and I looked up, and every boy was standing with candy stuck in his mouth. Some of them could not put another in. And then others came. The big boys took all my candy, and then I was deserted. They all played, and I stood there. For the first time I was out of my home, the middle-class, arranged-for home, out of the sheltering love of my mother, who was nuts about me. Or so I thought. And someone came over and put his arm around me and acted as my friend for a few moments, until he asked me: "Do you have some candy?" "No, I gave them all away to the other boys." He turned around and walked away.

Now I am giving out eggs. If everyone would give just a little to make the world good, we all would feel different. It has to come from those who have it, to do something good with it. We need each other,

Brothers, we need each other, we are again at the gate of hell, we will blow up the world if we do not love each other. I want to turn on the whole city, the whole country, the whole continent, the whole world. It is a hopeless task, but I will try to light a candle where there is little light.

I am boiling water for the third time—tomorrow, I will be in Tompkins Square Park again to give away the hard-boiled eggs. Yes, it is selfish. But it is my satisfaction.

Eggs have a magic quality. They hatch. They represent life. And they are good to eat. But if only a few people would remember to bring salt, that would be beautiful.

Sunday I took the eggs to the park and on my way, in the bakery shop, I bought yesterday's loaves of bread. In the park was a crowd of people. I asked a few of them to help me distribute the food but they looked at me and did not move a muscle. One man came over to ask: "Who gave the money for the eggs?" I said, "The local Merchants." I was standing with my big bags, the long loaves of the Italian bread sticking out when someone smiled and we started the process. Boys and girls joined us; it was beautiful as we broke the bread and we gave it out with the eggs to everyone who came for it.

Afterwards, I wandered on the grass and saw from the distance of about ten steps, two old ladies acting strangely. It was a dreamy sensation to watch them. They spoke words without sounds, eyes and mouths spoke silently, quickly, like movements of a rabbit's mouth and nose, and I went close to them. One of the old dried-up ladies said to the other: "They have a parade outside." Q: "What are they parading about?" A: "Discontented people's parade." Q: "What are they discontented about?" A: "They have everything, they don't know how lucky they are, they have everything, enough to eat. They are just troublemakers." I looked in the direction where they pointed and saw another bunch of boys and girls carrying large food bags. They were in costumes, the boys with Indian headgear, their hair shoulder-long, the girls with headbands, their hair to their waistline and floating around them in the gentle breeze. They wore long skirts, and even the boys had many long strings of colored beads around their necks. They came walking with healthy, smooth gait, barefoot. In the park, people showed indignation against them. Some laughed at them, some, saying the words shamefully loudly, "The hippies." I followed them and helped them with the bags. We sat on the grass and ate bread with cheese, drank milk or root beer. There were many beautiful girls among them and one of them had 'chiquita' written on her forehead, in the form of a blue label pasted on bananas. I called her over because she smiled at me. She had many little freckles on her face. But as she came close, I saw she had a tired blasé look. I told her my undertaking —giving out bread and eggs. She looked pleased and interested in what I was saying.

Patty sings for a career and makes her living teaching emotionally disturbed children. As we talked, we became immersed in the subject of the power in the individual's will to be expedient in today's society, where so much is needed. We didn't realize we were sitting alone on the grass, which the 'hippies' cleaned up after picnicking, contrary to those nice people, who despised them. We came to my house and I offered her some of the sweetest little bananas that I've tasted, which are sold around here; only the Puerto Ricans know about them.

After dining at her house, I kissed her breasts and made her body sensitive and said, "I will make you feel good." She put a blanket on the floor and I had a wonderful feast on this clean fleshy girl and she had to tear me away from her.

Women are so beautiful, and I love all of them. Their softness, it is something that all living beings need. Even the inkling of it is so sweet, the hint of their breasts, the slow or furious beating of their hearts. Something quite nebulous, a beautiful tranquilization, something that has nothing to do with words, with the intellect, with thinking. We are reassured, we become emotional, feelingful. Our breast tingles, within we feel shielded.

I have to equalize the effect of strain (which I endeavor to alleviate with the help of Dr. Ellis) from my work with the materialistic return from it. I can buy more eggs, and bread, and I will give them away again on Sunday. But in two weeks after the 15th of August, I will have a helper, we will buy bread, butter, eggs, and we will distribute buttered bread with the hard-boiled eggs, in the park. Recia called me! She said she is coming to live with me! She said she wants to take a part-time job here in New York. "We will do all the wonderful things. We will make a tremendous amount of pilaf, rice mixed with beans and chile, and other concoctions." She said, "We will give them away together."

With her on my side, I will gain back my endurance. I will be a happy Man.

2 August, 1967 evening

I was fired.

How did I come home? I don't remember.

There is this choking pain in my throat. On my job, the daily conferences reminded me of Visegrad and the memory of it compelled me to cry. I didn't cry and that gave me pain, to suppress it I needed much strength. The pain, by swallowing my crying, was so intense after yesterday's strain, that I couldn't work today, and I was fired.

Yesterday we 'Real-estate Representatives' gave our report to our District-Manager. I gave my account, reporting the situation of one particular building, because of some hanging wires in front of it. I described to my District-Manager the situation, informing him I had an appointment the next day with the landlord. "I will convince him to do something about the wires, and to allow TelePrompTer to connect his building to our network."

One of the salesmen said the condition of the building has nothing to do with the connection to our network. My manager was listening intensely. It was very tense. Then I screwed up that important formality by being loud to the salesman, who ignored all the violations to

129

that certain building. But I was afraid the assignment would be taken away from me, and I would not be able to get that order, so I spoke louder. In the conference room everyone became glum and serious. The assignment was taken away from me, given to that salesman, and I was very tired. That situation reminded me of Visegrad, it was real, the situation was *real,* and I *was really* in pain, and still am.

But now I am home I cannot repress my feelings anymore. So much pressure is necessary to suppress my tears and every swallow is a pressure, and it increases the pain in my throat.

I will have to see what happens if I make a collection for eggs.

Last Sunday, after I distributed the hard-boiled ones in the park, I bought again twelve dozen more. I will distribute these and wait for someone to ask where I got them, and why. Perhaps it will catch the heart of somebody. If this does not happen after five times, I will distribute leaflets, with the text of the miracle of the loaves and fishes from the Bible. I will do it five Sunday's and make collections to buy new eggs . . .

Shit—I cannot afford that now. I'll make collections immediately, while distributing the eggs. Let me give it an honest, unafraid try. An experiment . . .

I didn't have the guts. I distributed the eggs, but didn't have the guts to make collections. As I gave the eggs to grownups, it was a turn-on, and if I had collected money, it would have been a turn-off. But a bunch of young 9-10-11-year-old street-boys surrounded me. There was a driving urgency, an anger in that crowd. A desperation. I gave them a dozen eggs and they took them hungrily. One of them asked: "What are these for, to throw?" Although they were perhaps 8 or 9 in number, they took the dozen eggs from me, as long as I had any left. I picked up the shopping bag and started to give them out one by one.

With the eggs in my hands, I saw Raoul Kline from TelePromp-

Ter. He was there with his wife and child in the park. While I put on a big smile, I was desperate inside. On my way home crossing the Bowery there was a man, a colored man, crying, with blood flowing slowly out of his mouth. Seating myself beside him, swallowing hard, I stuck the eggs in his pocket, dried his eyes, wiped his face, and cleaned the mixture of slobber and blood from his mouth and chin.

I am finding myself again. I will make the trip to Recia tomorrow and tell her our dream to live together has to wait. Not for long, I hope. I will get a job soon, then start fixing my apartment for the two of us.

We will start a comfortable, beautiful, everlasting honeymoon in the fall. Or in the winter?

Recia was distressingly sad when I told her, "I lost my job at Tele-PromptTer. The pain in my throat increased to the point where I couldn't concentrate on my job—I was fired."

Traveling to Recia before daybreak, looking out the train, I sensed the magnitude motion of the universe, the slow emergence of the glowing sun. By the time I arrived at her town, the ruby-red glowing ball had transformed into a scorching, dazzling white-light.

We walked in the burning heat to a little cottage which is in the sand dunes. There I told her about my misery. "It wasn't a put-on for you to come to New York to live with me. It was my hope."

We parted at the railroad station. When the train got slowly into motion, she was standing by the track and her appearance was mystical as the sun sank behind her at the horizon. My fairy-queen disappeared in the absorbing darkness, and in the sky the evening star became visible.

Now Monday slides into Tuesday. I have put up my shelves. I am choosing out of all my possessions those I want to keep, the rest I'll give away, I will clean up my place. And after that I will take my peyote-trip back to Visegrad, there to cleanse my feelings, to relive those times. And I will start my life liberated from my memories of an everlasting yoke. I will be anew, for new times to come.

Washed down everything, cleaned all my windows, scoured the floor. I had my apartment clean.

Prepared three capsules. I shaved and took a bath. I was chilled and frightened when I took the bath.

At 12:15 a.m. I took the three capsules, swallowed them with iced tea.

At 1:45 a.m. I took three capsules again.

I slept a few hours; awoke with mosquito bites on my body.

At 3:15 I was gagging; my throat got constricted; I was very anxious; I was fighting it. I felt chilly with goose pimples. I felt restless, fidgety, my actions were sudden, choppy.

I walked to the corner of my room, and as I put on the guitar-raga, I fastened my attention on it. I knelt and tears slowly started to trickle from the corners of my eyes. I saw myself on the train coming from Budapest, then I saw a road alongside our train as we arrived in Visegrad. I saw cobblestones leading upwards, then steps, steps again, we followed them up, I and the lady who took me there. It was 'Visegrádi-Hegy,' the hill of Visegrad. Sitting among the boys, a little boy in shorts with blond hair. My name is 'csipetke,' the little pinch of dumpling, like the kind eaten in soups. I am just a pinch . . . I was kneeling in the corner—I felt the pain in my kneecaps. I was punished. Original sin! That is what it was. Something was wrong with me. Mystical stuff! The church. Catechism. Something was generically bad about me . . . I knelt in the yard, in the corner on pebbles. In back of me children were free, playing. I knelt for days that way. Every day when play was scheduled in the afternoon I was punished. What have I done? I must have done something! But what did I do? What did I do? My mother left—she left me. Why? What did I do? She left me, she didn't want me anymore. I must have done something! Why did she leave me?—Why?—I must have done something very bad—I am guilty—of what I don't know . . .

I was hearing words—Hungarian words: "The Jews drank the puddle in the railroad station. They broke out of the freight-train, ran to the putrid puddles in the waiting area and sopped up the filthy water there." I was disgusted . . . We were talking late into the night with the priest, one who liked to talk with us . . . Jews must be very disgusting. But aren't we Jewish? . . . Anyway, I was glad I wasn't Jewish . . . But where is my mother and father? . . . "Where are you?—Am I dead?—Are you Dead? . . ." I cried late in the night on my bed . . .

I noticed my image in the mirror—a big man. "I am thirty-two—not a little boy . . ." I seemed strange to myself . . . tears in my eyes.

It was then a quarter to four A.M.

We walked down only rarely from the hill. Like when we went swimming in the 'Duna' Danube. And once somebody escaped. Or two boys? He was brought back . . . He had to pull the priest all the way from the next town on a road which I first saw when the lady took me to Visegrad. Trotting, he had to pull the priest along the railroad, with rope tied to his waist, in the front of the bicycle which the priest rode, who went to get him from the state troopers.

I saw cobblestones leading upward on the steep hill, zigzagging . . . we followed it up the hill of Visegrad. A neverending road . . . Or were there two boys?

I look at the poster on the wall—the finger points. It is the only part of the picture I see. It is a symbol. The finger, the second points at me . . . I am guilty . . .

For what reason was I beaten? Why did I have to stand in the corner? At first I knelt on the pebbles . . . later I could stand or sit, but had to stay in the corner, separate from the other playing boys I had as friends, for several weeks . . . In the corner I had friends: large ants walking singly—longer than the nails on an adult finger . . . I fed them bread—saved it from my noon meal. I gave them morsels from my pocket, watched them struggle with the morsels, tugging them into the hole patiently, then disappearing into the holes where they could just fit in . . . They touched each other, they didn't touch me but I was one of them, they were my friends . . .

The war was beautiful. Exciting. Fireworks down below in the city. In the Monastery there was a window or terrace where we stood and all night we watched the 'Stalin-candles,' the flares, suspended in the air to mysteriously illuminate the sleeping houses below. Lights hovering in the skies. Searchlights from below pinned planes to the sky. Magic. Explosions. A spectacle. Very beautiful. I did not know that they were shooting them down all night. Next day somebody was caught—he had come down with a parachute. We heard about it.

I know now that I am in a drama, complete with as many acts as I dare to relive.

The music stops. It was the second time I heard it, still guitar-ragas, each of them are equally long, for the music holds my attention, and the memory travels in spurts. Phrases. Visions. And each time I put on the record, I go on to the next act, to the next segment in time.

It is four-fifteen A.M.

Act three:

The finger is pointing at me . . . this time it is the sink, leaving a shadow on the wall. My fingers, pulled together, were beaten with the whip handle and with pencils . . . in the dining room in front of everybody. For what reason was I beaten? . . . Did I make a toy parachute out of handkerchiefs? . . .

In the beginning my name was 'csipetke,' the little pinch . . . Then I am taunted with that humiliating name. I am so little that they want to put me in soup to eat . . . I am csipetke, just a pinch . . . later the pinched one . . . I am weak and I don't know the rules . . . They all had short hair. I wasn't like them, I had long hair. I felt terribly different. I said I wanted to get my hair cut. Completely off . . . I don't know where I got scissors, and I cut my hair in front . . .

I couldn't play soccer. I didn't understand the rules. Who are "we"? Who are "they"? Where is our side? Where is their side? Which way do I have to drive the ball? Perhaps that is why I was punished, and had to stand in the corner of the yard. Because once I almost drove the ball to the other side of where I was supposed to, for I couldn't distinguish the notion that now there were two sides, and boys whom I only knew as 'Janos,' and 'Arpad,' and 'Atilla' formed a group. Our side was 'against them.' I ran with the ball—all I heard was the cheering, the noise, and as soon as I took my direction the other side, our opponents, noticed where I was going and cheered me on. I almost put a ball into our own goal. But our goal-keeper caught it, and I was punished.

Quarter to five

I cried in the night in bed . . . in front of a window, under flimsy blankets, chilled, curled up in a ball . . . "I am cold . . . it is cold . . . it is winter . . . a long winter . . ." "Where are you? . . ." "Are you dead? . . ."

My toes froze on my feet. I walked in the snow without shoes. I walk to the refrigerator, pry open the freezer compartment. I touch the ice . . . the chill through my body, the shock of it travels perceptibly, with a certain fast speed, like when you shake a long loose string. I touch the ice with my lips. My breath freezes. It is real . . .

We ate well, very healthy when there was food . . . but we started to eat less and less. I don't remember meals. I remember sticking corn into the stove, and we ate it. When there wasn't anything, then we ate the host. "Desecrated host" . . . it was good. Sweet. Everybody got 7 every day. And then, a long while after, when I didn't feel anything but my stomach, the pain of it . . . sitting among the big boys, a little boy in shorts, in the winter, with thin blond hair . . .

The Russians liberated us. They petted us on our heads. They brought the sacrificial wine in buckets. There was only one cup. We stood in line, and everyone of us drank a cup of wine. They gave us host. Then they drank wine, and we drank wine. Then they drank with us, and petted us. They were good men. I got very drunk. I never drank wine before, didn't know what it was, but I drank a lot because that was the only 'water' I put in my mouth for a long time, except snow. Snow.

Five-thirty. The red candle is half as large as the white one. It was longer than the white one when I started. I am crying, I am pained. I am hurt and cold. I am crying, I am a man but I cry. It is all right to cry, I feel when I cry. Feelings? Feelings are all right, it is good to feel, it is better than to think . . . and not feel—the way we are taught from the time we learn that there are two sides, and we are taught to fight each other, are taught to kill each other. Little by little we are fooled into hate. Our species. "Rational Animal."

Down. Quarter to six. Part of me watches the tree outside the window take form. Slowly. I am looking for salvation, I have to feel again. Is this "healing"? I go to the Bowery one block away.

I see many men on the corner. I walk among the bums of the Bowery in my shabby sailcoat, the one Alfred gave me last winter. For the first time no one asks me for money. They are friendly, smiling at me, most of them with pained faces. I am a derelict like them. Some of them drink beer, some of them are sucking the elixir from the empty bottle. This is their alternative.

Slaughterhouse for ducks. The cases of ducks thrown by four Chinamen. The white man directs them. He drinks coffee.

Walk . . . Walk . . . I walk, I have to communicate with somebody. I call Cely but get no answer.

I walk to the 'Hare Krishna' Temple. I'm late, the singing is over.

I walk—a church where I find rest in the quietness. I go slowly home. I start to write.

People! We have to start to try to prevent wars.

The world is hungry for food, for love. Let us start in little ways, let us start a miracle before it is too late. Come, let us be one big family together. Walk together. Share together. Eat together. Only we can do it—we who have. You! You! You there, I too, each of us before it is too late for all of us.

I took my peyote and relived a lot by going back to Visegrad. I was back in Visegrad. I cried, for the last time in the night.

Depressed, awakening after a couple of hours of sleep, I saw Tulipe,

TelePrompTer Cable TV
MANHATTAN CATV
CORPORATION

425 West 218th Street, New York, N.Y. 10034 (212) 942-7200

August 8, 1967

Mr. Andrew Bihaly
217 Mott Street
New York, New York

Dear Andrew:

I am sincerely sorry the way things turned out and I
do hope that you understand my position. I, as well
as the other fellows, felt deeply sorry.

I would like to thank you for the wonderful jesture
that you left us in the conference room. There is no
other flower as beautiful as a rose and all I can say
is thanks.

If you need any help or any recommendations in any
manner whatsoever, please advise. I would be more than
happy to give you the finest recommendation I can.

Best wishes and I do hope everything works in your
favor.

Sincerely,

Ted

Theodore G. Sourlis

TGS:mj

Ho Chah's—my Chinese neighbor—beautiful 18-year-old daughter, sitting in the window opposite my window. I asked her down to sit with me. She came recently to the States, and we talked with the aid of the dictionary. I told her: "I bachelor," pointing it out in the dictionary. She understood it, and I explained: "I like being one, and will remain one." She didn't make a comment but invited me to eat at their house the next day at eleven-thirty.

Promising Ho Chah to put up their rope to hang their laundry on, I went over to them, and took a whole lot of books to Tulipe. I could only talk with her about silly things, like to a child. She is so childlike in a world of self-willed, skillful happiness, so discreet and extremely piquant and distingué.

Tulipe reminds me of Alma, the combination of being exquisitely innocent and so sensuous. I would like very much to be her friend, to love her and, of course, make love to her. But in that event I would love the Alma in her. I am still saturated with the idealization when I meet Alma's likeness.

We ate a tasty, beautiful meal. I complimented Mrs. Ho Chah for the superbness of the meal and expressed my gratitude to Mr. Ho Chah for having honored me with his invitation. He, in turn, said matter-of-factly that I was accepted as his future son-in-law. At the end of this direct declaration, I told him, I am sincere, therefore I must tell them that I am a bachelor who wants to be happy, and that (gulp) I like to remain a happy bachelor. Their soul dropped, but still they offered me a little ginger and dried fruit.

14 August 1967

Dear Ted:

I just returned suntanned and rested from a short Vermont vacation, and found your kind letter in the mailbox.

I understood your position when you fired me, and was only sorry that on the one hand TelePrompTer spent a great deal of money and human effort to train me—and didn't gain much thereby; and on the other I learned and knew much specialized information, now never to be put in use to the advantage of anyone. And that this loss to both of us happened because of my failure in one evening, as opposed to an overall ineptitude or undesirable attitudes on my part.

If ever in the future you will be in a position in which you can be more accepting of correctable human error than in the one you are in now, and you would like someone like me to work for you, I would be glad to hear about. Please do not hesitate to let me know.

I feel only friendship and thankfulness to have known you and your team, and wish you well. You and Lesly and Jack have done a great deal to help me. Thank you.

Very truly yours,
Andrew

In my life significant things do happen, but they do not happen all the time. I have to learn more to fill up those spaces in time, to learn to read between the lines of the book of my life. For subtleties. For nuances.

I will try to be more self-reliant than I've been in the past few weeks. I've felt very lonely lately and left the house every day to find a woman to communicate with. Women become a compulsion with me, and I try to have affairs with them, but it doesn't work because I don't think about what I am doing.

I do just the things which prevent women from relating to me or liking me. When our talk changes from our general discourse to intimate, personal subjects, and when the girl asks questions about myself, I tell her with sincerity about my life. Or when I see only the female in a girl, I ask her, as soon as I can, to make love with me and even try to paw her.

According to one report, from Mary, a girl whom I have known formerly and who isn't malicious, girls think that I am crazy. So I have to act like Alfred says, "Don't tell them anything about yourself."

Alfred and I are friends, but the more I learn by knowing him, the more I see him as a manipulator. He is in a way very naive, for it is easy to see the connections between the trends of his actions. Now his manipulations are centered on my car, and he works on me. For the past two weeks he has invited me to smoke hash in his house.

I declared a while back (when I lost my job in the museum) that "I'll keep my car and till I have the income to pay for its maintenance, I shall leave it in the country." He asked, "What about if you will not have an income?" "Then I will sell it," I said.

Twice within a short period Alfred asked me to buy one of his motorcycles, the one in which the wiring is burned out. I said yesterday (in his house, smoking hash) when he asked again, "Do you want to buy my motorcycle?," "I don't want to buy a motorcycle, Alfred." He must guess I have a little money saved from my TelePrompTer salary, because he said, "You have money now." But when I told him: "I won't buy anything until I make a studio out of my house" his voice became loud and hard: "Who is talking about buying anything! Listen to me for a moment. Do you want my motorcycle? The cost of upkeep is not like your car." It sounded like a suggestion for an exchange proposal. I answered, "No, Alfred, I don't want a motorcycle, I want my car."

But the trading-value for my car slowly impregnates my whole outlook. A new perspective starts to emerge. Maybe I can sell it. For such a price, I will be able to furnish all the needed equipment for my studio.

And then this past week, Alfred came down with the the idea that he is leaving the continent and will settle in the Seychelles Islands. I told him a long time ago of the magical tranquility which that place gave me in the short time I was there. He came asking for more specifications, more details about the place.

I went to the Public Library, found five books relating to the Seychelles and all the articles appearing in periodicals since 1949. Also I bought three magazines for $1.75 in a used-magazine store and brought them to Alfred.

Later in the week, he said: "Let us write a book together about the life of a very average Negro, who takes the leading role in the riots and racial trouble of the Negro Ghetto." He offered to furnish all my living expenses (including writing materials) in the Seychelles. I asked about travel expenses but when his friend Larry came with his chick, he left the subject hanging and we went to the beach, together.

I became very happy because I was in nature, something I haven't been in for too long. Later, my wet hair sticking to my neck, Alfred made a remark about my long hair: "It curls up above your ears like antlers." "Yes, they are my antlers," I said. "Life crowned me with them. It won't help me to cut them off to get a job even with short hair." And he said, "Now you won't need to worry about that, because of the book we will write."

After we came back from the beach, Alfred invited me again to his house to smoke hash. He talked about the Seychelles constantly. He made our trip sound very adventurous and exciting to the extent that, to finance it, I would be willing to sell or write the ownership certificate of my car to his name. He said, "The trip is worth an old Volkswagen." But I didn't say anything, and when he said, "I will go there without you," I simply said: "I sure will miss you a lot after you leave."

Yesterday, with a large chunk of hash, he came down and brought along his friend Larry. Alfred asked me, "What's with your car?" I answered, "I want to sell it." Larry said he wanted to buy it. I said, "I'll find out the price." And Alfred, correcting Larry said, "We want to buy the car together." I asked Alfred what plan they had for paying for the car. He started quibbling, so I told him: "The best for both of you is to come with me to your bank instead of writing out a check. Take out the cash right then and there, and pay me. Let me count the money, and then, and only then, will I sign the title to the car over to you."

I told Alfred that he had many personalities, and I wouldn't want my life to depend on some of them. After that last remark, he did not argue, agree or disagree, and with Larry he left my house.

In my pad, yesterday's heat backfires from the walls and fuses with to-day's heat. I drag myself out of the dispiriting atmosphere. On the street I feel freer and become, with the beads Anny gave me, a 'hippy' in the eyes of the neighborhood. A boy with a necklace and long hair. What will people think?—I don't care—I am myself.

I walk in the East Village, where I haven't been for a long-long time. People still know me, they remember me. The owner of the restaurant Engage comes to greet me. She says, "You changed." "I don't know how I seem to others. I don't know," I told her, "I always feel different. I don't know who I am from time to time." I sit there for a while. I hear people speak. "I am for this. I am for that. Oh, I am against that. I want something meaningful to do." The young. The hippies. Ism, slogans, formulas. Words—words. What can words mean? There are so many uncertainties today. I listen but I'm not there, I look at the table, a whole tableful of men, I look at the lovely young woman who everyone is speaking with. Her boyfriend pats her on her thigh at every opportunity. He speaks Spanish, she translates for him.

I am sitting alone. The late days of August heat combine with the burnt greasy smell from the kitchen, and the mish-mash, the male-female perfume, the sweaty-body odor makes the unrefrigerated air heavy in the Engage.

I sit in a small psychedelic shop on Avenue A, off Tompkins Square Park. It is air-conditioned. People sleep on the floor. I try to read the *East Village Other*, with one eye on a beautiful woman. Her eye catches mine. She sings the song that her accompanist is playing on an organ. It is haunting, meandering—it brings back memories from a church, a church in Visegrad. I look in the eyes of the woman, she smiles at me, I am unable to communicate with her. I am sad, I feel tears around the edges of my eyes. I smile, I am possessed by her smiling eyes, her beautiful lips. I don't know what to do. She sees someone, goes to talk to him. I close my eyes. When I open them she is gone.

I feel my emotions. My pain is real to me, it is intense, choking, prolonged. I am literally squeezing back tears. The reason for my feelings, I don't see the woman . . . Whenever I come in contact with a woman, I become melancholy, blue, sad. I feel tired, very tired. Oh how very much I want to bury my head in a soft woman's lap and cry and say how deeply lonely I feel.

I come home. It's drizzling. I cry a little, goading myself to let my feelings go; I want to be free of it, of this sadness.

My depressions are very forceful, but on the other side of them lies a world of adventure and fascination. Warmth, a friendliness for the world. But in my world there is pain and a consciousness that is gray and green and mean. Full of fear and worry and punctuated by a wish to commit suicide. It often comes in the morning, I wake up with it.

I write words in my uncertainties. What can words express?

I sit in the garden. The house is neglected now, no one sweeps it. I pick up the papers from the yard, but people on the higher floors throw down paper cups, bones, bread and cigarette butts, and I pick them up again. Alfred left a gas range in the yard, it has been here for many weeks. Then came a broken refrigerator and other junk.

I shall have to call up the Sanitation Department. I will put out the junk in front of the house, to be taken away, and I will sweep out the house again.

My exercises are lifesaving, perhaps literally, because when I do 19 sets of everything and sweat and feel my arms and chest aching and quivering in tight hardness, I feel myself alive for a few seconds, and the details of life become clearer. The mind is made of matter.

Now time's reflection is on Mira. In the spring she found a prospective boyfriend, the tall engineer from California, and I found Recia. She forgot her man. I am still deeply in love with my little girl. Since springtime, Mira is searching for an effectual partner, and I—is it a rainbow . . . ?

Mira and me: Our relationship is based on sincere affection and honesty, but the bond has been the biological force in which we are congruent partners, on a reciprocal basis, never hurting each other's feeling, or lacerating our friendship in case we find what we are looking for. I respect her and like her very, very much but she doesn't want or care for my love. But I know she must like me because she was so good to me. She understands my past but slides over my present. She is without the slightest trace of malice. She is satisfied with herself. She is absolutely content the way the world is rolling. She is uncomplicated, and her Puritan unbringing reflects her modesty, in her philistinism. Mira is charming in her happiness, which became complete since her awareness of the fact that she has the most sex-appealing behind. The realization gave her self-confidence with 'men.' She became outgoing (maybe outgrowing me), and a relationship developed between us which was detrimental because it left me more and more in loneliness since springtime.

Now it is the end of August, and I am tuning Mira out because she wants to be alone with her newfound boyfriend Edward, from Israel. She asked whether we could cease our love encounters conditionally. I felt the constriction of my inners, I squeezed my teeth together, slowly realizing the meaning of her word 'conditionally.' She wants our friendship to stay intact, but I said: "How do I know how I will feel in the future?"

We took a shower together. We tried to satisfy each other. She turned off the light the first time—for the last time in complete darkness. It was an effort in vain.

In the morning I took the few things that I had there, and kissed her goodbye. We walked slowly to the subway together, the way we did in the snow, and in the spring, and in the heat of the summer less and less. We parted at the subway entrance the way we did always, she for work. I said: "You will see me again, I hope." I heard the rattling of the subway and, sadly, came home.

The pain in my throat is quite regular now, and often very severe. I gag and it reaches down to the middle of my lungs. I am dawdling

144

away my days but searching for a source which will help me to escape these sufferings.

A rainy day. Autumn is here. I went for psychiatric help at the 'Medicaid' office of the Welfare Department. On my way I bought a beautiful $8 doorman's umbrella, just the kind I lost, the kind that accompanied me to the Be-Ins.

When I came out of the Welfare Training Center, where I applied for psychiatric help, there were leaflets distributed, urging everyone to go to the Fifth Police Precinct where Louie, who was busted, was being held on marijuana charges. I never met Louie, but to help another fellow, I went to the Fifth Street Precinct. There I joined a group of some well-dressed and some ragged hippies. Many wore no shoes, wore bells and beads around their necks, and a few had guitars, tambourines, finger-cymbals. We doubled our numbers by the time we reached Washington Square, where we circled around the fountain to the music played by the hippies.

We proceeded across the Village and marched hand in hand.

A cop-car was following us with a blond cop in his twenties in it. He was alone. "Stay on the sidewalk!" he spat at us. He almost hit someone with his car from behind. For him it was a revolution, it was cops and robbers, for us it was helping someone.

At the Federal Detention Center where Louie supposedly was, we encountered TV cameras, and high-ranking police officers. We stayed there for quite a while inquiring the whereabouts of Louie. The beautiful suntanned, long-legged girl who was under my new-bought umbrella and holding hands with me was taken away by one of two English boys, who was able to make a twosome with my girl's girlfriend. I didn't like to let go of the girl but gradually saw the beauty of two young girls meeting two young blokes. I saw how much nicer it is to stay alone and let them have a good time. So I wrote my address on a cigarette wrapper and gave it to her.

We, the group, proceeded through Canal Street to the Judicial Center in our search for Louie, who, according to the Detention Center information, was there.

The 'Palace of Justice'—a place I went many a lonely dawn to look at the ludicrousness of Western man's pretentions and posturing. A scene of Roman Splendor and foreboding, overwhelming stone buildings with elaborately frightening portals and cage-windows, telling me: We are very big and very powerful and very enduring and mighty. Mighty!!! And don't tangle with us! It is better for you not to.

There, in front of the huge columns and ascending steps, our tired little group, in wind and drizzle with excellent spirits, sang some songs and melodies. And there, in the strip of sunshine that had broken through the drizzle, stood Clair Nichols in splendor, a small, beautiful-faced woman, her black hair with a few strands of gray in it. I smiled at her simply. She smiled back and we talked. I looked at her pretty, delicate hands, touched her fingers and said, "I always look at a beautiful woman's finger for a clue." My arm was around her shoulder. She asked: "Are you always so friendly?" "Just recently," I said. "I wasn't always. But there was a song current last autumn which said, 'Reach Out! Reach Out for Me!' . . . and I am trying to learn to do just that." I stepped behind her and put my arms around her protectively. She touched my hand and our fingers intertwined. And thus we stood while the melody from the harmonica and guitar surrounded us and the crowd.

It started drizzling again. I opened the umbrella and Clair, with surprise in her voice, admired it. I told her, "It is new, brand new." We left the crowd with the melody of "We shall overcome" playing on the harmonica and guitar, which had a special meaning for me.

We went to the *East Village Other* office on Second Avenue. In the office, we exchanged addresses, then changing her mind, she said, "Wait for me." I waited downstairs a long time and kissed her on her lips when she came back. We went to eat at 'Paradox Restaurant' and she told me about herself, always searching for something unknown, she said, that was the reason she joined the crowd. Also, she said she had been earning a good-high salary in a schedule job, constantly keeping an eye on her wristwatch, but that it made her sick. Therefore she had to free herself from the pressures of watching the minutes and quit her well-paying job. "And since then I keep my watch off my wrist." Now she is her own boss, makes less money, but is happy. "I have a newspaper stand," she smiled.

Clair asked what I was doing. In the spring, I told her, I lost my waiter's job. Since then I've been struggling for existence, doing anything for bread, because I won't settle in the cubby-hole of steady work. Actually, I said, I hope I can do the things I really want to do, I hope I can become a photographer, and travel around America to photograph its summers and winters, the young and the old. I want to travel around the whole world, taking pictures of different countries. I will take pictures indicating tranquility.

I told her sometimes I am very negative and depressed, and if she meets me in that bag, not to be surprised or get frightened. It is the sick part of me, which is asking questions, Who? Why?—Why? For what? I told her I am sometimes doubtful, doubtful about the rightness of my actions, uncertain in myself about the purpose of life. She said, "You are so beautifully sensitive." We spoke late into the night-hours, because she could stay out. The man she lives with was working that night. But I was afraid to ask if I could see her again.

My bag? I couldn't say it completely—I didn't want to tell her all my doubts: Who am I? Who am I inside? I don't believe in religion, in country, in law. And yet I practice those principles from the Ten Commandments which concern my fellow-beings. I don't believe in country, yet I've settled down, I am making my house, constantly building a home. I don't believe in law, and yet I try to follow my own brand of unwritten laws. Who am I *really* inside? Am I very mean? Am I masquerading? Am I pretending? Am I pretending to write? Am I pretending to live? Death? Are we alone in the world? I am lonely. Does it matter?

Dr. Binra, my psychologist, shook me from the protected, jelly-fish-life and gave me back my backbone in 1965. I'm still on schedules but I am mostly free of confinements. I don't think as I supposedly should think, because a new world-view has opened up for me. Since I stopped school two and a half years ago, I face the challenge and gradually am hammering out a 'life-style'—I will gradually learn to float economically without being so very frightened. I am living in the present and yet consistently am united with the past and gradually my failures accumulate to the point that I am tired of trying, I am scared of trying to undertake anything.

'My plan'—to arrest on photos what I see and feel—to catch, after dawn, the awakening sun or the dragonfly with its vibrating wings searching for a fountain, then motionlessly sipping dew-drops from grass, leaves or wildflowers. Or, hanging on nothing in the air, a spiderweb, a spider waiting with bulging eyes for its prey in the center of his weaved hunting ground. I want to make perceptible a child's dried tears on his smiling face, or the bitter-smile on unshaven dirty faces of the Bowery. To become a photographer I need money, 'Money,' so I decided to sell my car. I have found out the average prices of used Volkswagens. $978. Considering a sales price based on this quotation, I will get around $500 for my car.

And now the question arises, can I jeopardize the vestige of my car? Should I risk the sale of my car? I am scared.

If only this pain in my throat would leave.

The closer I get to doing photography, the more anxious and frightened I become. I say to myself: "Andrew, you are afraid of success." —Of success? Or of failure?

Yes, I am. An inner fear . . . and yet I will succeed, somehow. Succeed at what . . . ?

> At being happy. That is all I want.
> I want to keep my home my nest.
> I want to be loved and love.
> I want to see a few places in the world.
> I would like to change the world a little.
> I am learning how to express my love—
> That others feel it and can love me.

I am getting free-er with woman. I am getting free-er of the past—of my symbol-addiction. The lonely gray years are getting counter-balanced. Beginning to become. Fancy-imagination—Illusion—Fiction!!! In fact, in my loneliness, I am doing stupid, difficult and self-punishing things, like buying roses for Pamela, waiting for her until 1:30 at Blum's on 59th Street, where she is now a waitress, just to find out that she doesn't work Saturdays. I got up elevenish, ate, and sub-wayed to Clair's house. I haven't spoken to her since we met but there I was, at her house, with the roses which I took out from the refrigerator, carrying them carefully in the humid, hot Sunday. I called her twice from a nearby phone-booth with my shirt sticking to my body, gagging, choking (I choke now too while I write), not to get any answer. I went to her door, rang her bell, she wasn't home . . . In the late summer afternoon in the heat, I walked to Mira's house, about 10 blocks away. She was surprised and negative on the phone when I told her, "I am here by your house." She didn't want to come down to the street. Edward, her new boyfriend from Israel, was with her, I waited a while—she came down quite beautiful. I kissed her lightly, gave her the roses and before she had a chance to open them, I left.

Pablo, from Hesse's *Steppenwolf,* has a namesake in a 'Psychedelic Community' on Bleecker Street right off the Bowery. There exists a small shop with clothes, beads, feathers, fifes, incense, posters, and postcards, all sorts of goods for the young. Behind the store is a medium-sized lot in which slide shows are held. Exquisitely rich and unexpected colors, dyes, paints, plastics, are sprayed on slides and intense light is passed through them, creating constantly blending unpredictable hues and shapes magnified many times. Slides are only one of their activities. Another is a 'dome,' constructed of wood and translucent plastics, which surround the viewer from all sides. On its many surfaces, slides are projected from the outside.

Columbia Broadcasting System gave Pablo a $20,000 contract to create a 20-minute spectacular with complete leeway as to subject matter.

And carpenters are needed to make screen-frames and other stage props in a large ballroom of an uptown hotel. I may work for Pablo as a carpenter. I am going there every hour to check on whether someone has made a decision about my getting on the crew.

In the morning, I awakened to the realization: "You have to meet the challenge of life." I looked through the ads in the papers for a job, then went again to Pablo's. There, a surprise meeting—Clair. We made a date.

I bought a rose and by the time I took it to Clair, at 7 P.M. at the *Village Voice*, I was uptight, turned off, hungry. We went to eat at the Paradox, then to her house. But the rose was wilted by the time I gave it to her. Still she liked it and put it in the middle of the table in a vase. We drank tea in the kitchen and then Norman, with whom Clair lives, called. "He will be at home two A.M.," she said and became fidgety because of her disheveled apartment. Seeing her distraction, I gave her a helping hand. Sitting again, sipping warm ice-tea, she smoked one cigarette after another. Finally I kissed her, but I had nervous cramps. My mouth was dry, there was a large knot in my throat. Despite my tremendous anxiety, I sat her in my lap and, kissing her, said: "Let's go somewhere where it's cozy."

We went into her bedroom, a small room with a large bed. I kissed and held her a long while with gnarled feelings of having a muscular, hardened manly body but without a flicker of life in my maleism. I was tense, my arms were stiff. I kept on kissing her, and gradually became a bit more relaxed. Soon my arms had the sweet feeling of holding her soft bundle of delightfulness. I caressed her fondly and brought her up into the clouds of soaring pleasure; she came to climax. Contented, lying in my arms, dazed, she was very lovely in the shadowy light.

But her mother called and she stopped being with me. She started washing dishes, wiping around, kept cleaning up. I was missing something. After her mother called, she put on the *Messiah* of Handel, she cleaned, she was casual and the whole affair seemed to her insignificant. I expected some sort of sign that she felt good, or that she liked it. Nothing. She was even distant when she said: "You have a date

with me for 10 P.M. for next Wednesday—I'll come to your house."
And she went to her room and left me alone. I felt again my grinding
nerves and left, saying: "I have a feeling it is best for me to leave,"
thinking of her man coming back. It was past three when I came
home.

In the morning the alarm rang. I was very miserable. I slept only a
few hours and had to go for a job without smoking, because I decided
to wean myself from hash. Despite my thirst for smoke, I went for a
job, a white-collar job, and I was miserable. Still, I will try to get by. I
have a couple bucks, and my rent in the bank (savings from Tele-
PrompTer) secured till the end of the year.

After walking long stretches, I finally came home. While soaking
my feet, I ate my lunch (stale bread but freshly soaked in good cold
water, and sprinkled with salt and pepper), and marveled about Clair. I
am finally in a love-affair where the woman involved is casual and
doesn't make a big deal about sex as I have. Yesterday Clair treated sex
as one of the routine, ordinary parts of life. Before, she put on country
music. But after sex, she picked up the phone, spoke calmly with her
mother, started cleaning, not even noticing me. No, she did notice
things. She gave me a rock from her rock collection.

Once more I've done it. I bought a rose for Pamela, and waited for her
till 1 A.M., where she works, and again she wasn't working. Rattling
home in the subway, I put the rose in the fridge. It was wilted by the
time I took it (between job hunting) to Pamela, the next day.

Pamela was cleaning her apartment; her laundry was soaking, meal
cooking. She looked tired. I gave her the rose, but the poor thing was
wilting; its head was hanging down. She stuck it in a big pitcher.
Never again will I give a woman an old rose; I shall take her a fresh
one some other time. But to take a piss costs you a nickel, a bitter
pickle costs a dime, you pay 20 cents for the chance to read 'Prepara-
tion-H against pain' whenever you look up into your fellow human
being's eyes on the subway, but you don't get a transfer gratis to go

further for a job. So trudging from place to place ("a token costs twenty cents"), I came to Pablo's at noon. Asking for work I got the answer:

"You want a carpenter job? Where is your Union book?" Then up to the Carpenters' Union. "You want a Union book? Do you have a carpenter job? —No. —Who is your recommender?" So Pablo's doesn't have a job for ME, but I'll ask 'someone' anyway tomorrow, and maybe I will see Clair, she often is at Pablo's.

Not wanting to go home to the tempting hash, I called up Pamela. Phil, the young fellow she lives with, answered: "She went to your house." I almost jumped from surprise, not having had her in my house since May. I ran home, and two minutes after I cooled down, Pamela arrived. She brought me muffins she had baked. I hugged and kissed her, and held her hand while we talked. She doesn't have prolonged friendships—"but we are friends since we met at Everything for Everybody in the spring."

We went to buy fish in the Essex Street fishmarket—mackerel, lettuce-tomato, and a few peaches. At home I somewhat stiffly, nervously fried the fish. She liked the meal, and asked questions. I could answer them coherently because they were coherent questions: "What are you doing, Andrew, since we last met?" —"Oh, I spent the summer searching for necessities." She said: "Andrew, you changed; why?" —"I am finding a life-style, trying to become happy." —"And what will you do after you find that?" —"I shall express something to the world with a blend of prose with photography." We ate, and before leaving, we hugged each other with affection. We felt each other's body. She is slender and brittle . . . and very pleasant to touch.

We then walked arm in arm to her house. She will come to my house Sunday, elevenish.

Clair came over at 9 in the evening, one hour earlier than expected. She had flowers all over her hair. She is a flower herself. She asked about supper. I said, "Fruit salad." And she flew into my arms, hugged me and, with jubilation, admired the "marvelous, clean, beautiful fruit salad . . . with mangoes, grapefruit, plums—and all cut up artistically. And oh, how I love cheese dressing, and apricot yogurt." We smoked hashish. I lighted a candle, burned incense in a trance. I saw a yellow diffused light everywhere; Alfred played his flute upstairs, trills, impulsive, irregular like butterflies in flight. We lay on the rug together, we kissed and caressed each other and a beautiful feeling overcame us. It was a delicious, magical evening. I carefully removed the flowers from her hair, placed them in the refrigerator, and undressed her, rejoicing in her smooth, velvety softness. Just to touch her body with my lips and fingers, the magnolia-like curves—oh, how I enjoyed her magnificent form! I told her about my joy, and she said she forgot love. She has a lovely, slender, faultlessly proportioned body, little compared to mine. She is so dollish, so fragile—a woman!

With a tranquil smile, she asked how she looked, and a feeling of love overcame me, a strong, indescribable, sweet feeling. As I kissed her body, she became newly aroused and prepared to receive me. I tried the impossible with my cold, powerless male-inability. In my limpness, sweating, in bewilderment, I felt the spasm. "I have to cry, to sob. I wish I could just let go." Then tears came and she held me tight to her naked breasts and caressed my back and skull. "It is all right," she said. "Everything is all right." Her words pushed me back, I was in the past again, I was in Apagy, my mother had found me, she held me, they were my mother's words: "It is all right . . . everything is all right . . . " and I thought in Hungarian: "I've been so many places and so many things have happened to me . . . it is so good to be held by you again . . . I've been lost, I lost my way, and now I found you." And sobbing broke out of me but I remained controlled with part of my mind, and gradually awoke from my doze. Clair said: "You look like a young boy, all the lines and wrinkles are gone." Everything was so clear: "I just came back," I said. "I was far away." I saw things in a new beautiful way. My house, her beautiful being. I felt the sweat cooling my skin. I was renewed, the choking completely gone from my throat.

153

I rubbed shaving-lotion over her back and massaged her with newly gained strength. She breathed heavily and caressed me and I her. I made love to her deliciously, stage by stage letting my excitement mount till we reached the crowning moment.

We looked at each other with wonderment, and she tried to say something about going home. But I took her in my arms and caressed her graying hair and said: "I love my little girl." I felt so proud as she fell asleep in my arms.

I couldn't sleep. After a while, got up and wrote, with flashlight in my hand, sitting in the armchair near the bed listening to the childlike breathing of my woman.

In the dawn she awoke torturedly. I cooked eggs and tea, served her breakfast in bed and tried to minimize her guilt about staying over and being a loose woman. She got dressed and I gave her the flowers which I placed with care in the fridge. She didn't want to go back to her life, I could feel it. She loved to be catered to, and cooked for, and loved. We walked slowly to her house and sat down on the curb and rested. She smoked a cigarette, settled down within herself and when we parted I kissed her and said, "I love you."

I feel it, I am tasting the love in my mouth, in my sinews, in the sun that touches my skin, in the salt of my tears, in the songs I hear—I feel the love surging up in me.

She is so beautiful, and she has lived so much.

I called up in the evening, after I missed her a few hours, I took a brush, paint and paint thinner and went again to her house. We talked over tea. She talks very fluently, and I listen, but often I don't understand the words because I listen to her expressions and her inner being . . . her totality. I listen to her voice, I listen to her music. She gives my mind and soul a hard-on.

I plastered the holes in the wall in her kitchen, and she got turned on as I plastered and painted. She reached out and breathed on my navel and kissed it and made little remarks that I look verrryyyy good. While I passed by her, I took a taste of her neck, the little fuzzy part close to her hair. She is so very beautiful in her lightblue country dress, her waist and slender shape not stated but suggested, her soft little ass so nice to reach out for.

She took a bath and rubbed herself with lotion, next to the plants that grow near her window. She is the bloom of the plant, her graceful movements like flowers swaying in a breeze, the upswept lines of her legs are the perfect holders for her arched loins. She is so feminine, little but beautifully proportioned and graceful in the old-fashioned sense, and she turned on the flame of passion in me, that is how she is. I carried my pleasure-lily into the bedroom and we made delirious love.

We relaxed and the dawn crept into the room while we slumbered. She awoke startled, sitting up suddenly, looking into the corner. I was adrenalized in a second, but there was nothing there, just the mysterious dawn's light.

I got dressed, kissed her and wonderingly said, "I am falling in love again . . . it has happened so suddenly . . ."

I walked home in the empty awakening city, feeling my sweet feelings, hearing a song by the Beatles over and over in the rhythm of my steps and whistling its caressing, blending music. Life is so magical, so complicated.

It is a tranquil day of sunshine. For me, thoughtfulness. I didn't get to sleep until 1 A.M. so I went up to the roof to sleep in the sun and to write. But I was restless. I brought down my bunny rabbit and dug up the garden. It is black earth where I will have the spring flowers blooming next year. I sweat a little from the healthy muscle work but it freed my mind, and could think clearly. It is joyous how lovely little things are. When Beth's man, who was connected with an army hospital, was transferred to Alaska, Beth followed him as his 'secretary' and left me her bunny. My cat, Tom, and Harvey, the rabbit, became fond of each other. They are very good friends. Harvey hops where Tom is, smells him, thinks him his mother, wants to cuddle to him. Tom grabs him with his paws, not his claws, not roughly but gently. He starts to chew Harvey's head, the play becomes ungentle. Harvey lets himself be bitten and kicked without moving even an ear, and Tom starts licking Harvey's nose and forehead. Harvey closes his eyes and goes contentedly to sleep. At night they chase each other all over the room while I am asleep. Only vaguely do I know in my dreams that something is happening down there. When I finally awake, after a long time of restless sleep, I see them at full speed galloping all over the room, chasing each other, Harvey chasing the cat, then the whole thing reversed, Tom erratically changing directions at every turn with marvelous unexpectedness. At other times Tom stalks gracefully and gradually forward, tiger-crouching, taut and completely fused mentally with the motionless Harvey, then a lightning jump, and a headchewing which inevitably ends in a gentle lick, and then Tom jumps away bashfully.

On this doing-nothing day, things happened. The junk which Alfred left in the yard all summer long was cleared away. Alan Doner helped me. We took all the large pieces outside, and the Sanitation Department (which I called) carted it away.

I think of Alfred a lot nowadays. He changed my life so much. He helped me . . . and yet he does things that baffle me. When he proposed that we go to the Seychelles to write a book together and then, when he didn't get my car, he went off in a huff and there was a long silence.

This week Alfred reappeared. He came into my room on two consecutive evenings and 'laid on me' two pieces of hashish. But he came in afterward and would have smoked my hash which I bought from him, but I told him I didn't have anymore, although I had saved one piece. And last evening he came in again with hash as he was hurrying 'to work,' and asked me for $5. I told him, "You have 20 dollars in advance for the stuff, and I have only 10 dollars." He said, "I'll get some change." It was my last bread. (Except what I have stacked away while working at TelePrompTer—for rent till the end of the year, but Alfred does not know it.) But he took my money. At night I tried to see him in his room twice, and each time it was the same answer, "It is the wrong time." But after his junk was carted away, he came down, and I asked for my $10 back, but he only gave back $4. He still owes me $6. I feel I was taken, or the hash and his asking for more money is somehow connected with his wish to make me smoke more. He knows I'm on the 'tapering-off road' and, therefore, came with his hash on my 'turned-off days.' I think maybe I better change the practice of letting him into my room only on my 'turned-on days,' which will be gradually rarer.

Yesterday I had an anxious day. The day before, I had tried to go to sleep early—"wake up early and go get a job." It was impossible to fall asleep. I went out, bought two cans of beer, which left me with six dollars and fifty cents in my pocket. Coming home, I walked through Chinatown; almost every block had a lonely man asleep in a doorway . . . Why? How?

In my garden I saw my tree—unrecognizable, it is without foliage. It got completely mauled, chewed up . . . And this summer I feel the same. My past came back with all its ferocity and made my inners rot. Yet I am alive like the tree. New twigs still shoot up from its bare branches. I am alive, I am keeping my body my own, my sanity.

I came up to sleep and met Frank. He was carrying a lot of clothing in his arm. He told me, he came back yesterday from New City, from Ethel Hage's house (where he left my car after I lost my job in the museum). He said she was asking about the car, and that Ethel is now divorced, is in keen need of a man, and recently he turned her on to pot. He said she is the only turned-on person within that neighborhood.

In my apartment, I went through my downward spiral of trying to fight my paralyzing fear of getting a job. I wanted even a dishwashing job today, yet the thought to wash dishes in a 'cubby-hole' again brought my guts into rage. It was the fear-shit, every ten minutes or so—I had to let it go, my throat was gagging viciously, I couldn't go out of the house. I debated in myself with facts, I reached a point, I had to make a decision: "Tomorrow I will sell my car." Then I took one long breath of hashish, held it for a minute, and started to feel the

157

life seep back and listened to a beautiful Raga. I noticed the lovely reflections on the ceiling and walls, the exquisite shimmer of light filling my little room.

Today, in the morning at 6 o'clock, James from the next house knocked. We ate breakfast, and I turned on before we left my house to sell my car. James drove his Porsche (which is well worn and not babied), alongside Palisades Parkway to New City to pick the car up.

In New City we found Ethel Hage's idyllic house hidden in the forest. Ethel is a well-tanned, nicely rounded, very healthy looking woman, who I was curious about, because of Frank's remarks about her, and her friendly voice on the telephone when I announced last evening: "I will pick up my car tomorrow." We exchanged a few natural, relaxed remarks, while her children were running around with loud, happy hollering. Her oldest, a sexy 15–16-ish girl, was thrilled at our coming.

Ethel Hage was very helpful. She showed me where my VW was and went back to her house. I was in severe anxiety. I blew up the tires and, while the battery was being charged, I just stretched out in the forest. I thought of 1962, the time I had my accident with my motorcycle, and nearly lost my left hand. After it healed, my mother had given me this car. It felt good driving it.

The battery recharged, we drove away from New City. I drove in and out of about 8 used car lots, but no one considered the $500 I wanted to sell it for, they wanted it for a fraction of its value. James followed me everywhere with his car, and I suggested we eat somewhere. There I told him, "If I cannot sell it for its value, I'll drive it to Cely and leave it there." So I did just that. I drove to Cely's with the plates still bound with wires. She wasn't home. I left her a concise, desperate note, telling her among other things, do with the car what you want, I don't want it anymore, in myself knowing that even though I was penniless, I wasn't going to screw myself *or* my car. So I left it there and felt settled and relaxed, the choking was gone. I cut the umbilical cord: the car.

Yesterday Frank came in and asked how I liked New City. I said, "I couldn't enjoy it." And I told him, he belongs there, he looks like Robinson Crusoe, his beard is full, his coarse canvas pants faded, his shirt fringed, his sandals worn. And I also told him, "I got rid of my car." He asked me about Ethel Hage. I said I liked her but wouldn't want to have relations with a mother whose sexy daughter is there—it would be a wicked situation. Then he asked me in so many words whether I wanted to have sex with him. I said, "No." He made allusion to the possibility of his harming me bodily, and with fright's bitter muck in my mouth, I said again, "No."

I paid my rent and remained home. With automatic reflex movements I tried to put my pad in order, while in my guts Visegrad echoed, "We are going to do it to you!" and the idea of bodily harm immersed me in terror. "My mind" searched for an escape route: "You are in America, you are grown-up, he didn't force you, he is a good man, he accepted your "No." And slowly I marshaled myself into the mellowness of planning.

I prepared the ground in my little spot of garden for next spring's blooms and pampered my wounded tree with solutions and, seeing the new offshoots of tender twigs, I dilly-dallied my time till dusk, when the star of hope winked at me.

Today, true to my schedule of petering off my habit, I visited Alfred, and he asked, "You want to see me about something?" —"I want one day's supply for high." —"I don't have time for idle talk." I got up and said, "So, I'm not a good customer, but you are welcome in my house anytime," and walked out.

I contacted Marty Forat for a supply. He sent it with Frank. I was

159

sealing the wall and he was making subterfuge remarks. I understood them. I told him, all men are homosexually capable. It depends on whether each one of us decides to act it out. It is one's own private decision. I myself chose not to. He changed the meaning of the words "us" and "act." I didn't stumble, or stammer, just continued and told him that every action had an effect on me, a consequence in my life. I wanted my reality to hang together by being consistent in this respect. I know that is difficult sometimes, for there are so many selves in us, but as long as we know that certain trips are good, others bad, we should take only those we want and avoid those we don't. He stepped close to me. I didn't 'lose my cool.' I was leaning against the wall, my arms folded in front of me, and he touched my arms and shoulders. My mouth became dry but I didn't move, and he said, "Relax, nothing will happen to you," and he stepped away.

Then I told him I had friends with the same inclination as his, but I made a deal with them. As long as they allowed me to be a friend and respected my feelings, I wanted them, I needed them. I said I accept him as a friend. The only thing I ask in return is to be accepted as a friend. He asked what I did when I don't have a woman. I masturbate, I told him. With women my sex trips tend to hang together, recently more than it used to be.

I haven't been seeing much of Alan Doner my neighbor either. He became sexual towards me, and I don't want to have sex with a man, I told him. I love the love of women, but I never would have it with a man. Please, don't frighten me, I said to him. And from now on, I have to avoid Frank . . .

But as my days pass, I corrode some more. I cannot write when I am miserable. Every day I'm anxious, I'm many mentalities away from myself.

Monday, I went to Clair's house. It was a long, hard walk and by the time I arrived there, I had to rest. I sat on the street curb, leaning against a fire hydrant, aching from tension.

Clair came out ten minutes later. I went with her to the back of the house, in a beautiful untouched garden where the vegetation was left fallow for years until it became entwined with woodbines, long tendrillar manes like hair grown long and shaggy. We sat and in a short while Norman, Clair's man, came down. A lanky, dark young man, he was pale, not very handsome, but gentlemanly and unassumingly cultured. "Norman, this is Andrew." I got up to shake hands and sat quietly while they exchanged some almost inaudible words and drank their coffee. After Norman went to work, Clair gave me breakfast in the garden. She showed me a few poems she wrote, very poetical poems, expressing anguish.

Later, in her bedroom she touched me, caressed me, and left for uptown. By the time she returned she had seeped into my spirit, not only from the poems, but from her things. The posters, the plants, the little talisman-like amulets hanging on the wall, and my feelings limbered up and surged forth. I looked around the apartment and saw the flavor of life on the walls, in the cracks, in the little used corners. The same kind of life I lead, human, imperfect.

I stayed with Clair all day. In the evening Norman and I and she ate supper together (which was a turn-on for me). We were tensely reserved at first, but, since I was calm, helpful and friendly, by the time we finished eating, we loosened up and conversed while we listened to the end of the Ninth Symphony. I loved them both, Norman and Clair. When I left around 1 A.M., Norman took my hand into both of his, then he hugged me and I clutched him to my breast like a brother. We accepted each other, bound by our love for the same woman: Clair.

But now a few days have passed, and I haven't touched her nakedness or anyone else's. I am frustrated and feel rotting inside. I don't get life in my lifeless life-tree. It is without a flicker of heat, it is cold. But my mind is burning with lust, my mind is always under women's skirts, between their white, soft thighs.

Yes, Clair was over. She said she wanted to make love with me. In spite of my inclination towards her, I couldn't make love to her—and she wanted me to. We talked a lot, reasoning with one another. Now she wants me as a friend, but things aren't right between us. My desire for her is growing but I'd have to wait for the time when Norman doesn't give her the good loving every woman needs.

She is very helpful. She mentioned an international settlement not far from here, and a girl friend of hers, who stays there, would like me. Meanwhile, she helps me. I sell newspapers from her stand. And meanwhile . . . one day while I was working with her, the tree in front of my window was cut down in my absence! A metaphysical blow. Whoever cut it down covered the stump of the tree with a cloth, as if it was an arm or a leg cut off. I was sick to my stomach. After its leaves were chewed off by the tent-worms, it had started to grow shoots again. My tree loved life! It tried to stay alive! I will plant yet another one.

I am very depressed. I am growing unhealthy in many respects.

Recia Mahler, my little girl, wrote me a beautiful poetic song-letter. She is kept home by her parents, but she feels miles apart from them and alone. My spine tingled as I stood reading in the street.

"Mist covering land and sea, and pain within the lighthouse of my eye. Why is it that a dream is so hard to follow, that I am more willing to believe the ugliness of myself, that I know nothing of love and you are love itself." She sent a little lace to me in her letter. I came home and I read her letter over and caressed that little black bead she gave me and placed the piece of lace with it.

The Welfare Department, where I applied for Medicaid psychiatric help, did not answer, and I have to cure myself. Maybe then I can keep a good job, and call Recia to live with me.

The thrill of realization. When Alfred moved into the building last year, Mignone had just left me and I was down. Alfred used to call me to his apartment and I got high for the first few times, and started to realize how beautiful *people* are . . . and sunlight pervaded my insides —a great joy in life. I read Steppenwolf's sublime description of diversified pleasures, and Alfred was constantly talking to me about sex.

I got acquainted with people and on my days off from the museum we gathered in my house. We smoked plenty of pot, and I met the go-go girl from Buffalo. And I smoked more pot, and the thrill of life was welling up in me. I started to feel very happy. I was high all the time, not only from pot, but from life. The adventure in it. The idea that you don't need therapy, that you could do anything and you could be anyone and still you can have friends. I was happy, doing the things I wanted. I had a good steady job, I adjusted myself to my new status, I didn't owe a cent to anyone—I felt the surge of independence. But I lost my job, and the big failure of nerve came. Now that I've been living hand to mouth for a while, and having free days galore, I still love them. But now I am ready to finish my plans and because I can't get Medicaid I contact Mac Rattof. He will get me some peyote. I have to free myself from the shackles of these memories of mine. I want to work. Work for Recia. I am finished with Alfred's life-style.

I get up 6:30 A.M. and in spite of my neck-cramp, I goad myself, "Go look for a job." It is hell, but I make myself do it. And I came home disappointed for the thousandth time—more and more depressed. Because it seems if you don't have an 'influential daddy' or you are not an ass-licker with your boss or your superior, and you don't pay him (compliments, favors, money: 'corruption') for your advancement, you will stay on the bottom. We are slaves in this society. I discovered that 'in the labor market.' I fill out employment forms, take tests that standardize my intelligence, pass them easily, and then am told that the position has been filled. This happens again and again to me. After looking at my 'employment record,' I am asked a question: "Why, with your education, *are* you 'only a laborer'?" "Why did you lose or leave a previous 'position'? Your record is sketchy." It all points to the labor market slave system. In effect, you are asked: Will this man remain in our employment and remain *our* faithful employee? And this is measured by his performance in the past. My past performances are my chains.

163

We, the 'intellectual' laborers, are the prisoners, and the prison doors won't open for us. We are all in a labyrinth and we have to discover by our own selves that we are in one. We have to accept the fact that we have to *work* our way into and through the maze, for we are unable to break through the walls and partitions. They are made that those who enter a downward spiral sink into and are ground up in it and the whole system of insuring our paranoia is such that we never can escape the maze. Those who are bewildered and angry and try to force themselves through the walls are thrown further and further back. Why? . . . Why? ? ?

Oh, she is so beautiful. She is Eurasian, her mother Japanese, her father American. She has straight long black hair reaching below her shoulders, and eyes that in the day are more Caucasian looking than at night. At night she becomes Oriental. She is slender, olive-yellow skinned, muscular, almost childlike, in her slim bone structure—doe-like.

At the Be-In in the park I glanced at her; immediately she reminded me of Alma, and observing her for a while I became very hung up, mesmerized. But in spite of the fact that I wasn't relaxed, I went and spoke to her, offering her my tangerine. We touched each other, I kissed her in the park, and soon after we came home.

I was very tight and anxious. When I am anxious, my lips become dry, my throat constricts. I choke. So I smoked a tremendous amount of pot. Slowly I became tranquil, cooked some tea, and while she drank it, I, in a semi-trance, caressed that shiny black hair, following with my fingers the line of her heartshaped face and felt electrization in my whole body. She took off her little sweater and with my open hands I held her divine torso and felt the silkiness of her golden skin on her slim shoulders. I took off her bra and kissed her little breasts, listened to the sweet beating of her being, and kissed and licked the groove of her navel. She didn't stop me at all. She wanted what I wanted, love, to be loved.

CAN YOU DIG IT ?

A GIANT BE-IN

THIS SATURDAY, SEPT. 23rd

CENTRAL PARK SHEEPMEADOW
SUNRISE UNTILL ? ?

CELEBRATE THE BEGINNING OF AUTUMN

DO YOUR THING IN FREAKED OUT COLORS

DIG THE TRIBAL RAP - AFRICANS,
INDIANS - HOBBITS - GURUS - DISCIPLES -
SAINTS - SINNERS - WANDERERS
DROPOUTS - DROPINS - CHROMOSOME
MUTATIONS, ETC., ETC.

BRING GOODIES

AND LOVE

After a while she said, "I have to go home, to feed my kittens." We walked to her home in the deepest Lower East Side, the lowest of the neighborhoods. She lives with her boy-*friend* (a friend, she told me). He is from Cornell and shares with Angela his apartment, so she does not have expenses. We were together in her room just a short time, and a whole world of experience happened between us. She showed me her art, she told me of her family and her past. This is the first time she's away from a small town in upstate New York. She is in a fine-arts program at Cornell University, her next to last semester. She'll be in New York until January.

We smoked pot. She told me she doesn't smoke much anymore, much less than I. She smoked a lot at one time, but she went through that stage . . . she can take it or leave it. Also she went on two LSD trips, one good, one quite bad. She said she is a hippie. But she is not really a hippie, more hip to life, not even that. She likes luxury, she wears the latest fashions: simple, undecorated cowboy boots, thin-striped purple sailor pants that are wide at the bottom, and a sweater, which brings out pronounced the beauty of her shape. She wore a bell-necklace to the Be-In and a light canvas jungle-jacket, with "warmth" pinned to it in the form of an orange button.

She undressed herself. We were in bed. I loved her body and I could not have enough of it. After we made love she said, "Now you must go home. To feed your cat."

Little Angela has moved in with me—until she finds another pad. She and Jack, her boy-friend, were run out of the neighborhood. They were among the very few whites living there. His almost new car was stripped and vandalized and finally burned. He was beaten and robbed on the street, and the next day in the afternoon while he was studying, was surprised in his apartment by burglars. He left everything in the apartment and moved to friends. Angela came to me.

This is the 21st day since Angela and I met at the Be-In. So much has happened between us since then that whenever I start writing, I feel emotionally alienated from these events. Just now I am beginning to right myself to balance, am getting used to the idea that she is the very image of Alma. Today we were talking about it.

She is catlike. She is very beautiful, her face is a child's face. In that slim gamin-like body, a flame is always burning. In her unsaturable hunger for love, she has shown me that I make good love to her, that I take her into spheres of quivering ecstasy. When she is satisfied, she becomes more Oriental than otherwise. She stretches out like an open flower and is a lotus floating the surface of a mellow lake, lovely, beautiful, motionless.

I make love to her, she doesn't make love to me. Not yet. In her dormancy she is like a baby and I tiptoe to the bathroom, in privateness to quench out my burning flame.

We laugh a lot, and sometimes I am very happy. But we have a stormy relationship. Last night she was very unhappy and took a bad trip on hashish. I didn't know what to do. I was desperate, thinking she would leave me, that we would separate. *But* I had to *accept* it. Very soon, I accepted the fact that she is a wanderer.

What I want to do is to be very very nice to Angela while she is here, and keep her love for me after she finds a home for herself. If she moves out, I want to be her friend as long as she is in New York.

But now is also a difficult time for me because I am off-balance because of no job. I, avoiding getting one, put it off day after day. But I know I will get one soon . . .

I am in love. I love Angela. I can see her faults but I'd be unhappy if she would leave me, for she is a flower. The innocent violet, the slender graceful narcissus, the smiling morning-glory, the luxuriant rose, the enigmatical orchid. She is very beautiful, exotic, slender, boyish, little-girlish, and yet her behavior is self-assured, full of aplomb. She is quiet, speaks only when she wants to say something, and she has a lovely way about her. She loves doodads, wears a bell-necklace and has an anklebell on her ankle, a tiny bell she bought in a psychedelic shop

—we go to many. And she spun a string out of sewing thread, put the tiny bell on the end of it and made a puller for the ceiling-light by the bed. She loves lavender, so we bought a lavender-colored sweet incense, and I found a small old rusty box in the cellar, which we rubbed with silver paint on the outside and painted gold on the inside, and she put this lovely colored powder into the box. She is very patient and was willing to copy a small poster to make a larger one, to simulate age by charring it over a flame ever so slightly. She worked on it for a day and a half. She likes to caress little things: Harvey, the rabbit, is her darling, then her little cats, Orio and Tim. She likes my Tom too, but I am the one who takes care of the pets. And I have to guard my pet Angela, too—to protect her from Alfred. But how can I do it while I am working?

Yes, I am working again. I got a job and the people seem to relate to me as human beings, not as machines.

While going for an advertised messenger job in an office building, I met a middle-aged lady on the elevator. The machine didn't start until both of us made a move towards the buttons. I said: "Must be the circuitry. We had to incite it simultaneously." We arrived on the 19th floor. Holding the door for the lady, I showed her off the elevator, and she smiled at me. As I was filling out the employment form, thinking it 'sketchy,' and with doubt handing it in, there was the lady from the elevator, Mrs. Patterson. She recognized me, greeted me, and gave me the job.

I am learning about life. I am learning, for example, that people want 'something-beyond,' something that isn't in the strict rules, that if I do something thoughtful, something pleasing, something human, they will allow me to get ahead, they will 'like me,' like Mrs. Patterson, get on the human level: person to person. And everything has its symbolic equivalent, its gesture. If I learn to know people's gestures, and read them, I will know 'where I am at' in their eyes. It is not the content that matters, it is the form.

Like the form of Alfred, his performance. He flirted with Angela as soon as he saw her. He did it slowly, methodically. He 'exposed' himself to her by indicating something pleasant or interesting about himself or his friends. He made remarks about his plans for helping Negro musicians with their pay-demands, by organizing a union. He associated himself with these things, he said. He stops at nothing to get as much as he can. He is a rapacious user. I have to stop him from using Angela.

After I came home from my first day of work, during which I almost choked to death from tension, I found my house empty. Angela left a note saying she was going to sleep at her girl-friend's house. I spent a tortured night, the first one in two weeks without Angela, turning on all night. I went to work in the morning without breakfast. But when I came home Angela was in bed, greeting me with that enigmatical smile. Seeing her back, my inner-storm subsided. But as soon as she touched me with her caressing hands I started to cry. I got into bed with her and put my face next to her warm breasts. She embraced me with her slim arms and for a while I thought I was in Apagy, and I said, "You came back—you came back." She held me close to her naked body.

Since Angela moved in, my state of mind has improved. I've started to work steadily but it was quite difficult, so I asked for psychotherapy and got some tranquilizers. I've taken my tools from Alan Doner and will start to finish my darkroom and reactivate my lighting system. I have started to get out of myself, and have written down some very materialistic plans, plans that I can follow through week by week. My list is close to the body. I'll buy some shirts, a handsome jacket, and an overcoat, which I haven't had since I was robbed two years ago. I'll buy good-quality food because our meals are splendid when Angela does the cooking. I know she lives with me for the requirements of her body but I serve her with joy because I love her.

Angela is often tense and transfers her tension to me, perpetuating the condition. For one thing, she refuses to speak about her doings, her thoughts or her plans. She surprises me with her decisions. Last evening she said, "Now that you are working, I intend to take a job." When I asked what kind she became irritated, and said, "A job, a job, a part-time modeling job which pays well."

Secondly, Harvey my little rabbit, caught the fleas, presumably from my cat Tom, who catches fleas often on his amorous outings. So I used Tom's disinfectant-agent on Harvey, rubbed it into his skin one evening, and the little white rabbit went into shock, shitting all over the room, instead of in the box in the toilet. There are white spots of dried urine all over and it is disgusting. We stepped into it with our bare feet as we stepped off the bed in the dark. Harvey has started to lose his fur, it is all over the rug. He has sores on his body where he rubs and scratches himself because of his itching. His poor behind is bare and his springy leaping hind legs are stiff. And Harvey endures his pain mutely. To free him from his suffering, I wanted to take him to the A.S.P.C.A. but Angela acted horrified. She forced me to keep him.

Angela is often upset and tells me she will move out. She is irritable and contrary. So Harvey must live to suffer because Angela would move out of the house otherwise. She keeps this source of tension between us alive. I bought some cream to put on Harvey's skin and it is pretty disgusting to smear the salve on him. I do it so gently, but it must hurt him. The creature of patience stands it with such meekness. Angela was really pleased by my reversed attitude in keeping the rabbit, but even smearing Harvey doesn't help him. A few days have to pass. Meanwhile I'll have to make a cage for my game Harvey, because Angela doesn't like to step into his droppings.

Angela wants to become a famous model. She thinks she can walk into *Vogue, Harper's,* or *Look* and immediately get a lifelong high-salaried contract and a glamorous life. After finding out that wasn't so easy, even with her beauty, her spirit dropped. She became dissatisfied and irritable.

170

Then, Sunday evening, I said to her: "I know a job for you." And I gave her the ad. It was in the *East Village Other*. A photographer was looking for a skinny model.

SKINNY MODEL, under 23, over 16, must be photogenic, junior figure, 110 pounds or less, B-cup or smaller, must have clear complexion, light or dark. Established magazine photographer planning significant, quality photo book devoted entirely to one girl. Experience not necessary, but mature attitude essential; several poses will be nude but within strict limits of good taste; models who expect to pose for pornography need not apply. Project will take at least three months, two or three nights a week, one or both days each weekend. No conflict with daytime weekday employment. Low pay, possible fame. Additional compensation will include all expenses, meals, make-up, clothes and costuming purchased for model throughout project, plus complete model's portfolio of at least twenty 11 x 14 prints. Chuck, 760-2871 eves.

She read it and became excited. Instantly she raced down to phone the party despite my begging her to do it the next day. When she came back she was calm and spoke charmingly while dressing herself in pants and her new sexy lavender-colored sweater. She was enthralling in her simplicity. I was ready to escort her but she stopped me with a short "No." Her voice changed as she was leaving and she said, "Here I go into the big city." I didn't get a kiss as she left. So I aborted our love—she went there and stayed all night.

She called around 10 o'clock, telling me not to worry. But her voice was hard and abrupt. Missing her the whole night, before going to work, Monday I left a note on her incense box: "I missed you, I love you, I need you."

Monday went by with numb feelings while running errands, but in my shock, like sleep-talk, over and over my inner voice said, "Angela went to see about the modeling job I called her attention to. She remained out all night. She slept with the man and I miss her terribly."

By evening, Angela was home. When I saw her I smiled, but inside there was pain. She said she was offered $1 per hour for posing. She asked me to come meet the guy and get an impression of him. Tuesday I went. He is a phony, a real businessman. I told Angela not to go to him anymore, and we went to the Gracie Mansion where the three rivers meet. We stayed there to exchange warm kisses. Her passion awoke. Whisperingly, she urged: "Come home."

When I touched Angela's Mount of Venus it was like sandpaper. She had shaved herself. It felt horrible and turned my desire into shame, for I still loved her. I knew I was crazy.

I blew up my air-mattress. The long night was very long and I wrote a letter:

"Dearest beloved Angela:

The only reason I write is because I cannot speak to you with words.

I made a mistake. It was a mistake to give you the ad, and the only thing I must *do if I want to try to undo it, or at least minimize its effects, is to communicate my thoughts.*

Please, please, please, don't get into that project with that man. He is a phony. My feelings after I spoke with him, and the things he did, and the way he approached that project, was a disfiguration of you, just like go-go dancing was when I met you.

His image of you is disgusting, and in complete conflict with the way I know you to be. I am in love with you and he wants to USE *you. The photography, the ad was just a gimmick, and he wrote it that way because he wanted to avoid those kinds of people who would recognize it to be what it is. I was fooled, but my foolishness affects another human being,* YOUR *life, you, whom I love so much. I want to avoid, while I still possibly can, your following my unthinking, whimsical, destructive advice. Please don't go to that man anymore, please don't do it.*

I feel toward you as a lover-friend, who is partially another 'you' inside of me . . . I want to be a nondestructive friend to you . . . one who looks at life from the point of view of what is good in the long run for you. That is why I say all this."

After I finished my letter, a terrible restless sensual feeling got hold of me. I woke her up and clung to her body for warmth, but she didn't respond. She just lay there. I asked: "Angela, why are you so mean to me?" "Because I like to be mean, that's why. I like to be mean." And in quick succession: "There are several things in our relationship which I don't like," she said. —"What?" —"Do you want to change it, or do you want that I move out?" —"What do you want?" —"I don't want to be hindered." We looked into one another's eyes. The longing for her lips became so great that I kissed her lips. She just looked at me, and didn't kiss me back. I walked back to my air-mattress.

In the morning, I moved quietly in the room while Angela slept. I prepared myself for work, and while shaving, I practiced a calm smile in the mirror. I kept the smile-mask on the whole day.

In the evening, just when I was coming up the steps anxiously, not knowing what would await me at home, Angela was leaving. I gave her some cashews which I bought for her. She loves cashews, but took only a few. "I read your letter," she said. "You'll find my answer, it's in the room."

I found as an answer to the letter I'd written last night, a book, *The Prophet*, by Kahlil Gibran, inscribed: "For Andrew a *beautiful* book. Love, Angela." And within it a note: "My favorite part talks about not only a perfect *marriage,* but how any stable and beautiful relationship should be by 'giving of yourself with joy.' "We can be together but we have to have spaces in our togetherness."

She didn't cut me off from her friendship. She just has to have "spaces" in between. To be with her new man.

"My Beloved," I wrote:

"I know my self-destructive insanity. Only an insane man will show his beloved an ad which says 'several poses will be in the nude.' Only an insane man would say, after reading such an ad, 'I know a job for you.'

"But you underlined the words: 'giving of yourself.'

"I know of giving, do you? Have you ever come and rubbed my back? I did it for you many many times! Have you ever been awakened by me if I had a bad evening? You did it many times! Have I ever awakened you to satisfy me? Have you often washed dishes?

"I yearn for your love.

"I love the book, because it IS beautiful . . . But I also live outside of books and symbols, in the reality of feelings and emotions . . . which hinge on something *besides* poetry and the idyllic charm of it all.

"I need your skin and warmth and you send me phrases in a book! I still love you. Perhaps this hell can pass."

Angela is tense. She wants to put our friendship on a fighting phase. We fought over the rabbit and over her job. She told me that John, her new man, promised to pay her the $1 per hour, plus 'fringe benefits' while posing for him and a good percentage of what the project may gross. But I answered, the man who supposedly wants to create a photographic essay about her is a square, an alcoholic middle-aged phony. The man is cunning and the ad was used as a way to meet a gorgeous chick. But Angela said, John is a successful executive, and Sunday she received $10 from the 'executive.' I told Angela: the man purchased her, her pleasure-hair she shaved off at his asking. When I touched my little hairy mountain, I felt a stubby little nakedness instead, mutilated somehow. In bed I kissed her on her cheek and she kissed my lips, but as soon as I tried to kiss her again, the moistness of her lips became dry. I felt I was kissing a stranger. She refused to sleep with me.

She said we have to break up, and we fought over my rabbit. I wanted to take him from his cage, but Angela said he was disgusting. At night I found him cold. He was dead. I didn't take him to the A.S.P.C.A., but took him to the little green spot next to where my squirrel Peanuts rests in my garden. The next day I noticed that Angela had bought a new tube of contraceptive jelly, so I know she was at the man's house before our fight.

We broke up. It is over. Angela moved out.

She slept here Friday, Saturday and Sunday. But wouldn't let me near her and I couldn't touch her. Monday *I* told her: "There are several things in our relationship which I don't like. I arrive home tired but you are not here. You spend your evening hours with him, the man who told you to mutilate your body. Since Friday you slept in my bed with me in sweaters and panties and you made me frustrated—do you want to change all that?" I asked her. She hedged, said something about being disgusted with sex. But I asked her again: "Do you want to change?" And she replied: "I don't think it is possible to change it." —"Then move out!" I told her. —"I intend to," was her answer. I got out of bed, prepared the air-mattress and told her, "That is your bed." But I felt horrid, went to her, kissed her and told her to go back into bed. I went to the toilet, masturbated, took a bath, and turned on. I decided to make some eggs. But as I was clattering the dishes, she said: "I spent at least $30 for groceries since I was here." —"How much of it would you like me to pay?" I asked her. —"Thirty dollars. When can you pay it?" —"When I get my salary." I agreed to everything she asked. "My things will still be here, and you will see me during the day for a few days, until I find another place," she said. —"No rush, but you would have continued torturing me, so I kicked you out of my bed."

Then she jumped from the bed and started to get out her Cheerios and milk from the refrigerator. I told her: "I was just getting ready to fix some eggs for us." —"I'll eat cold cereal, thanks anyway," was all she said.

At noon I came home for lunch and found her packing in a rush. I'd 'caught her.' After she finished, we carried down her stuff. I tried to help her open the door of the car, but she didn't let me.

We came back for the rest of her belongings. I held her hand and told her: "I was happy you stayed here. You don't have to leave forever. I am glad to know you and thank you for the book. I read it twice." She was in a tremendous rush, almost as though escaping.

She left without a goodby or a hug. I yelled after her: "What is your address?" She told me and I wrote it down. Before she stepped into the car, she looked up. She was beautiful with her Oriental eyes, her long smooth black hair, in her warm-colored orange sweater and bluejeans. A pretty girl stepping in a new fancy American car.

The first thing I did as I rushed back in the apartment was rip two documents off the wall—a flyer I'd kept, an announcement for the Be-In where we met, and the advertisement in the EVO about the modeling.

She left me a note, very cold, factual, materialistic, asking for the $30 she spent while living here. She only spoke of money.

In the summer, after I was fired from TelePrompTer, I tried to get a job with the government by applying for training as a 'Public Service Career Trainee.' Yesterday I got the telegram for an interview. It would have been a six-month training program with a weekly stipend of $70, at the end of which they would have given me a job, helping people to fill out forms, teaching them to present a good working appearance, etc. etc. . . . That is how the government is in the 'business' of maintaining the status quo, maintaining the wage-slave system.

We who look for a job aren't slaves, but we are chained *in* our minds and in the number of choices that are open to us. We are aware, we can perceive the larger picture: 1) A man is tempted to have dreams . . . paradise-islands to travel to, status-aiding organizations and groups to join, mass-produced activities to partake in. He is tempted by the media with luscious appeals to his emotions, long-haired women smiling and caressing, golden voices couched in harp-tinkling music, allusions to the clean and wholesome countryside, in forests where he can find peace and harmony. 2) A man is encouraged to get into debt. To have him *owe* his *future* to the system. He purchases on installment equipments and gadgets. He gets credit cards. He can borrow if his bills are unpayable or if he bit off more than he could chew. Yes, these are the chains which produce corruptness. Consequently, if you don't show promise for the job, the heartless position-holders, with over-specifications, will push you deeper in the despairing stink-hole. And when you ask why you didn't get the job, they don't tell you.

I was rejected and afterwards felt very demoralized, very sick. And yesterday and today I didn't go to work. Instead, I spoke with two women social-workers and a male psychiatrist in the Community Service Society, where I was prescribed tranquilizers and advised to take psychotherapy, which I already applied for through Medicaid, and is in the process of being approved. It was strange to be asked questions by people who seemed to want me to respond as a sick person: What is my trouble? What do I do on the weekend? Do I have any friends? Do I like girls? Do I have a girlfriend? What did I get out of psychotherapy two years ago? What insight did I gain into my situation? I made my answers sound pat and complete enough to reduce the need for more questions. I wanted to go into as little detail as I could, yet satisfy the need for their interview forms.

Yes, I'm sick. But I am getting certain insights into what makes me feel so sick inside. The same thing that happened with Alma, happened with Angela. When living with a girl, I become insecure, fear that I will lose her, fear her leaving me so much so that I abort our relationship. I must, in my illness, cause her to leave me . . . as it was with Angela now. This teaches me something: 'Do not try to live with anyone.' I must relearn enjoying living by myself. Because, when a girl leaves me, I relive the trauma of when my mother, during the war, sent me to Visegrad to save my life.

But now, I am ill and have to get help to be well again:

Dear Sir:

I am not receiving public assistance. My source of income is being a messenger and my income is $71 a week, $57.22 net pay.

I was under psychotherapy for two years, ending 1965. Ever since I have tried to be on my own, instead of depending on anybody or on the GI Bill, which sent me through Queens College. I should not have interrupted my therapy. My doctor advised me against it. I interrupted this process because of a lack of funds.

I worked for nearly two years as a waiter, but was fired in early spring. Because I could not find a job, I was begging on the street. I found food in garbage cans, and once in a while friends fed me a meal.

In June I got a sales-representative trainee position (a well-paying job) with TelePrompTer Corporation for six weeks. But as I was working, I became very anxious on my job. My throat constricted to the point where the pain became so great that I could not concentrate on my job, and was fired.

Recently, I started to work at the Urban Renewal Management Corporation at 38 Park Row as a messenger, and the same symptoms continue as on my sales-representative job. I can only keep my job because, through the Community Service Society, at the 'psychiatric walk-in' of the Beth-Israel Hospital, I was given tranquilizing pills (only one month's supply which I take on my job three times a day). The doctor there who gave me the pills advised me to go under psychotherapy as soon as I possibly can.

At night, and also sometimes on my job, I cry. But I do not know what the reason is for my severe throat pain, and anxiety, and crying fits. Only a skilled doctor can help me to get better, but I cannot afford the price.

I wish very much to remain, and to become a constructive member of society, a good citizen, and I have not accepted public assistance, *because I want to try to learn to fend for myself economically.*

That is why I asked help from Medicaid during the summer, when I was down-and-out, and a beggar for several months. Now I would like to get well again, and I cannot do it alone. I need a doctor. Kindly try to help me through your office to go into psychotherapy again, before my life completely disintegrates.

Very sincerely yours,
Andrew Bihaly

After my work, I cleaned my refrigerator and took out the old food-stuff Angela left here. Alfred came in and asked about Angela. He said she wants to buy hashish from him. I was jealous, and told him I was going to see her tonight; so he gave a piece of hashish for her. He wants to make love to her, and this is one of his ways of doing the hooking . . . I will keep the hashish, and will give it back, saying: "I forgot to give it to her."

I visited Angela. I went to her with a present, a tray of grass for her cats. But in the middle of the tray, I planted a lavender flower, for she likes lavender so much.

Angela was sleeping in her clothes at 7 p.m., and she seemed alone and somehow down. When she saw me, she asked, "What is this?" and as I said, "Cat grass for your cats to stay healthy," Tim, one of her cats, started to eat it, and she became pleased. I made compliments about the roominess and attractiveness of her new pad. She asked whether I'd like to eat, and cooked me an omelet with peas and curry; she gave me bread and butter, a cup of tea, and some very fine cookies. It was true hospitality and perhaps love on her part; I felt a great deal of intense and kind warmth. I only expressed my gratitude towards her with my eyes.

While I ate, she showed me a snapshot where she sits on her new motorcycle, a red shiny, fancy, sharp machine . . . she rides it in pants, a blue sweater, and sunglasses . . . (She rides the cycle/She wears boots and pants/She rides the cycle/Rides over soft flesh.) Her long hair hides half her face. I gazed at the picture and longed to have it but was not sure whether she meant to give it to me, and didn't ask.

She told me about her job. Modeling, but sometimes she goes only to buy scotch tape, "doing things to help the project." She gets a lot of money: $5 an hour. The guy, John, buys her things—everything she ever dreamed of—takes her out, makes her feel important that she is a model. Whatever she is doing it is for the "project." And the project is just another aspect of their relationship—her getting money, respect, attention, and the hope of perhaps marrying a rich man became the chief points for Angela. "John is successful, very rich . . . by the wife from whom he is divorced." And John, a rich man under the guise of making a book, finds himself a love-relationship, which might have been his aim in the first place.

Angela was open and friendly towards me, she burned some incense, and showed me a letter her father wrote, all about God, a well-intentioned and loving attempt of an estranged, old man, trying to communicate with his young daughter. "Here I write the essence of my wisdom: Love God, put Him in your daily life, and all the rest of the pleasures and benefits of life will come to you . . . God is everything that is good in men and in life: God is Love of men for each other."

She showed me her reply, a long, thought-out, composed one, about individual liberty to have one's god, one's own kind . . . and hers is *anything* beautiful: "BEAUTY." She told her father something about the god of love. And that he has to accept it, pain being part of love and life.

It was all quite somber and serious. I read it slowly, although she expected me to just skim through it.

I kissed her several times; she didn't pull away but didn't return my kisses either. I was a little frantic to let her know I still cared for her. She asked me to come to her, she needs me, she said. But Angela is now with her new man, his photograph is pinned to her wall. But I bet she will leave him, too, for she is a wanderer. I must relearn to enjoy living by myself, and must feel happy living with Tom, my cat.

As I walked toward my job I thought, I have to see the world in a rosier light and in one of the psychedelic shops on Avenue A, I bought a pair of red glasses, and saw how everything changed, the contents of the wastebaskets, the rubbish, the litter, the filth, the seediness—everything became rosy, and my whole consciousness changed.

As I walked home from work on Avenue A without the morning's rosy feeling, I saw everything had changed to dirt. Everything. All my life my feelings have depended on my consciousness. Even my facial expression changes when I am in a good mood.

And now, where am I? After my rosy morning, I lost my job today, on the 10th of November, 1967.

Being again jobless, I had an arid weekend. Saturday, in my solitude, I got centered a few times and cleaned my house, and listened to music. In my loneliness, in the afternoon I subwayed to the Botanical Garden in the Bronx, to be outside—in nature. After I came home I cooked a meal, and warmed up near my fire.

Today, Sunday, I took the subway to 68th Street, to visit Evelyn in the mental hospital. She is the girl who I met last year when I was a waiter. Since then she was admitted to a mental hospital. I visit her often and between my visits she sends me letters, some dealing bravely with her toying with the idea of leaving to work in some high-class department store—that is, in the jungle of economic hustle. Her letters show her changing mood, some frightened by the gigantesque outworld, some happy in the embracement of the hospital. But all her letters are written on self-cut colored papers, decorated with tiny pictures from magazines, and all have a kindergarten style. I visited Evelyn but couldn't see her. The head nurse told me, "Evelyn is resting. No, we can't waken her."

Yesterday morning, I thought, I have to look for another job, but instead kept myself busy with ruminations: I have tried to live independently, I wanted to join 'Society.' I thought I could. But now I realize I won't be happy anymore in the mainstream of society, because I am not like everyone, I am not 'average,' so I am dropping completely out of society. But instead of falling out and landing on my ass on a hard surface and breaking my bones, I am gradually tuning out, gently, even kindly. And all because I wanted to be a grown-up, to grow up by myself, to live independently.

But again I thought, go for a job and took quite a bad trip of fear and sleep-hallucination. By noon when I awoke and quickly ate, I felt better and went for a stroll. I stopped by an office called 'Resistance,' where I overheard conversations: There is a belief that there is a right way and a wrong way. But if people do not compromise, the only alternative will be war, open conflict, the destruction of one party by the other. This alternative is not acceptable to my point of view.

The new way of doing things (the way of the future) will find another alternative to open conflict. WAR is perfected now. It is my feeling that the best way for man to change himself and his rottenness in some *other way* than the outright killing of his 'enemies' is to make his 'society' aware of the profit motive of war. PASSIVE RESISTANCES, NONCOOPERATIONS, BOYCOTT . . . Making it so unpleasant for the warmongers that their system *will* gradually but definitely go out of kilter.

After I listened to these people's talk, I electric-typed some more. For several hours.

Life is difficult anywhere but it becomes especially so when we become progressively more sensitive and perceptive. We learn to look for ways to find what is *not* written out in bold letters. There is a surface and that is like a theatrical scene. Behind is REALITY. When we read the daily papers, we can find out about the truth when we learn to read between the lines. Some things are never seen by anyone, for we simply do not have access to the insides of certain systems. Those who have access to the inside will not help anyone to know what goes on behind. I cannot be specific, but the more I take different jobs, the deeper I get into different systems, the more I feel that anyone who enters anything seriously finds that he loses part of his integrity, part of his 'innocence.' It is the old word, 'compromise,' which is the 'I give a little—you give a little and we both stay in the game' system which is a remarkably stable and enduring way of behavior, which permeates the business-minded bourgeoisie everywhere where Western-type success is achieved. This way of life became stable here. But it has a Price this stability, the price is: life here in general is sterile and hypocritical and hysterical . . .

The hysteria that people feel is, in my mind, a separate issue from sterility and hypocrisy. It is the result of the two, especially the result of hypocrisy. People feel a great disparity between what they see around them and what is hidden from them. The difference, which cannot be defined, makes people anxious; some people more, some less, but most people who are sensitive, who are in contact with what is happening, they feel it . . . especially those who are in positions of leadership, who are in contact with the intellectual part of life, in contact with theoretical things. They have equipment to do it with the mental capacity, the leisure to brood and reflect on the information at hand, or with methods, they find out certain specific areas of life's problems. And they are most often those who are creative, writers, photographers, educators, men and women involved with *other* people, from different parts of society, moneywise, agewise, educationwise, and residence wise. Maybe I am too specific about this because I feel in common with such people lately, and I am trying to delineate where I myself fit into all this. Anyway, I often feel all these things, anxiety and a resulting hysteria. Also, as I write, I constantly have a feeling of uncertainty about the notions that I express, for whatever is 'yes' is also 'not-true,' it is just a matter of a continuum, a matter of *more* true than not true. These things, anxiety, hypocrisy, sterility, are modern-flavored concepts, they are simple, but coalesce into syndromes. They are not isolatable, definable. No one can put them into a little neat box, they are volatile, very personal, and so new that one doesn't even know *whether* they really exist. I especially refer to anxiety.

The manifestations of it are everywhere, they crop up unexpectedly. Once, in the Guggenheim Museum, I saw an exhibit of the paintings by Edvard Munch. Among them I saw a painting which previously headed an essay-article of *Time* magazine, on Anxiety. It is called the 'Shriek,' and it shows a human figure of undistinguishable sex, crossing a nondescript quiet bridge that cannot be placed into any specific place. This figure puts his hands to his temples and is wide-eyed, and his mouth utters a silent, anonymous shriek. Two other persons stand on the bridge looking into the nondescript, empty, calm distance, completely unaware of the inner conditions of the person screaming. Above them swirls a turbulent, red, coarsely brushed sky. In the article, there is a Kafka-esque little story, describing a man who enters an elevator every day in the building in which he works and pushes the button of the eleventh floor. Midway between two floors, the elevator gradually stops, and a loudspeaker in the ceiling of the metal box speaks in a crisp, cheerful, impersonal voice: "We are very sorry, but we cannot expedite your ascent any further. Please remain calm. Further instructions will follow this one. Do not call for assistance. We will contact you at the next opportune moment." The man becomes frantic, presses all buttons available to him, but the machine does not respond. Hours, maybe days pass, the man shouts, sobs, beats and scratches the walls and doors of the metal box. He caresses the black, plastic buttons. He falls asleep exhaustedly, awakes in a shiver, and kneels down under the loudspeaker in the ceiling of the shiny metal box. He places his palms together in front of his chest and prays towards the ceiling.

People are trapped in a complex machinery about which they are just beginning to know. This large machine was previously named by Hobbes, Machiavelli, and Saint Thomas, but its individual parts were never as interchangeable as they have been in the twentieth century, never as easily in communication with each other as they have become through the modern mass media, never as controllable as they are in the age *since Hitler.*

Men become first dumbfounded, then confused, then start doubting the sincerity of others. They become progressively unaware of how others feel, then start doubting the reality of absolutes which men in other ages could rely upon in their most extreme hours. Then they discover that they have to deal with their contorted inner selves hiding within their own breasts. Their deeds crop up when they are with strangers or friends, or during intimate relationships with innocent loved ones, and in their own nightly dreams. They turn to phony cultists, to readers and advisers, to 'Scientologists,' to 'Swedenborgians,' to 'Keristans,' and frantically join 'action-groups' of every description, involve themselves in weird and unrelated religions like the 'Ba'hai.' They read the *Reader's Digest* openly and in corners pornography for eroticism. Their children giggle when they see that their fathers want

184

to feel the asses and breasts of their secretaries or of the lovely beatnik-sirens walking down the street. They see their mothers pop TV-dinners in the oven 5 minutes before daddy comes home from the office, they see how nobody really cares. They start shooting up all sorts of chemicals, pumping them into themselves through all their orifices; goofballs through the mouth, glue and pot through the nose, heroin through the veins. They go wild, dream of Peanut-Butter orgies, pile into phone booths and Volkswagens for fun, and run amuck in their LSD-induced trips until they 'wander' into the mental hospitals half dead, and confess their 'experiences,' gratis, for headshrinkers there. A few rich get the hell out of the country before the Draft takes them to Viet Nam to 'hunt Cong' in the jungle. Others quickly join ROTC groups and cram to get high grades in science courses so they can stay in college, others join the ranks of Graduate Students to get more education (Daddy can afford another 5 years of NYU or Columbia) instead of offering themselves to their Country, to the great Plans of LBJ. The poor join the Army and the Marines, because there they can learn a trade and stay out of trouble. Girls who realize there isn't a chance to find husbands worthy of the name in the cities (above a yearly minimum of $15,000) and go back to Paoli, Pa., to join the YWCA and turn to their girlfriends to get pure, good Baptist sexual satisfaction. Some go to Alaska as secretaries (like Beth did) to find men at Tuli Air Force base, in the Arctic wastes.

Thousands of young college graduates are rejected from the Peace Corps because they are not politically reliable, and go to serve in the welfare-system and get locked in the 'Machine' of the Megalopoli. Thousands of college graduates are rejected from their places to work from behind a desk. There is not yet a place for them in the intellectual work-force, and there is no use to strive to fight for the right of entering the world of bread and butter and totem-pole-climbing. Life here is sterile and hypocritical and hysterical. But where do I fit in . . . ? In today's REALITY.

But where are we? We, the lonely ones, we who are bottled up in our self-made prisons, we in small apartments with bathtubs in our one room? Where are we? The marginal producers who have to sell our labor on the market because we (I) starve otherwise but work as little as we can. We try to tolerate and we get high and then laugh at the scenes uptown, and when we are high we have the guts to say to a lesser or greater degree, "Fuck off with your plastic world, give me back reality." But, after the high, we go back into waves of insecurity. Where are we who cannot feel?

After my typing I visited Angela and gave her the last $5 which I owed her. Angela was talkative. Her mother will visit her this coming Thanksgiving weekend. She will meet John and will sleep over at his studio, a new one they are fixing up. A marriage scene is taking shape.

Angela told me: "Out of the little ad which you gave me, there might be a marriage." And I might keep knowing her at rarer intervals but stand by to witness whether she goes into the finale.

I got very depressed when I came back from Angela, and all the things she described, the meaning of it, that I was instrumental in causing it. But I will continue to reach out into the world and find someone!!!!

Part Three

Dear Mother,

Whenever you send me a postcard you make me emotionally sick for a few days. That is because I am neurotic. Because I choose to live honestly, by and for myself. Not for my past, and I am not alone.

Life is difficult, I don't have to tell you that. I know you don't want to make it more difficult for me to live independently by sending postcards.

At least face the possibility that our "family" has broken up, that in these times I barely communicate with Cely or her husband. And with you not at all. This is so because of my own shortcomings only. I shall have to deal with them. No one else can.

Surely my situation and feelings will gradually change. Meanwhile, I wish you well.

Andrew

Dear Cely,

A day alone at home, for me, like many days nowadays. But when I went out to take a walk, in the mailbox, your letter. A warm letter. It felt good. You ask how I am, whether I need anything. And you say you miss me.

I answer, I fluctuate, and I am amazed at my resilience, my capacity to come back from dour, despondent regions to the sunny side. I am very sensitive to atmospheres, emotional vibrations sent out by presences of others. Life is quite eventful in the city, there are a lot of new people.

I am changing within from a young man ("a youth") into a man. I don't know how I know this, I cannot think of any single thing as evidence . . . it is just a nebulous feeling . . . but I know that that is happening.

I am independent, I am living alone . . . and maintaining a quasi-equilibrium after a long history of living in the protective custody of mother, and mother-replacements. Three decades of it, to be exact. Visegrad, Apagy, Mother's apartment ("home"). After the flight from Hungary, Modena, Soriano, and a zillion temporary underground-railroad stops, 2 IRO-camps, mother's apartment in the Bronx ("home"). Then the USAF, the Concord Hotel, and Queens College (GI Bill). And there in the middle of it, Alma and a near nervous breakdown. Then in therapy at Dr. Binra's. And a sudden super-wish to eject myself from the spine-softening womb of that life-force-shrinking, life-force-wilting woman, my mother. And my discovery, and struggle against the inner hollowness she tenaciously fostered (and still attempts to) within me. A vacuum which filled me with dread. She insured the perpetuation of her "role in life," the best she could, and I stayed embroiled in her net, my consciousness clouded, for three decades, half a human's life.

But somewhere near my thirtieth year I paid off my immediate economic debts to you (with a lucky check from the wrist injury) and left the jelly-fish-spine-life. Got a little place of my own and have been at it for nearly three years already, "being on my own," living in the city, as opposed to the dependent bondage in which I was settling for half of my life.

The contrast is often very great. But I am doing it and no matter how marginally I am successful, I know one thing: that in essence that is what I am learning, by practicing it, a seemingly simple thing for others, alas, for me arduous: BEING ON MY OWN.

You write about the car. I left a note when I was leaving it. I revealed my inability to intelligently get it out of my life and asked your husband to do that and to benefit by it as much as he could, financially. That is how I think about it still. And any time any legalities have to be attended to (like signing my name on the release paper) send them to me. I will promptly *do it. I am so glad I don't have to think of it anymore.*

I am ragged and my diet is limited, but I am facing myself, and improving my own lot tangibly and with deliberate assurance. I am learning how to type professionally on an electric typewriter in the office of the Mobilization against the war in Vietnam on 17th Street near Union Square. Those people allow me to "pay" for the use of their typewriter by my mailings, and other simple office-chores. As soon as I am able to, I shall get a typist job . . . then I can have a steady income. Perhaps I can even type at home, if I buy a big typewriter, privately. And then, after I have picked up the pieces financially, I shall get into photography or movie-making, I am not sure which . . . perhaps both. My rent is paid up until the end of January, and I still have $14 to eat on, and I started out on $25 on the tenth of November. I take vitamin pills and make sure my body is well-fed, protein, phosphorus, calcium, iron and niacin-wise.

Blessed be my house. It is warm and friendly and versatile. I make a fire daily, and all I need is here.

And blessed be woman, for they love me, with all my hangups and inconsistencies. A Cornell student from Upstate lived here with me for a while recently. She was delicious. Others stay with me for a weekend, or an afternoon.

And finally, blessed be pot, for it is a (literally) life-giving catalyst. I would have choked to death without it or gone berserk from the pain long ago.

Why do I say blessed? Is that religious? No, I am not religious. But life is, when beautiful, when calm . . . and these things are part of my beautiful life.

If you like, I shall spend a few days with you after the 16th of December. All I'd like is to be picked up and brought back and wouldn't want to stay more than 4–5 days, very likely less. The change would be good for me since I haven't left the city for a year now. All I ask is to be accepted and feel I would be, from your letter. But if my Mother is there, forget it. Will make other arrangements in that case, to get together.

Love,
Andrew

I will copy this letter and send it to Cely. But my Mother will never receive my letter. I cannot send it to her. But I will keep it for my book, it records my feelings.

> In the winter of our lives
> Something freezes in us
> We forget the fresh warmth
> Of our childhood.

The feelings of expectant curiosity, of the surprise of outcomes change. We grow to know a little something of our surroundings, enough to create a 'so what' attitude. Then, one day we look at a black cat drinking white milk at a sunny window next to a white rose in clear water in a simple glass.

We realize the terrible way we adults look upon this marvelous, marvelous world. Symbols, slogans, formulas, ugly, mechanical symbols supplant the loveliness of feelings which real things, real, soft, warm, alive things gave us. Moods and atmospheres, which long ago we had ears to listen with and were curious about, the little sounds, the inner adventures. Oh, people, let yourselves be children again!

Writing is partially my subconscious desire to perpetuate the events in my life. And the flavor of writing, when I am capable to record my thoughts, is in the form of positiveness. But for a long time in a fog, I sluggishly let days pass with my slurred thoughts unable to think. I couldn't write. But the letters woke me up. Now I am writing on scrap-papers.

Special paper, special feelings. A night without sleep, and finally, after attempted yoga exercises, masturbation, and writing. I see the 7 a.m. dawn light as I once used to feel it, when I first moved here, out of college, into "independence." I want to make it, to work to make it, to break this independence-lock, this special horrid feeling of not being able to live alone, support myself financially. Of having to depend on support, for help. But now it will work. I will finish my apartment and get myself going with a part-time job, after buying some work-clothes. It would be fun trying to be with kids, not having to regiment them, perhaps having adventures together. Or a neat little job, where the guy next to me is a good fellow, and we help each other whenever we can.

15th of December 1967, on Friday, the day before my *33rd* birthday, through an agency, I landed a job as a 'teacher's helper' in a Day Care Center Nursery. In two weeks, up to today, I taught the following assignments: 8 hours in Upper Manhattan, 4 hours in Lower Manhattan and $3\frac{1}{2}$ hours in South Brooklyn. The salary is $2 per hour, which will be all right as soon as I get a steady job in my vicinity. Then I won't have to travel 2–3 hours and spend carfare for a four-hour work day. Anyway, I made $30 in two weeks, with $15\frac{1}{2}$ hours' work.

One of the things I realize while working with children: as we grow, the inside in us, the I, and the outside self, separates. Is that what the world calls growing up? We lose something, I think, somehow, when we are becoming adults. As we grow up, we gradually grow into our invisible sack, psychically enter our invisible cage. Actually, it is a private world that we all have but can be explained only partially to others.

All of us have a complicated-simple machine, a memory-machine we called it when I was a kid. I remember when I was a little boy, I could "play" i.e. read anything, play an instrument, or, with other kids, we could sing, or no matter what they or I did, we could do it when someone was not there, when we weren't conscious of somebody looking at whatever we were doing. We also brewed some strange adventures. For us certain phrases had certain unique meanings, we had all kinds of languages and images. But aren't kids great? Aren't kids much more imaginative, more good-natured than grownups?

In the Day Care Center it occurred to me as the kids were painting, or scribbling or playing something, that someone always went to them and said pedagogically, "This is very good, but if you really want to do it better, do it this way." And because that person could do it that way better, and shows it that way, the kids automatically assumed that is the way it should be done. And the kid starts to think it must be done in a certain manner. The same in schools. They have to learn to make sentences to sound a certain "literary" floweryness, and gradually, with painstaking accuracy and 'pedagogy,' they start thinking that when they write something it has to somehow differ from the way they talk, or the way they think.

And they start to use a kind of language they think you want them to speak. Also whenever they sit down to write, a tension creeps into them. Why do I say this? Because the PUBLIC LANGUAGE THAT YOU AND I LEARN IN THE SCHOOLS IS A PHONY LANGUAGE. YOU LEARN IT AS YOU GROW UP BECAUSE EVERYONE YELLS AT YOU AND REPEATS WHAT YOU SAY IN A DIFFERENT WAY AND YOU CANNOT HAVE WHAT YOU WANT UNLESS YOU REPEAT AFTER THEM THE WAY THEY SAY IT. SO THEY BEND YOU TO THEIR WILL. I WRITE IT THIS WAY BECAUSE WE ARE MADE TO LEARN TO SHOUT.

I have to find an identity, a conscious identity. I am a beatnik, a rebel, I will not, and try my damndest not to be pedagogic.

Today is the first of January 1968, and 'no schools,' no work. Oh! . . . I yearn to be in the forest.

The forest is like a womb. It holds me yet never touches me if I do not move. It is silent but has voices which even the guts can hear. It is stern as God. It is silent to culture and unaware, it speaks only to the fundamentals, the beingness of being, and makes your life, gradually, a clear waterhold of a brook. It makes me naked in front of myself, for I cannot run away from my own self. Everything settles down in me; the cultural, the city poisons ooze out of my pores. I feel health, sanity, SANITY, SANITY!!! oh-oh-oh sweet sanity coming into me bones.

January the 2nd and 3rd. Working with beautiful encouraging kids, but my days were very sad. My poverty bothered me, it showed in my clothing. And after two days of 16 hours' work, all I got was, "You will get the check by mail."

5th of January. I worked in a different neighborhood, half a day. There were rough, neglected, antagonistic kids and I also had a very bad, authority-ridden lady to work with. I tried to show the kids my postcards (I bring them from home) but they made a fight of it, tearing them out of each other's hands. But one nice episode occurred. I met Martha there, a pretty, plump girl who told me I am good with children. After 4 hours' work, the nursery paid $6. I asked for $2 more but did not get it.

Monday the 8th. The agency wanted to assign me to West 129th Street from 3 p.m. to 6 p.m. I would have earned $6, minus tax and carfare, plus more than an hour's travel by subway, plus the thirty minutes' walking time to the nursery, which is in deepest Harlem, where even mugging in daytime is a way of life. And I would have to walk there in the dark. So I refused to work there. I took out money from my savings account, now leaving $21.32 in it.

In spite of my daily telephone inquiries, the agent couldn't give me an assignment till the fifteenth, from 9:30 a.m. till 5 p.m., at a nursery on Second Avenue near 98th Street. But I was late and the supervisor lectured me. It is good that she warned me, because it could become a pattern.

In the playroom I introduced myself as Andrew, instead of Mr. Bihaly. The teacher didn't like that, it was against her wishes. The kids were marched around at her command to the music of a scratchy record. Later the boys were left with me. I played them melodies and got them mad by not letting them touch my harmonica. They ran berserk, throwing things on the floor. It was so surprising, I didn't know how to handle it. Finally, the teacher scared them into quietness.

In the afternoon I was completely alone with the kids and showed them postcards. They didn't tear them out of my hands, and there was a little boy who actually tried to follow the lines in a calligraphy, and remembered things in the pictures. I had a beautiful exciting day, and next day I received my pay; $15, for 7½ hours' work.

On the 16th I got an assignment in a friendly, liberal kindergarten. We, the 'teachers,' were addressed by first names and by the children in the same way. My work lasted only from 2:30 till 6 p.m. $7. "We will send you a check."

The 19th. A 'Nursery Group.' The children were poor, but clean and not neglected. I was in good spirits, but in the afternoon, during their sleep, the old spinster woman who supervised me got on my nerves. The way she looked at me, I felt she was pointing out that I needed better clothing. After my 8 hours' work, I got my $15 pay, which helps me enormously, because of my expenses for telephoning to the agent, and the carfares.

For a week I checked with the agency and did not get any assignments. It was depressing and difficult because I emptied my savings account to pay for gas and electricity and had no money for necessities, i.e., for rice.

Monday the 29th. Greenwich House; 7½ hours, with a beautiful teacher, Jessica. The children were hostile, but I showed them my postcards through my rose-colored glasses, and I made friends with

195

them. They were actually a sweet bunch of four-year-olds and I enjoyed working with them. During my lunch break, I bought Jessica a flower for her hair, and she said it cheered her up during the dour, gray day. 7 hours' work—$15.

On the 31st, I checked with the agency. I was proud and happy! *I was asked* to 'Greenwich House'! 5-year-olds in the morning, 3-year-olds in the afternoon, and the kids liked me. I saw Jessica again and on parting she said, "I will see you." I got my pay—$15. 7 hours' work.

February the 3rd. A cold, rotten day. Subway to 103rd Street and Lexington Avenue, and half-hour walk to 416 105th Street. But the children were intelligent, positive and curious about the postcards I showed them. I also played my penny-whistle, and they actually danced to my music. $15, 7½ hours' work.

Finally, February 8th, got work but afternoon only, from 3 p.m., same address, 416 East 105th Street. Five-year-olds. I tried to turn on the kids to music with my penny-whistle but had a difficult time till 6 p.m. $6, 3 hours' work. I arrived home at 8 o'clock.

Today is the 16th of February. Got work Second Avenue near 97th Street. I refused to spy on the children in the toilet when ordered by a huge old spinster. But wasn't afraid of her. The kids were responsive, yet authority-ridden, but I showed them postcards and played my harmonica and they loved me. "You will receive the check, soon as issued."

Monday, 19th of February. Church of All Nations. 7 hours' work. A magical, luminous sunny day, with 4-year-olds. Charming, loving children of varied races and bright faces. A beautiful, sweet, brownskinned teacher, Linda, who encouraged me to teach the children songs. In gym I walked around, and the kids joined me. I held their hands and by the 5th revolution I started to play my penny-whistle, and we danced and marched together.

But a little fight broke out. So in the middle of the gym we sat in a circle and put our heads together and had a 'peace-meeting.' I said: "No fighting, no kicking, no scratching each other. We are one peaceful family. We love one another." So it went all day. I'd love to teach there permanently. "There is talk about it," Linda said. I will inquire about it tomorrow. I seem to have won (perhaps).

While the kids were fighting, I thought: "The games children play become serious when adults play them. Real tensions build up. Real rage awakens. Real hitting. Real pain. But the pain would go away if we grew with the one who 'hit' us, because we would have a chance to hit him back, then the pain we received feels less painful. But if we are subordinated to the 'games,' the pain, and the wound or bruise hurts even more if we cannot hit back. The 'pride' hurts the 'ego'."

And there is the big 'game,' the game of life, which no one plays according to the rules. Rules are seldom spoken about . . .

For months, my whole concern has been to find a place where I can fit into 'society.' I tried to earn my living, while working with children as a teacher. But in REALITY, I can't even approach the level of being a 'teacher's helper' on a steady basis.

Today is the 15th of April and after four months of my 'teaching' assignments, my whole earning was approximately $350, minus telephone, carfare, and the 20% tax deductions. And very seldom was it paid promptly. A 'teacher's helper' has to wait a month for half or one day's earnings.

But I want to make it! I want to break the independent look, so I've decided to join the free trade market. Today, I got a peddler's license for $5. Paul MacLanaham lent me $10 for wheels, then made me a tremendous, well-designed sturdy cart out of scrap-wood from the streets. He finished it today, and I can start making $ on my own. I am in business for myself. In the flower business.

16 April 1968. Bought carnations and iris for $6. *I made $6*, the first time out with my cart. It is handsome and rides well. This is the year of my thing.

Inasmuch as my mother wrote me so many letters, I finally answered her, asking her to visit me. She was here. I was quite emotion-filled and listened to what she had to say. I told her only: "I am healthy and happy." What could I say?

18 April '68. Bought carnations and cornflowers for $8, and made only $3 (although I sold out). I gave wrong change to someone, and so gave money away.

Friday, 19 April '68. Bought flowers for $15, and sold almost all. $10 profit.

Thursday, 25 April 1968. Monday and Tuesday the weather was bad. Barely broke even two days in succession. I haven't been able to make money. Yesterday I couldn't go out in the bad weather. But I went out and collected empty cans from trash-baskets. Painted each one with different colors to have nice flower-vases for my business. While doing the painting, I was in the house all day, rained in, isolated from the world with my thoughts.

Today I left the house early bound for the wholesale market to shop for flowers, and arranged the cornflowers and peonies in the new vases. They looked like a beautiful flower-show and I proudly pushed my flower-cart to my street corner. The raingutters had dried but viciously cold winds drove me home to put on long, warm underwear.

Around noontime a flock of little pretty girls surrounded my flower-cart. Susan Brown saw me and covered my eyes with her little cold hands. We met at the Be-In so long ago last year in Central Park when the snow was still in patches on the grass. She gave her phone number, and came a few times to me. After she moved to a new place I couldn't find her, and she vanished from my life. I held Susan close to my body and felt her youth swirl through the marrow of my bones. She said she lost my address, that was why she never came to visit me again. I gave her my address and shared with her and her friends my sweet date-nut-bread lunch. I took off my warm outer insulator-jacket (I wore two), put it around her shoulders, I kissed her lips and cheeks, and said, "This made my day worth staying out."

If she would just love me enough to stay with me occasionally . . . I know it would be disastrous if she'd move to me permanently, we have almost nothing in common beyond skin-games . . . If only I could reach her interests with mine, and if we could be lovers for a few years, maybe we could love each other into old age. After Susan left, I got very depressed, lonely, full of longing. I stood on the corner with my flowers, but no one came to buy them. As darkness fell, I took home all the flowers which I had bought in the morning. It is late. I know they will be unsaleable tomorrow. Where will I get money to buy fresh ones?

In the morning I pushed yesterday's flowers to my stand; they were heavy. I tied a rope around my waist . . . and pulled the cart to my corner. I stood there till twilight, and then asked the passersby, "Do you want some candy?" And with a rush they took all my flowers till I had no more . . . And I stood there deserted with stiff limbs . . .

My throat constricts in pain, repressing the urge to cry. I did that for so long that I cannot unlearn it . . . But perhaps someone trained could help me to travel through certain emotional terrain easier than if I struggle through it alone. I keep eluding remembrances of whatever 'I' bothers me. I am thinking of going back into psychotherapy, or perhaps peyote is the better way?

Meanwhile, little by little, I do something about my house. In the rain I planted three kinds of morning-glory seeds. Red, white and blue in three boxes next to the wall in my courtyard. Also, in two other boxes under the outside rear window, next to my loft-bed. I will have flowers around my window, but I have lost my flower business, and all my hopes to ever become a photographer.

But what I was after was illusory, a sheer wishful dream. I pursued dead matter. I haven't gotten beyond 'survival' since 1965 when I dropped out of college. I tried to settle down to sink roots into one place . . . alas the place I sank into is sand, sifting sand, morally putrid and exceedingly anxiety-producing . . . And I am still locked into society.

We in Western Society are all hypnotized into the premise that the getting of objects is, should be, the purpose of life. I woke up to the reality: I will be happy to the extent that I can dehypnotize myself of this premise. Photography was my reality, a voile woven out of my vain dreams. I wanted to photograph! To immortalize my creation for the betterment of the future? Basically, to make a living. It was materiality-objectification. I hypnotized myself to be a perfect photographer.

How perfect is perfect? How perfectly can we do whatever we choose to do? How much effort do we expend on the object we create? If we live ourselves into that which we do, it will merit the test of time, it *will* endure. But is that what matters? So what for a Colosseum? a Parthenon? a painting? What happens within the human beings in the meanwhile while they build it? Are they happy? Are they sad? Are they admired? Do they 'better' others' lives? Is there a talent to see into the future? To see the needs of future people? Are we allowed to speculate? Or is the *now* the process, the feelings of the people traveling with me on the spaceship-earth at this time more important? Societal processes cannot be measured.

How about our masks? Is the Caesar his mask? Who lives behind it truly? Who is the Caesar? Johnson, Hitler, De Gaulle, Kennedy? Imagemakers do it for them, an image-industry, makeup man, script-writers, speech-writers. And Gandhi? And Churchill? Were they real? And Nietzsche? And Dracula? Superman? Who were they really? Wagner? Spinoza? Jesus? Muhammad? Who and how were their images (masks) distorted, manipulated, used? Did *they* know that would happen? Riddles, riddles . . .

And what about the little balloon man on the corner who smiles at the children? Or the flower-pushcart-man, who shows the loveliness of a cornflower or peony? Or the lonely-sad adults who speak with tinkles, shapes, forms, ephemeral moods? The ones no one knows about? Or cares about? Are they saying less important truths than those who can *afford* to spread their falsehoods? The Hearsts? The megalomaniac potentates of industry, the Astors, DuPonts, Fords, the Shahs and Pashas, the Rubirosas and Andy Warhols? The rich tricksters? The phony gallery-owners and museum directors? The tastemakers, the feeders of the culture-hungry industrial cogs and bolts-nuts? Riddles—riddles.

I am going to a psychiatrist today. I almost committed suicide four days ago.

And I let my mother visit me yesterday. She was asking me how am I. "I am fine, healthy, and happy," I said.

How about our masks? How about taking them off to those who know us? Or to those who never met us (personally)? To dare to do that, to take off our clothes (the facade we hide our souls behind?)? Is that daring valuable? Or is it better to put more and more masks on, to elaborate our masks to try to become more and more 'admirable'? 'Likeable'? Riddles, riddles.

My psychiatrist asked for a description of my sex life, event-by-event. He wants to follow methodically my sexual history from early boyhood into the present. But I feel something frightening, and I want to overcome it.

I remember a fear which used to fill me. I have to concentrate on the past and see what the fright is.

LIGHT UP THE DARKNESS—YOU FIND PEACE THROUGH CLARITY.

Only that can hurt me which I do not know. I have to conquer each part of remembrance by penetration and erosion. I have to shine a strong light, I have to discover the syndromes which keep me in the bondage of misery.

Senator Kennedy was shot. I tried very hard not to let it suck me into despondency and bewilderment. The murder tried to, but I didn't let it get me down. CAMUS: *ENGAGE*. Cleaned and washed everything and by being purposefully energetic, I associated myself with my apartment. My quest was to de-thinkify my life, to peruse and not to be involved with the murder. I covered my possessions with an attractive textile in fresh-clean colors and I tried to infuse my thoughts with their spirit. Now they do not look humdrum and dull but lovely in the light. The lovely motifs bring forth and emphasize shapes as they come through my two eye windows. They are Epicurean, Japanese in style, where every place is meant to beautify life, soul breathed into everything.

But still, I had to escape my mood, so I rode on the subway to Brooklyn. Homeward, the subway was monotonous, a dreary place as I looked at the boring, anxiety-producing ads and waited for the rotten subway stops to pass.

I came home, and started to write: "Dear Mother, I never really told you anything about myself while you were here to visit me. I let you observe. I knew you could see for yourself. Things are going badly with me, my life is going downhill. I am in constant financial troubles, although I need relatively little money . . ." I wrote a long letter to Mother for help. But the written word is only a tool. An inner thought spoken is better for me . . .

Now I am high. I took some puffs and can write anything. I can write about my friends. I can write about my soul. I can write to Mother and I can say to her anything. I can be pretentious, but I have to write to her more concisely. I wrote to Mother a note to visit me.

My mother again came to me. I told her: "I'm healthy and happy but I am becoming different in important respects. Since I got into the Yoga scene-religion of Swami Sachtidananda, I'm doing on less; and yet being cheerful and clean and healthy." Mother said: "Everyone leads a different kind of life, and each tries to influence the other. But there is a total amorality, unless it is communicated." I realized, I hadn't communicated with her for such a long time. I said simply: "I am well." My mother explicated: "If people's subjective reality doesn't mesh they avoid each other, but when formalities are exchanged, mistakes in relationships can be corrected. But it is difficult to make one's life work, or to be masters of one's fate, in spite of the several labels that people live by. They are the syndromes of today."

(And I am in Scientology, drugs, Indian Yoga's, Western, Judeo-Christian, Oriental-eclectic, Puritan, existential cults. I am a wanderer, mendicant. I am concocting and constantly oscillating, ever changing. Labels have their meaning for me, but they are taken from many sources and others would call them lurid, weird, exotic, crazy. They are all of these. "It is where *you* are at." The perceiver determines the values he judges others by.)

Mother continued: "We are in America, maybe you would still like something? You look thin." And then I asked for $1,000. I said to my mother, "I will invest the money in not expensive but good and necessary food to have at home. I will buy some paint for my house and some clothes so I can go to work comfortable. Then I will look for a 4–5 hour job which I *can keep*. 'I'm trying to find a job where I can work with people who will like me, and whom I will like, or maybe I will try something on a free-lance basis, and the $1,000 will last, till I will find a steady income.' And Mother: "You should do whatever you like to do, whenever, wherever, but eat well."

Wherever I am, I am just one of the boys; or just one of the children. They are (each one) my equals. They cannot throw me out, and do not want to get rid of me.

I am not bad. I did not do anything bad. My mother did not leave me because I actually did something, or failed to do something. She will not leave me again. I can do anything I want, it had nothing to do with her. I am independent, I must not be afraid to do, to accomplish anything! My mother's leaving me will not depend on whether I will fail or succeed at doing something. I can relax. I can feel wanted . . . on the street, everywhere.

Mother has sent me $200 already. I live on what I purchased. Inexpensive foods. Oatmeal, rice, lentils, onions, cabbage, oil, margarine, wholewheat bread, tea, milk, canned fish (tuna, salmon, sardines), green peppers. I intend to buy small fish, which I will fry. Yellow perch, or butterfish. I have had broiled smelts already on pointed chopsticks and they were delicious.

As for work, till I feel ready for it, I'll remain busy doing my house painting. And I shall try my flower-wagon again. Perhaps if I show up someplace with $10–$20 worth of flowers for 3–4 hours a day, I can make $20 a day. If that does not work, I shall try to do modeling, see how the shoe fits. Then I might string some beads, and see how beads sell on the street. Finally, I'd enjoy getting into carpentry. I'd enjoy making for other people lofts, fundamental furniture, doors and windows. And when some of this keeps me going, I shall start photography. Not commercially, just for *me,* for my own pleasure.

I do not go anywhere that costs money. But I would like to (once a week) have a bowl of rice for 30¢ at the Paradox. And I shall take at least one Yoga class a week ($1), and perhaps this will come through the 'Ashra,' a Yoga-retreat. I want to leave the city for a weekend once a month, to be in the country, to be in the green. Then, hopefully having longer and longer stretches in the country, perhaps move and stay there for good.

And most important, I am going to find a woman to sleep with regularly at her house or mine. (She shall keep her pad.) She will be attractively knowledgeable, understanding and affectionate. A younger woman, so *I* can have enjoyment when I give her joy with my slack ability. I hope she will love my body even with its shortcomings, and love me enough so she'll *want* to satisfy me and *enjoy* my satisfaction. Then, if we get along for a while, she can come and live with me, sleep with me here in my room. If she wants her own scene, she can have the apartment next door (which is empty since Alan Doner moved out).

It is amazing that I haven't completely *lost* my former dreams at T H I R T Y T H R E E. I can pick up and perhaps have a new beginning.

Therapy: My psychiatrist asked about my sex life, and I told him the many relationships I've had during my stay with the Air Force in Germany. I talked about the numerous love affairs I had in Europe (many more than in the USA) and some, the ones *I tried* to make satisfying, were indeed that. (Perhaps it could be worth my while to look for another European girl. Like Mignone was. Those women can love a man better than American girls revealed to me.) I got up to the end of my stay in Germany, and my return to the US. Then I veered off to the present and told him, I am afraid to look at what I will be like, I am afraid to look at myself when I get old, I am afraid of reality, the future. I am afraid to love an older woman whom I met recently, I am too much in love with my dreams. And I am changing. In the neighborhood certain people have stopped existing for me. I don't want to see them anymore. An old Italian man with a cane in his hand, when I see him now I fix my gaze at a faraway point in front of me, he isn't there for me. But I used to like him before, and nowadays when he calls, I tell him point-blank that I don't have time, and keep on walking. This frightens me.

Some of my days get very troubled, but only because *I* make them that way. Such was yesterday after I came home from my psychiatrist. On my way home, being *generous* to my own self, I bought canned food, adding to my food supply. At home, I got things done, cleaned and secured loose screws on my bed. I was building the *island* where I am now living, but hoping to go to the country.

At the very end of the day I decided not to go with my mood—"resist it and wrestle with it." I got high and left the house with my umbrella in the rain. Ate at the Paradox. There I saw a plump girl with smiling blue eyes looking at me. I walked over to her: "Andrew"—"Nina." She filled me with good vibrations, she seemed to be balanced, healthy, active, a talented country-girl. I'll try to see her every second day for a while, then we will see . . . because she has a "quasi-boyfriend."

I have different notions now. I am looking for *my* woman. *A* woman. For whom I will be the only man, *her* beloved. I haven't met her yet. Nina? I won't push.

If Nina will not want me, I will go out, I will be on the lookout, I will find a girl. And now back to work on the apartment, by myself; for myself. An island. Helped by my mother.

I went to my psychiatrist. I had told him already about my relationships with girls, and wanted to go into the present. What is most painful to talk about is with my wakeful introspection of homosexuality, relating to myself. It is frightening and conflicting, and I have not yet squarely faced it. The more I realize it, the more frightening it is that there has been a 'boy' in my life twice, 'using-me,' in the sense that both 'held me back,' i.e. influenced me not to do things independently for myself. Both I thought were my best friends. Al Hillers: we met in the Public Library in my high school years, while we both were working there, who kept telling me, I accept you, it doesn't matter whether the world does or not, do not strive. And Alfred who steals my tools I need for my work as soon as I start to do something. Just recently when I mentioned how nice it would be to become a professional photographer, he said: "Don't start anything new. We'll go into a business partnership. We'll make darkroom furniture." This kind of involvement. Though, no one does anything to me. Rather, I seek out such relationships, and keep them until it becomes evident what is going on, what is really happening.

Actually I am de-escalating, phasing out my friendship with Alfred. For four days already I did not open my door for him. But he saw when I helped Neal move his belongings into a Vantruck, also, I helped clean a neighbor's backyard and we planted grass, flowers, bushes in it, and Alfred made some remarks about it. I asked: "Is it bad to do something little in the world? Or to do what others around me can enjoy?" Then he called me up to his apartment, "for a friendly smoke." He started to speak about his business and, carefully modulating the atmosphere, offered me hash and spoke about wanting me as a business partner. He spoke in detail about investments. I knew it. He saw my mother, afterwards saw me shopping, so I simply explained the difference between having money or getting some money for necessities. But he tried to put me uptight by my 'misunderstanding' him. He was double-talking. He just kept talking, garbled, and I didn't take his smokes. But I kicked Alfred, so what?

But how did I get this way? I wanted to build an apartment, settle down, get into photography. I met new friends whose help loosened me up, away from what I originally wanted. I smoked a lot of pot and neglected myself and now I'm in therapy. Oh yes, I am getting money from home, my only work is my pad. And I'm my only admirer. I'm finishing my dream with my mother's help, her money, in defeat of my old self. But known by no one but myself.

Who am I? What am I? I have doubts about myself all the time. Am I 'Babbitt'? Am I Robinson Crusoe—Thoreau? Am I a true man? Is it possible to be a 'true man'? Are there 'true men'?

Therapy again. Things went all right at first—a chronological account of my sex history. Then I told my Doctor I want to speak about the present. He said fine. I told him about my two anxiety-ridden days, about my throat pains and the irresistable urge to cover my head with a blanket and sleep, my confused attempts to do something with my chaotic apartment, how all the time I thought of the country, of running away, of starting a new life somewhere in a sunny, healthy, friendly place. But all along I knew that what I wanted was to run away from what was inside of me, and I could not run from it.

I came home to work on my apartment, but became extremely anxious, my throat constricted and felt in pain. Towards the afternoon I got high, a desperate high on hashish. I walked down through the morbid Bowery to eat an ice cream, and that calmed me down. A few moments standing on Second Avenue in the chilly, gray, drizzly atmosphere brought me to realization that nothing changes in the world, only in my inner self.

My greatest pleasure is *sleeping* under a warm, soft blanket between the breasts of a large woman. But I am a grousy thirty-three-year-old man. My fetality is my fatality.

I am anxious. I overslept. It is a beautiful, sunny, warm day. I am anxious because I am almost finished with my apartment. I will have to go out and work. And I don't want to go out and get a job and work. But I am working myself closer and closer to that future I asked for, the future of my hero self. My future is knocking on my door.

My cat Tom comes and I see his ear is full of scabs. He scratches himself so I try to cure the cat and carefully take him in the beautiful sunny day up to the roof. I see his scabby internal-ear and gently squirt mineral oil in it. He shakes it out and I say to him, "So you don't want to be healed!" I see my life. The loathsomeness of it which I can't cure. And my fist, involuntarily and to my utter surprise, descends upon his head, then again. He spits, he scratches, it is horrible. I want to stop, I do. But I am surprised and amazed at myself. I am two people in one, a violent sadist beast jumps out of the meek 'good' man. And I want to work with children. (Of course, I shouldn't.) And on the roof I remember I was a child in Visegrad and I feel the pain and cry. I remember what was done to the child me in the monastery . . .

My psychiatrist wants me to function in life, to go out and meet all those nice people. But I am afraid that I sometimes act what others would label 'crazy.' Am I afraid of being crazy? This question is a real fear—that I am crazy, really going crazy. Maybe I am too afraid and want to run away from such imaginings. And the light around me slowly is turning into darkness. The evening stars above me are shining unchanged. In my apartment I cover my head.

And I dreamt that I was in an insane asylum, and had to follow a nurse. She was going to show me her ward, where I would be kept. I followed her, but she was going too fast for me to keep up with her, so I tarried after her. She did not care, I just stayed behind. Occasionally I caught a glimpse of her in the distance, and tried to follow her in a general way, but she disappeared. I started to follow my own whims and entered an avenue, at the end of which was a tunnel. I entered it and at the other end was a wildly flowing torrential river. There was a rocky ledge upon which I sat. And enormous stone figures of gargoyles and other stone figures were sitting on either side of me, constantly splashed by the white froth of the tips of huge, powerful waves which were in slow motion. And the gargoyles crouched, leaned forward and backward in contorted positions, but unable to move, were green-gray from all the moss and other tiny vegetation that grew upon their faces and shoulders because of the contact with the water. I sat there among them at the end of the tunnel, mesmerized by the mysterious atmosphere. I stayed there for many hours. It became dusk by the time I walked back through the tunnel to the other side where the terrain of the insane asylum was, where I was supposed to be led to my ward by the nurse. I saw in the tunnel pink smoke, ephemeral, heavily oozing around my feet. I walked through the heavy smoke, waded in it, not knowing where my feet were stepping.

At the mouth of the tunnel, where I originally entered, I saw in the distance the nurse whom I was supposed to follow. She sat in her white uniform on the first steps of a gently ascending row of marble steps leading gently upwards. Each step was so easy to step up to, for its elevation was short. We walked up to a large building and entered a small door where huge enormous portals should have been, for the proportions of the structure were majestic, and such a style called for large, impressive portals. Instead, there was just a simple door, large enough for a man to enter. And the nurse said: "This is the insane 'asyly,' welcome to the realm of the madmen." And there they were, men eating and drinking, sitting on pillows and benches and boxes which were translucent and gave light. The men ate fruit, exotic, juicy, ripe, varied, plentiful. They ate them with great gusto, the juices of the papaya and melons and cherries and grapes running down the sides of their mouths, into their beards and laps. And they fed each other, and some who ate enough fell asleep in each other's laps, resting their heads in each other's arms. Some of the men were bald, and others had long, curly hair. And the women were busomy and curvacious, some of them were bald, some had long flowing hair. And there were little monkeys playing among them, some hanging on their shoulders or arms with their tails curled around their limbs, resting.

And the psychologists, who were the doctors, sat in comfortable leather chairs. They were very old men sated with the joys of life. At the head of their throne-like leather chairs were dried-up masks, made of shriveled human skin and hair, with glass eyes. One of them said:

"We know what you want, come eat and drink with us, and feel at one with us. We are all in the insane asylum." And a lovely woman embraced me and fed me papaya and grapes and cherries, and took out her lovely soft warm breast and gave me milk to suck. And I was satisfied and slumbered in her lap. As I awoke, a youth with beads around his neck and on his wrists brought a typewriter to me and said: "We know what you want to write. Do you?" Then I woke up.

June 25, 1968. After therapy. During my session I kept saying to my Doctor: "I feel I am different from other people. I don't belong in society, I don't want to take a job and join the mainstream. I want to go to the country to live there, my reality is there." But he asserted that I live in self-deception, that my reality is an inner reality. Basically, he said, my fear of being different is because of my style of dressing. He suggested that I wear a suit, instead of the kind of clothes I have on. Then I won't feel different and will have confidence in myself. It would also be advisable if I cut my hair short.

Last year Alfred said about my hair, "It curls up above your ears like antlers." I said, "At least they are *my* antlers." Now my Doctor wants me to cut them off. Shall I then go and take a job? Will I stop being afraid to work where the crush is? Where each protestant minute is used and not, repeat, not wasted? Yes, nothing must be wasted, especially time . . . Time is money! Whose time? Everybody's time. That means that everybody's life is worth money. To whom? To each individual? When I start to look at myself, look at my own life as a business proposition . . . So you better take a job, buddy! If not, you won't be a productive member of society! We'll label you a bad little boy, a bad member of society! We'll label you a vagrant, unwanted! 'undesirable.'

When you 'conform' to a certain vogue, dress a certain way, wear a clean toothpaste smile, will you have a life to match? Will you have confidence right away? Will you forget Visegrad and whoever fucked you up in that place? Before the Second World War, when I was a little boy in Budapest, I had wishes, I dreamed the kind of life I'd like to lead . . . that people in my life, myself included, should be honest. None of this weird interaction, trying to impress others with clothes. A suit would be a cover-up, my smile a mask. Wouldn't it be pitiful to masquerade constantly? And keep on playing a game with people? It would be like going to Times Square, an amusement area, where your photograph is taken behind a cardboard image of carefree, happy people, who say, "Hoppla, hoppla, I am the happy! I am happy! This is the way of life!" When you go behind such an image and stick your face into it, you look grotesque, you feel grotesque. But when you cannot take your face out of the guy you stepped behind, inside of you are still trapped your emotions and feeling, and you would like to rip off the mask, yet the front continues, so you must continue masquerading, and your mask becomes a yoke.

I have these years worn sandals and, on my body, my clean but well worn-out dungarees with a sweat shirt. They weren't hiding my identity, they were me, my second skin. My wish was to grow hair and I grew it. But I couldn't live my wishes, I realized that yesterday, Tuesday, 25 June 1968. And today I bought a pair of black conventional-looking shoes, took out my suit from the mothballs, my white shirt and necktie from the box, shed my second skin and put on the phony outfit. And I cut off my hair just now. Yesterday I was *me*. Today, 26th of June, 1968, Wednesday I look phony and feel phony. The transformation was very difficult. In between I almost committed suicide. With gas. I was working on it.

June 28. My Doctor, surveying my dress-up and short hair, sees signs

211

of advancement in my condition. He wants me to go to a former patient of his who will see to it that I get a suitable job in pleasant working conditions.

It is a crazy world which tries to make you believe the myth that you are not a failure, but that 'you are a success,' after having tried it three times without success. And I must not, should not continue to believe this myth, no matter where the stimulus comes from. I cannot live in 'outer reality' because I would be 'living in a deception.' So I may have to give up my reality for a while and return to where other people are at, operating through their self-deceptions in order to live the life I want to lead. I realize my own wishful desires—to live a healthy, simple life in the fresh air, away from all the psychological obstacles abundant in the city.

As soon as I came home from my Doctor, I doffed my clothing, changed it to *my* other clothes and got high.

Walking on Cooper Square I see a sign, 'Free Store.' In its windows, hand-drawn placards, invitations: 'Come Lonely,' 'Come Homeless,' 'Come Lost,' 'Come Hungry.' In the store, hippies. A young man gave all the information he could. It is for the young people who've left their homes, or were homeless, who need help. The Free Store is sponsored by The City of New York, under the aegis of the Human Resources Administration. "What are they eating?" I asked. —"It is not organized." —"What are they doing?" —"Just sitting around." —"Where do they come from?" —"From all over." And all over the store, boys and girls just sitting around, some eating sandwiches, others looking on. They could be fed good nourishing food bought for practically pennies—maybe I could help.

After dark, as I was going home, the children were playing on the streets, while the nearby lots were empty, were filled with litter. They could be cleaned, planted with trees to be made into little parks for the children. Maybe I can start doing it.

So, today I gave my application for a job in the Free Store to the Director, and told him I can help. I have the ability to work and want to work for the people. He promised his intervention in my getting a job there. Meanwhile I say to Mother: I am fine—and take her money . . .

My mornings are dreadful. I awake depressed. I put on my monkey suit to go to my Doctor's former patient for a job. I am scared to go for a job. I come home, rip off my suit, cover my head and sink back into the immobility of sleep. After a while I arouse myself and walk to the rookery of the Lower East Side. I peep over wooden fences, searching for empty lots to make parks out of. I see a tiny clean plot with an elevated flower-garden, a kid's swimming-pool and a bench. A long, narrow lot with light foliage, a few trees. A church, behind it an empty clean lot. I speak with the priest about planting trees. "Whatever you want," he says. Next building to the left, a Synagogue, behind it a tiny plot with ailanthus trees, foliage, bushes, with a green strip for a sidewalk. On East Fifth Street, a garbage-filled small concrete area looks uninhabitable, but could be cleaned: milk boxes filled with soil to plant bushes. It needs a sandbox and it can be made into a cheerful playground. East Fifth Street is the slum of slums, one of the bamboo-fenced lots is an official dumping lot with a blue sign which says: 'Disposicion de objetos bultosos Lot #1, 2 p.m.-7 p.m."

But most of the lots are neglected, filled with rubble and household refuse, the breeding place for germs and rats. I inspected forty lots and plots, and every one of them could be converted into little parks for community use. It needs a great deal of manpower, but in the Free Store the people are idle.

After my exploration, I go to the Free Store. I saw the hippies' hulking muscle and became more and more convinced that together we could accomplish the park-development. But also, hardworking people need nourishing, solid food, and I could cook it for them.

Mr. Moore, the director of the Free Store, measured my suggestion to make parks, to cook for the people. He gave his assurance. I will get a job in the very near future as program and food organizer. I should give him a definite plan (in writing) and he will submit it to the Human Resources Administration.

Just back from my psychiatrist. He said that to make parks, to cook for people is not realistic. These ideas, he said, are out of tune. His former patient will get me a good steady job. And so, I promised I will follow his advice and take the job wherever they send me.

Oppositions against individuality are producers of deceptions. As long as I do not fall for these deceptions, and *keep* my own images about life *in spite* of the fact that it is 'out of tune with reality,' I can realize *my own dreams.* They are realizable. I just have to live otherwise for a while (*act* exactly as is expected of me), yet meanwhile, I will deceive my employers and take their money to get out of the bag they want to keep me in. When I take a job, I must act the part, and take *their* deception seriously. I'll show up punctually, in the 'correct' dress and appearance.

But while in 'their' job, I must, I will, work against them, behind their backs. Every evening in the Free Store I will work with what my Doctor calls 'those people.' It will be my *own* activity. I will act upon this duality as long as I can stop myself from being disturbed by the deception. I will work on my *act,* I will have all the props ready.

Such difficult times that I almost give up writing. I get very depressed, and I cannot always climb out of it, especially when it comes on me in the morning. At those times, independent of the weather, I want to commit suicide, death hangs over my head like a heavy blanket. When I turn on, it goes away, that feeling. My psychiatrist says it is because I have nothing to do that day, therefore comes the dread of it. So today I did several things. I inquired in the Free Store for my job, and I got it. It has been approved. Then I shopped for lentils, oil, and discovered noodles that can be cooked in 3 minutes and eaten immediately, and cost 12 cents per serving. They can be cooked with shrimp and sea-soned oriental. I am working with rice and lentils right now, and once I have assimilated them into several dishes, I will add potatoes, and split peas and beans. With spices, oil, margarine, onions and cabbage I want to create several dishes that are filling and cheap and tasty. There is an oriental bean which sprouts when I add water, making a fresh vegetable called beansprouts. After these staples, I will enter the region of noodles and sauces, into which all kinds of things can be mixed, from eggs to cheese to fish.

Imagine! feeding great masses of people on next to nothing. Quite a few beautiful things could be done for the needy to ameliorate the hunger everywhere. There will be food for practically anyone who wants it in the Free Store.

During my weekend experimenting with cooking, I had an assortment of delicious food. So Sunday evening I went to the Paradox, looking for someone to lessen my solitude by inviting her to my house and share my meal. There I met Nina, the blue-eyed girl. She came with me, and I told her the reason for having so much food prepared. She was thrilled by the idea of making beautiful parks, and that I will feed people. She promised she will be my constant visitor in the Free Store.

The Free Store has to be organized in several respects. 1) Cleanliness. 2) Orderliness. 3) Behavior. To make an effective progress, I made myself a working program: Clean up the place, collect dirty dishes, the dirty clothes, wash greasy tables, couches, and chairs. Sweep and scrub floors, and do the bathroom. In the kitchen, scrub walls, windows, stove, sink, wash usable dishes, clean up filth, prepare the facilities for cooking (what about fridge?). And the people are in keen need of a washing-machine (from where?). It can be placed in the basement. I spent several days cleaning up the place, but the kitchen is unusable and until the plumber and electrician fixes whatever has to be fixed, I can't cook. But the people are hungry. The Administration provides the Store with $7–8 for the daily dinner expenses (25–30–35 people), so I'm going with this amount of money to do my shopping. I go with my large shopping-bags to the Houston Street bakeries and Jewish delicatessen stores and collect leftover breads, rolls, and whatever I can get. Every storekeeper is generous, but 'Katz's' delicatessen is the most generous among the merchants. With the money I buy margarine and mayonnaise for spreads and the ends of cold-cuts and cheeses. I purchase very reasonably and go loaded with food to my hungry folks. Nina is surprised at the amount of sandwiches I'm preparing and is amazed how quickly they disappear.

We try to discover each other while working together. We prepare illustrative regulation posters, and decorate the walls: 'No Youngsters,' 'No Oldsters,' 'No fists,' 'No fights,' 'No guns,' 'No gambling,' 'No alcohol,' 'No narco,' 'No crashing,' 'No yelling,' 'Please,' 'Thank-you.' By the door we have posters: 'Welcome,' 'Please introduce yourself,' 'What do you want?' 'Please use ashtrays.' And slowly we are coming together.

August 14. The Free Store. I received my third salary—$45, take-home pay $38.82. It feels great to be liberated from degrading dependency. When I saw my mother, I told her about my steady job, my income, and that I will get a salary raise soon.

Our Director, Mr. Moore, seeing the orderliness in the Store, promised me he would submit his recommendation for a pay increase. I am working 8 hours regularly. But while I'm off, I do the shopping with the 7–8 dollar grant, and for the needed supplement, a collection. And behold, the Houston Street merchants fill up my shopping bags with bread, rolls and whatever else they can give. So, when I am in the Store, the folks have ample food. While I'm at the Store, we work together. We decorate the place with murals, paintings, some sculptures done mostly by the girls. We, the guys, post them on the walls, with interesting newspaper clippings. We also have poetry and prose readings, solo and group singing, and some of us play the flute, pipe, mouth organ, guitar, tambourine, or whatever instruments are available, sometimes it is only whistling or clapping our hands in rhythm. The Store has a dignified atmosphere without being snobbish. We have a comradely relationship and a common goal, our park-development project. I made all necessary notes about the empty lots and we are now working on the plans for planting them with greenery, and the project is about to become a reality.

I contacted Village Green Productions. They will make a film of all the lots in their present condition. They'll show all the phases of our work until a park emerges.

24 August '68. Long time no write. The radio is on. Wars are spreading rampageously. In our country uncertainty is growing. In New York City, corruptions infect the Human Resources Administration. And all the news affects my life.

According to Mr. Moore, the Human Resources Administration is under investigation—a big fraud has been discovered. The Free Store funds have been stopped, including the food and occupational grants. Now the folks are hungry and worried and seek reassurance from each other—they start to migrate and go on the road again. I am working in the Store—where all employees get salary punctually except me. I work, but since the 13th, I haven't gotten my pay.

My life has changed. Diametrically from a month ago. I am on the borderline of killing myself, yet I see the cosmos from a new point of view, as a region of new life.

I am struggling out of my old consciousness into a happier one. To change the face of this earth, yes, the methodical lies, the fact that we think only of ourselves and forget how others feel. The sordid defraudings have to be corrected. Ultimately, everyone has to buckle down and be aware of the futility of the old ways—the futility of one-upmanship, the futility of competition with your brother and sister instead of working alongside with them for a common good.

Meanwhile, all around me, America is dissolving in its mire of sloth. Some people in comfort. But lonely creatures are drifting hither and thither in attempts to alleviate their confusion and bewilderment. Our lives, hours, days, become only a value. We buy and sell ourselves and seek clarity and contentment in weird ways. Mine is Yoga at this time. It might keep me alive, until I am sixty-five. That will be difficult, because the world is against life now. We are having wars all around us, labeled with the names of the places they take place in: Algeria, Viet Nam, Thailand, Guatemala, Czechoslovakia, Tibet, Sinai, Birmingham. Most are lied about and are fought for irrelevant reasons, and the world is hypnotized into it. And I am torn between living here or leaving the whole mess, hiding away in the mountains, finding my own peace and contentment, my inner peace. On the other hand, I am rooted to the city, this horrid place which must be changed unless we do not want to live anymore the way life can be. We must try to perform a miracle, where we let go of past ways and embrace truer truths, where we can unite in the love and understanding for the individual's needs, and help each other for one common goal.

I have led a life of hell since I stopped getting my salary. I could not get up in the morning and was fearful and neurotic, self-punishing. Didn't take a bath for 4-5 days at a time. Walked the streets by myself, aching for someone to place a kind hand on my skin. I was very, very anxious, struggling with the idea of asking my psychiatrist for the job which he suggests that I take. He is kind. He loaned me $10 to buy fruit juice . . . and I did not ask for a job. I've thought about suicide, by gas, very many times. I threw my cat out and when I found him on the street, I scared him away. He let out a cry, and I was lonely, very lonely, but hung on.

This Saturday, after writing, after an oatmeal breakfast-lunch, as I was drinking a cup of tea in the quietness of the afternoon, Nina walked in, and we talked. She knows of our hope to do the parks, and the troubles we have. We talked about them. She quieted down my bitterness. She convinced me, we will make the parks. And I promised her that on Monday I would pick up my bicycle from the dealer, for which I gave a deposit. In my cautiousness (money) I still had not picked it up. Soon I will have my bicycle. I will then communicate easily to the people who will film our park-project, without having to walk long stretches.

Nina told me her problems. She wants to settle down in New York and is looking for a place of her own. I told her about the place next door and that she can move in and all I wanted was for someone to live there who would be happy there. That I had no demands of love from her and if she chose some man to live with her I would try to be his friend, would treat him with courtesy.

Nina, seeing the apartment, liked it, but said it has to have a stove. We went to see about a gas range for her and as we came home in the sticky, muggy heat, she said: "Let's go under the fire hydrant." I had never done that. Reluctantly I changed into swimming trunks, and we both had a refreshing shock of cold water right on the street, and a cup of warm tea immediately afterwards. We kissed, she kissed me warmly many times, and all my troubles were suddenly over. I knew that I would always be in love with this healthy, blue-eyed girl who came like a ray of sunshine into my disintegrating life. I didn't express my feelings with words—only with my eyes. I gave her one of my pocket-watches as a welcome-home present. And now I will help her to settle down, to make her life happy.

Last week started according to our agreement with Nina. Monday I finally made my purchase, with a $30 payment—the full price for the (secondhand) English Rex 10-speed bicycle. We signed the bill of sale with the store-owner before a witness on the 26th of August, stating that the bicycle is my legal property.

My week was eventful, but not exhausting till its last day. My cycle took me everywhere with ease and speed. To the Free Store, where we are coming together with the new fellows who have arrived there. I was cycling to 48th and Fifth Avenue, where I had a meeting with the Village Green Productions representative, about photographing of the motion picture for our park-project. My cycle took me back to the

Lower East Side, to the lots where I was looking for a good visual spot, to start filming for our project. I then sped to East Fifth Street, and as I was looking over one of the fences for a good location, my bicycle, which I had left leaning against the fence a few feet away, was jumped on by a young man in a white shirt, dark pants, and long oily hair, who rode furiously away. I saw him only from the back . . .

I reported the robbery at 2:30, 1st of September 1968, to Patrolman badge number 13264, 9th Precinct, E. 5th Street:

"I hereby certify that on (date) the 10-speed racing-bicycle of Mr. Andrew Bihaly was stolen while he was performing services necessary to find a location for the photographing of a motion picture.

"This was duly reported to Patrolman Gilmore of the 9th Precinct on East 5th Street 20 minutes after above incident."

Not having my bicycle, I trotted home and felt a rope around my waist. I was pulling a cycle with a heavy load.

Under my blanket I felt safe, isolated from all troubles of the outside.

In my engulfment something warm and soft and marvelously delicious happened. Nina spoke to me. She enlightened the whole situation; the bicycle is a loss, but it can be replaced. Bikes don't make parks, *we* have to make them. We will make them!

1 September 1968

FROM: Mr. Andrew Bihaly
        Youth Chore Member
        217 Mott Street
        New York City

TO: Mr. Herbert Moore
      Director, Free Store
      14 Cooper Square
      New York City

Dear Mr. Moore:

I wish to make some suggestions for the improvement of the Free Store Program, so that more young persons who now exhibit some degree of inactivity will be motivated to contribute more of their creative natural energy:

1) The Free Store should serve an oatmeal breakfast and a cup of coffee for two (2) weeks to anyone who awakens by 8:30 a.m. and desires food.

2) This needed nourishment might just motivate those who are hungry to start their day early instead of awakening later in the day.

3) This food will satisfy the hunger for a whole morning.

4) This food will supplement the health needs in relation to vitamins, minerals, and bulk the body needs to enable it to do hard physical labor. It will create the capacity to exert bodily effort, and to strengthen both body and mind.

5) It is my assumption that those being fed and rising early will be strongly motivated to participate in projects aimed at the cleaning up and beautification of the neighborhood. Some of these projects might entail the removal of the rotting garbage from the immediate vicinity of the Free Store, filling wooden boxes or milk boxes with soil, and perhaps starting by planting trees, and other decorative foliage, in the storewindow and other nearby visible locations.

6) With the permission of the neighborhood landlords a program might be started to empty these eyesores of rotting garbage and replace the rubbish with bushes and small ailanthus trees (a wild tree which needs no water or other maintenance other than its transplantation after the fall leaves fall off them), leaving space for the children of the neighborhood to play in, or providing the young people of the Free Store a nearby garden so that they might have some contact with the nature and enjoy the city on a more personal and intimate level than the concrete cold pavement with which they now live.

7) A great deal of free publicity will result from these endeavors which will supply tangible evidence to those negatively predisposed towards the Free Store and hippies in general to modify and possibly change their ill feelings and destructive intentions.

8) The publicity might also add the needed degree of good feeling to the atmosphere of the neighborhood so that the local residents and merchants might be given the incentive to offer food and other material help to the Free Store. This might also create a means for communication on a person-to-person level so that information may be spread in an effective manner throughout the city and probably throughout the country.

9) The officials responsible for the monies needed to continue the Free Store

would take notice of the long-term constructive activity started as a spontane-
ous effort which might permanently affect the lives of the inhabitants of our
neighborhood, on a physical as well as psychological level, and alleviate some of
the oppression of the people of the neighborhood experience because of the neglect
and corrosion of the appearance of the Lower East Side.

10) PROGRAM EXPENSES.

(I listed all expenses, 12 ounces Thermoformed plastic cereal bowls, and the
food items. TOTAL EXPENSES: $14.76.)

I recommend the above suggestions for your consideration, and hope that it
may be of some help in the work we all started here in the Free Store. It is of
utmost importance that this program be commenced in the immediate future,
for the cold weather will soon be upon us and deter the fall promise of the
above mentioned.

> *Very sincerely and respectfully yours,*
> *ANDREW BIHALY*
> *Youth Chore Member*

September 3, Tuesday. Mr. Moore read my letter and said: he likes
the proposal, but doubts that we could get $15 daily for breakfast. I ex-
plained the $12 is for plastic bowls and the money for that will be
spent only once. All that I'm asking for is a two-week try, and we can
call it Project TOGETHER. Then I told him that I have been working in the store since 22nd of July and was promised I would get more
salary, but instead I haven't gotten any salary since the 13th of August.
It will be issued right away, he promised. He himself will see to it.
And as soon as I get it, I will pay $10 to my Doctor and $10 to Toby
and John, which they kindly loaned me.

Mr. Moore got the answer from the Administration! We can start the
Project! It was approved for a fifteen-day experiment. Yesterday the
stove and sink were repaired and today I have to start the begging for
needed stuff.

Begging for your own self is degrading. But I feel satisfaction and pride doing it for the Free Store. So I'm collecting from the Houston Street delicatessens whatever is needed. I got a huge pot, a stirring-spoon for cooking the oatmeal, and a large scooping-spoon for serving it with. From the Administration we got $10 for two days. It will be only enough to buy food for breakfast. So I brought 18 juice glasses (my own property from home), paper bowls given by the YMCA (we will need them for the cereals), and spoons were promised by one of our members. I bought one luxury: a pot of geraniums for the table (55¢) to underline the festivity of the occasion. And tomorrow, Friday, we start. I will go to cook breakfast early, very early.

September 6, Friday, 1968
Summary of Project TOGETHER, for the first breakfast:
The breakfast was a failure from the point of view of someone who expects fast change in human beings and who does not accept my, or anyone-else's, human fallibility.

For breakfast a great many people arrived. Orange-juice powder was not prepared all at once, but in quart-intervals (there being only 18 glasses). The oatmeal was ready, prepared only in fifteen bowls, because only fifteen spoons were available. But before the food could be arranged on the table, the juice glasses were taken, no more glasses available, no more juice prepared; the people became panicky that there wouldn't be enough to go around. The people grabbed things for themselves and complete confusion reigned.

After all the hungry ate, about 8 people remained behind, and I made a little speech:

"We come together to eat, get up early in the morning, and do our 'Thing.' The more people can cooperate, the more is their THING, the more can be accomplished and done. Please spread this word. I speak to you as an Indian, not as a Chief."

We then sang songs, I played the flute, and by 9:45 everyone left the room. I cleaned up with one of our kind friends who had eaten with us.

$12.32 was spent on project TOGETHER.

I 'overspent' $2.32. Bills were submitted for purchases.

I gave the summary to Mr. Moore. I asked again for my salary. His telephone rang. He didn't answer me, maybe he didn't hear me. He spoke with someone on a private matter. I left his office.

Saturday morning. I'm here in the Free Store. It is still dark outside. I am working. Everything is clean. Pots are on the stove. I am living for a few indeterminate moments in SLOW MOTION; this seems so because of the infinite number of movements that I made while preparing breakfast. It's also due to my keyed-up-ness and my hunger and the pain in my body—and my fatigue.

Phrases overheard in the Metropolitan Museum restaurant last year come into my mind:

"WHAT
IS WORTH TO WHOM
HOW MUCH
WHEN"

"It may be essential to certain of our decision-making . . ."

"If I were there, I wouldn't have put it in the back seat. It is my fault. I would have put it in the trunk."

"What is he afraid of? I mean, what is he afraid of?"

"He'll outlive his little nest-egg."

"Can't you tell him he is wrong, all wrong?"

The breakfast is ready. People will be here but I will serve at eight o'clock.

Summary of Project TOGETHER for Saturday, September 7, 1968:

Breakfast of oatmeal and orange juice (imitation) was served in an empty room on the floor. We sat in a circle and started to eat all together at 8:00 a.m. sharp. Breakfast was over at 9 A.M. The mood was quiet, none grabbed food this time, as they did yesterday. I made a short speech: "This is an experiment, and it will go on for thirteen more days. This is the second day of it. We'd like to help anyone who gets up to eat to start their day with a good stomach and good feeling. We hope that it will dawn upon some of us that we can cooperate on some projects, to make the Free Store and the surrounding area more beautiful. Or if you want to do your own thing, whatever that might be, a full stomach and early start might help that too. We can also learn to know each other better. This is not a charity undertaking. Thank you for coming, have a pleasant day."

The mood was cheerful and one of general helpfulness. One young man offered to help wash all the dishes.

Legal hassles were discussed only by three persons.

It would be helpful if some of the leaders of the Free Store would join our breakfast to initiate specific discussions on things we might be doing together. One man (myself) cannot make all the speeches . . . All I can try to do is catalyze the situation.

No coffee was served for lack of cups. Approximately 10 persons did not get fed, for only 25 bowls of oatmeal were prepared. Only a gallon of milk was available. To continue this project, we need two gallons of milk, (30) cups for coffee, and 10 pounds of oatmeal.

Up until now I have laid out $2.35 of my own funds to continue the project. This personal outlay of funds ended yesterday.

Thank you, and respectfully,
ANDREW BIHALY

I gave my summary in the office on September 9, Monday, to have it forwarded to the 'Center' and asked for the daily grant for further shopping. But I was informed: Project TOGETHER will not get any more funds. Then I asked for my salary, which I hadn't gotten since the 13th of August. "We must go," someone was calling, "there is no time to lose." And I was left standing there.

"WHAT IS WORTH HOW MUCH TO WHOM WHEN?"

And I stood in the office and after a while the words came to me:

> "There is no time to lose," I heard her say.
> Catch your dreams before they slip away
> Dying all the time
> Lose your dreams
> and you will lose your mind
> in life unkind.

225

As I started to clean up my home, Nina came in. I thought she wanted to help me again, but she said she can not move into my apartment, because she is going back to the farm. She came just to say farewell.

After Nina left, I calmed down. I knew that I didn't belong in the city anymore. That the country I was trying to transplant, activate in the city, was mere scenery, an illusion. If I want to make it a reality, I have to go and live in the country myself. I started finishing cleaning up, but just before mopping the floor, I hid under my blanket for 25 minutes only but remained there for 12 hours, unable to face the reality that I can't achieve anything. I took a tranquilizer in the dawn and finally arose at 11 a.m., calm.

Why can I not do anything? I'd like to know what holds me back. I am trying to do what I like best yet do not do what I want, because something in me doesn't want to let me, part of my personality doesn't let me. I am sitting here writing and part of myself is bugging another part of my personality, it is playing hide-and-seek. I am in great conflict and it pains, it hurts to talk about this area, something doesn't let me. Something in me doesn't let loose my potentiality. Why can I not accomplish anything? Why can I not write? Why can I not do anything? I have these beautiful relationships, but I am afraid to bring them into the sensual 'phase.' Why? Because I don't want to remember something? I cannot accomplish anything, I cannot do anything because somewhere in the past when I was very young, when I was in Visegrad, something painful happened, something so painful that my mind doesn't let it go? Visions, memory fractions suddenly shape up, I want to run away from them but these things begin to jell around me —"Make him eat it." Then I vomited. Someone forced me to eat it. I did. I vomited again. It must have been horrible. "Eat it" and I walk my days with this memory, and I can't accomplish anything.

I belong in a place in society. I have set up programs for myself in order to fabricate a life for myself, a life of great dimensions, a life to exhibit among the great wonders of the earth, a marvelous edifice. But something in me hasn't allowed my potentiality. I don't know what to do with myself, my inner fabric has shriveled away, my inner motivations have atrophied. Could it be that this is a disease, like a lead-painted room, like the way the painters, Modigliani and others in his time, died? Lead poisoning? Slowly and surely I become crazy, it is hateful and spiteful, a person who sees sanity through other people's sanity. I want to run away from the truth. Yes, I have become ill. Thoughts, thoughts with visions, memories suddenly come, yes, memories do drive me crazy. It hurts very much. I refeel the pain I am integrated with, how can I digest my childhood in Visegrad?

Anne Frank died. But what happened to the living? The living must go on living. The living must learn life, learn it while they are living it. Their fate is not as easy as simply dying. How does one live one's life in spite of one's memories? Fissures incite, fissures in the self, in one's self, in *my* self. I must swallow the fissures, swallow them once again and chew them and digest them and shit them out and eat them again, my fissures. One must live with one's fissures. One can't simply lie away one's fissures—*especially* to one's self. I know. I tried for 10 years. Oh yes, one must integrate emotionally, integrate intellectually, integrate culturally, integrate racially, integrate viscerally, integrate. And one must cry one's own tears. No one can cry anyone else's tears. One must do it for oneself. The tears must filter out of one's guts, with a huge heavy lump in one's throat, behind and around one's Adam's apple, and finally they must seep out from around one's eyes, and trickle down on one's nose and cheeks. If it happens, once in a while, then one is integrated a little more. That is how I eat my fissures, my shit, which Anne Frank didn't have to do, wasn't privileged to do. I am, we are privileged to do it, we alive people. We, the living.

The facts are simple, they are simply facts. Ridiculously simple facts. Have you any feelings left for a tearjerker? Hey, you-all! Hey, public! Hey, have you any feelings left? Without feelings you gonna become a vegetable, a houseplant! All you gonna do is just grow. You won't feel nothin'. I urge, I urge you, public, I most solemnly urge you to have feelings. Myself included. Especially myself included. You see, I even let you into my little secrets, you looked behind my little alienation effects. I hope my effects are effective, for *your* sake: otherwise you gonna be nothin', grow into a houseplant without any feelings

The New York Times

Life and Death in the City

SEPTEMBER 23, 1968

By TOM BUCKLEY

. . . . .

Andrew Bihaly was a quiet man who lived in an immaculate flat in that vanishing emblem of slum life in old Manhattan, a back tenement, built behind the tenement at 217 Mott Street.

He was 34 years old, slender, with aquiline features. He was born in Hungary and told his neighbor, James Patton, that he had been confined with his parents in a concentration camp during World War II.

"He wanted to help people," Mr. Patton, a figure in the East Village hippie world, said, "but he was afraid people wouldn't like him. That was one of his hangups. He was seeing a psychiatrist. He worked at the Free Store on Cooper Square, and it bothered him that he didn't get paid for it when other people who worked there did."

That morning despair overcame him. He dragged his mattress onto the floor next to his two-burner gas stove. He fixed a rubber tube to the jet. Then he fastened a plio-film bag around his head and ran the tube into it. Then he turned on the gas.

. . . . .